Global University Rankings and the Politics of Knowledge

EDITED BY MICHELLE STACK

UNIVERSITY OF TORONTO PRESS
Toronto Buffalo London

© University of Toronto Press 2021
Toronto Buffalo London
utorontopress.com

ISBN 978-1-4875-0454-0 (cloth)   ISBN 978-1-4875-3041-9 (EPUB)
ISBN 978-1-4875-2339-8 (paper)   ISBN 978-1-4875-3040-2 (PDF)

Library and Archives Canada Cataloguing in Publication

Title: Global university rankings and the politics of knowledge / edited by
    Michelle Stack.
Names: Stack, Michelle, 1967– editor.
Description: Includes bibliographical references and index.
Identifiers: Canadiana (print) 20210154497 | Canadiana (ebook) 20210154586 |
    ISBN 9781487523398 (paper) | ISBN 9781487504540 (cloth) |
    ISBN 9781487530419 (EPUB) | ISBN 9781487530402 (PDF)
Subjects: LCSH: Universities and colleges – Ratings and rankings. |
    LCSH: Education, Higher – Marketing.
Classification: LCC LB2331.62 .G66 2021 | DDC 378–dc23

This book has been published with the help of a grant from the Federation for the
Humanities and Social Sciences, through the Awards to Scholarly Publications
Program, using funds provided by the Social Sciences and Humanities Research
Council of Canada.

University of Toronto Press acknowledges the financial assistance to its publishing
program of the Canada Council for the Arts and the Ontario Arts Council, an
agency of the Government of Ontario.

Canada Council   Conseil des Arts
for the Arts   du Canada

ONTARIO ARTS COUNCIL
CONSEIL DES ARTS DE L'ONTARIO
an Ontario government agency
un organisme du gouvernement de l'Ontario

Funded by the   Financé par le
Government   gouvernement
of Canada   du Canada   Canada

GLOBAL UNIVERSITY RANKINGS AND THE POLITICS OF KNOWLEDGE

Edited by Michelle Stack

For many institutions, to ignore your university's ranking is to become invisible, a risky proposition in a competitive search for funding. But rankings tell us little if anything about the education, scholarship, or engagement with communities offered by a university. Drawing on a range of research and inquiry-based methods, *Global University Rankings and the Politics of Knowledge* exposes how universities became servants to the rankings industry and its impact.

Conceptually unique in its scope, *Global University Rankings and the Politics of Knowledge* addresses the lack of empirical research behind university and journal ranking systems. Chapters from internationally recognized scholars in decolonial studies provide readers with robust frameworks to understand the intersections of coloniality and Indigeneity and how they play out in higher education. Contributions from diverse geographical and disciplinary contexts explore the political economy of rankings within the contexts of the Global North and South, and examine alternatives to media-driven rankings. This book allows readers to consider the intersections of power and knowledge within the wider contexts of politics, culture, and the economy, to explore how assumptions about gender, social class, sexuality, and race underpin the meanings attached to rankings, and to imagine a future that confronts and challenges cognitive, environmental, and social injustice.

MICHELLE STACK is an associate professor in the Department of Educational Studies at the University of British Columbia.

Contents

Acknowledgments

Thank you to André Mazawi for the many hours at the Vancouver Public Library (pre-COVID-19) discussing this book and a second book we coedited in 2020. Thank you for the always collegial, intellectually dynamic conversations, along with excellent coffee and humour.

To the Peter Wall Institute for Advanced Studies at the University of British Columbia, who funded an international roundtable on rankings and journal impact factor that led to research collaborations which continue today. A particular thank you to the interim director of PWIAS, Kalina Christoff, who has been steadfast in her support of this research.

A special thanks to Mayumi Ishikawa and Chuing Prudence Chou, who I met at the Comparative International Education Society Conference in 2015. The excitement of meeting two scholars who were at the forefront of critical writing about ranking was exhilarating and led to applying for the roundtable and eventually this book, for which they were generous in providing advice throughout the process.

A big thank you to all the staff at the University of Toronto Press, in particular Meg Patterson, who stewarded this book through reviews, funding, and finding a way to make it freely available. To Barbie Halaby for her outstanding editing abilities and patience, and to Suher Zaher for taking time over her holiday to create a stellar index for this book. To graduate research assistants Jingwun Liang, Sameena Jamal, and Sonia Medel for the exceptional assistance they have provided from the roundtable to this moment of finally submitting the acknowledgments.

Thank you to Annette Henry, Bathseba Opini, Heidi Janz, Hartej Gill, Deirdre Kelly, and Mary Lynn Young for their scholarship and teaching on racism, colonialism, ableism, and sexism that are central to the many critiques offered in this book.

Last but not least, to the wonderful group of 2020–21 Peter Wall Scholars that I am fortunate to be a member of.

Abbreviations

HEI	higher education institutions
ARWU	Academic Ranking of World Universities (sometimes referred to as the Shanghai Ranking)
THE	*Times Higher Education*
THEWUR	Times Higher Education World University Rankings
QS	Quacquarelli Symonds
"Big Three"	THEWUR, QS, and ARWU
IF	Impact Factor

GLOBAL UNIVERSITY RANKINGS AND THE POLITICS OF KNOWLEDGE

Introduction

MICHELLE STACK

Rankings play an important role in guiding parents, students, policymakers, and investors in engaging particular higher education institutions (HEIs) and their programs, but the impact of university rankings goes far beyond university campuses. Doctors learn how to be doctors, teachers how to be teachers, and lawyers and judges to be lawyers and judges at HEIs. People support HEIs in various ways – public and private – as volunteer research participants, as patients at teaching hospitals, or through taxes that provide monies for research and other grants that are impacted by rankings.

Saints, generals, and royalty – along with cars, toothbrushes, and ice cream – are ranked. Our fascination with and use of rankings are not new. James McKeen Cattell served as the president of both the American Psychological Association and the American Eugenics Society. He also started a ranking of US universities in 1906 (Usher, 2015). Similar to today, most of the institutions he deemed to be at the top were predominantly wealthy and white and began to accrue large endowments through their participation in slavery (Wilder, 2013). However, corporate university rankings, which purport to be global, are a relatively recent phenomenon. The Academic Ranking of World Universities (ARWU), also known as the Shanghai Ranking, began in 2003. The *Times Higher Education* and Quacquarelli Symonds joined forces in 2004 to create the QS-THE Ranking, but in 2009 the two separated and the Times Higher Education World University Rankings and QS came into being as separate rankings. The ARWU, QS, and THEWUR are often referred to as the "Big Three" rankings and are frequently cited by government policymakers and industry and university leaders. The Big Three also have a number of spinoff products, including regional rankings, consulting services, and software aimed at helping university leaders make hiring and other decisions that could improve an institution's ranking. In addition to the Big Three, there are approximately 150 national and specialty rankings and over 20 others that purport to be global (Hazelkorn, 2015).

The central objective of this book is to expand the conversation about what a good and worthwhile education could be and to look beyond the argument that rankings are here to stay. This book expands the critical literature on rankings to consider questions of how knowledge is produced and shared and what this means for who and what are seen as "world class." These are not technical questions but central to imagining futures that confront and challenge cognitive, environmental, and social injustice.

Education is big business. The number of students travelling abroad to study has increased by 50 per cent since 2000. Rankings play a central role in where students go to study and therefore which universities benefit from the revenue they bring (Lynch, 2014). The Chinese government has created the C9 League and provided these institutions with US$1.86 billion to compete with US Ivy League schools. Russia sets aside US$152 million for students to study in a top 200 world-ranked university, and India only partners with universities in the top 500 for joint degree programs (Taylor et al., 2014).

Which students get selected for which programs and who teaches them are affected by rankings. A recent study out of Stanford surveyed 100,000 high school students (Challenge Success, 2018). It found that rankings play a significant role in the decision-making of students and their parents. However, rankings do not provide them with reliable information about well-being, student learning, or future job satisfaction. Gallup-Purdués (2014) Index found that students who had good experiences in higher education reported higher levels of well-being and job satisfaction after graduation. Good experiences included mentorship from professors, internships, projects that were engaging and lasted over a number of terms, engaging professors, and extracurricular activities. The authors found that students who attended highly selective schools did not have higher levels of well-being, but those with higher student debt loads had lower well-being.

The impact of rankings is not limited to student selection of university or the metrics used to evaluate research. Their effects extend well into the global economy. Studies consistently point to the impacts that university rankings have on trade (Cantwell, 2016), immigration policy (Ordorika & Lloyd, 2013), the flow of graduate students, faculty hiring, and philanthropic and financial support (Badat, 2010), tuition fees, and in some cases even university presidents' salaries (Yeung et al., 2019).

Muller (2017) argues university rankings are a form of rent-seeking in that public higher education institutions redirect "social surplus toward private actors (of various sorts)" (p. 59). Rent-seeking behaviour includes spending resources on rankings or reallocation of resources to maximize the possibility of a high ranking without regard to whether this activity serves a larger social value. Increasingly governments are moving away from block funding of post-secondary education and instead requiring institutions to compete for resources with private and non-profit providers. The result is that many systems provide more spaces for students to participate in higher education; however, as Cantwell (2018) argues, this does not equate to more opportunities for all.

> In HPS [high participation systems] two processes of social stratification are brought together. Unequally ranked and valued students are matched with "appropriate" unequally valued educational opportunity and the unequal social outcomes that follow. An imagined world of free choice and open possibilities is translated into a real world of social allocation and life closure. (p. 27)

The efforts of the Chinese and Indian governments to move up in the rankings appear to be working. At the same time, both countries have cracked down on academic freedom (Scholars at Risk, 2019b). Countries with numerous top-ranked universities including the United States (Scholars at Risk, 2019a) have also been critiqued for infringing on academic freedom. This book questions who decides what and who the university is for and what this means for society.

How much is known by policymakers, parents, students, and others about the rankings that have become central to decision-making? Who should decide what makes for a good education and if our educational institutions are meeting our needs? How do rankings shape political cultures, and with what implications for democracy? I hope this book opens up conversations around these questions.

This book came to fruition after twenty-two researchers from five continents spent four days together in Vancouver, British Columbia, Canada, discussing and debating the impacts that university rankings are having on student selection, research funding, and faculty hiring, and on HEIs' missions and marketing strategies. The authors in this collection address these and other important questions.

The chapters are organized around three themes: The first theme touches on geopolitics. The reader will note the use of the terms "Global North" and "Global South." These concepts come with issues, but alternatives used thus far raise significant problems – for example, the use of the term "developing countries," which is essentializing and stigmatizing. Global North and South are used by leading scholars in higher education and comparative studies including Boaventura de Sousa Santos, Walter Mignolo, and other critical and decolonial scholars. Speaking about the privileges of the Global North is not to say that all Global North universities are privileged or highly ranked. As an anonymous peer reviewer for this manuscript stated, "In the context of global rankings, lesser known institutions/institutions with a different mission to the elite universities are geographically in the north, but metaphorically in the south." Indeed, universities which often serve groups structurally excluded from top-ranked Global North universities are constructed as institutions focused on equity and devoid of excellence as constructed by elite, predominantly white and upper-class universities. The authors in this book point to the need for an understanding of global rankings in different contexts, across and within societies, and particularly how these differences are mediated by the media in reinforcing top-ranked Global North universities as more desirable and of higher quality. The authors also demonstrate the importance of understanding that the impacts of rankings are global but not devoid of context-specific implications.

The second theme touches on questions associated with knowledge. The three chapters in this part show how the business of rankings and journal impact factors (IF) are connected and the impact this can have on the education we receive and the research we use, directly or indirectly, to make decisions.

The third theme touches on the privileges that rankings enhance or reinforce as well as the anxieties they provoke at the level of institutions and individuals. Contributors analyse the connections between mental health and rankings and the influence of rankings on how institutions collect and use data for decision-making.

The book's concluding chapter synthesizes the main themes and offers suggestions for a future research agenda that considers possibilities for expanding conversations and policy alternatives beyond "rankings are here to stay."

Theme 1: Geopolitics, Rankings, and Journal Impact Factors

Rankings are part of a global education industry (Verger et al., 2017), which a major player in the industry, Holon IQ, estimates will be worth $10 trillion by 2030 (Holon IQ, 2020). Sadlak (2014) maintains that rankings allow prospective students, funders, and government to sort through a diverse and stratified higher education sector. For others, the classification systems raise questions about equity.

Mittelman's (2017) research concludes that the focus on winners and losers by many nations has resulted in the top-ranked HEIs in a country receiving an annual average budget of approximately $2 billion, which is often money redirected to them from HEIs who serve the majority of students. Schultz et al. (2001) show that some Danish firms have very "sticky" reputations, which means that even if they are not very profitable, they have a good reputation and therefore are assumed to be profitable. They propose that "reputation is not necessarily about actual economic performance but about perception and interpretation of cues" (p. 37). Drawing on this work, Esposito and Stark (2019) show that, regardless of changes in indicators used by rankers, Yale, Harvard, Stanford, and Princeton will always be at the top due to this "stickiness" (p. 20).

Ranking critics also identify the circular logic of focusing on reputation rather than on what is actually occurring within an institution (Bowman &

Bastedo, 2011; Marginson, 2014). Such a circularity does not contribute to improving teaching and learning. The Matthew effect (Merton, 1968) can set in – leading to individuals or institutions receiving accolades based on social capital while others, equally or more capable, continue to be ignored. Others have argued that university leaders who use rankings for decision-making do not have an adequate understanding of methodological issues related to rankings (Hosier & Hoolash, 2017).

Higher education encompasses a wide range of institutions, with diverse academic and scholarly traditions. Some researchers have, therefore, critiqued the logic of comparing universities with different missions and traditions within the same ranking logic (Olcay & Bulu, 2017; Paradeise & Thoenig, 2013). Small differences can have a significant quantitative impact on how an institution is ranked and, subsequently, on how it is funded (Fowles et al., 2016). In other cases, some higher education institutions manipulate data in an attempt to improve their ranking (Barnard, 2018; Bhattacharjee, 2011; Jaschik, 2018). Temple University's business program, for example, was ranked number 1 in the US for four years in a row, but after an investigation by the Pennsylvania attorney general and US Department of Education, the university admitted to falsifying data for its business school and six of its other graduate programs (Evans, 2019). Soon after the Temple scandal hit the papers, eight other colleges admitted they had sent incorrect data to *U.S. News & World Report* (Morse et al., 2018).

The 2019 admission scandal that rocked the US school led Pulitzer Prize–winning writer and University of Southern California (USC) professor Viet Thanh Nguyen (2019) to conclude,

> USC suffers from the same desire to climb the rankings as other schools, which drives it to raise billions in a fundraising arms race. The rankings also reward "selectivity," which is why schools try to gain as many applicants as possible, knowing that they will reject most. No wonder parents are desperate enough about the admissions system to reach for various forms of corruption: coaching (expensive), bribery (even more expensive, and obviously illegal), and the ultimate power play, the massive donation (the priciest, the most visible, the most lauded and therefore the most acceptable form of corruption).

In 2006 an organization called the International Ranking Expert Group (IREG) was formed and developed guidelines for rankings and to give the IREG stamp of approval to rankings the group deems adequate. Rankers sit on the group, which has led to concerns about its independence from the interest of rankers (Taylor et al., 2014).

Three companies dominate the global university rankings. The "Big Three" include the Times Higher Education World University Ranking, the QS World

University Rankings, and the Academic Ranking of World Universities. They also have numerous spinoff products (Stack, 2016), including a suite of rankings (e.g., best student city, regional rankings) and software tools that promise university administrators the ability to make tenure and promotion decisions that align with metrics used by rankers (e.g., InCites).

The QS is particularly entrepreneurial, with its "QS intelligence unit" that provides services to assist universities in improving based on QS metrics and through an audit (for a fee) could receive up to 5 stars that can be used for marketing. QS also provides assistance with setting strategic direction for an institution, student recruitment, and external strategy.

The majority of the top-ten globally ranked institutions are located in southern England, California, the Tri-State area (New York, New Jersey, Connecticut), and nearby Massachusetts (Stack, 2019). Pusser and Marginson (2013) argue that the rankings legitimate growing inequality and "reinforce both new and older forms of power" (p. 563). Alfredo Garcia, dean of the School of Law at St. Thomas University, refused to file data requested by U.S. News & World Report ranking because of its deleterious impact, particularly on institutions with a focus on serving racialized and Indigenous students. Within the American context, PK–12 schools that serve predominantly minority students are under-resourced compared to predominantly white schools. White students are often provided greater resources through schooling to prepare for university admission and more often have families that can support them financially. Rankings do not consider these factors and penalize Minority-Serving Institutions, which may take students with lower test scores and spend resources to support them to successful graduation, as compared to predominantly white institutions (Richards et al., 2018).

The Big Three are also an important factor in the pressure many academics outside of the Anglo Global North experience to publish in English. Not only is English necessary, but they also must focus on topics that Global North journal editors will find relevant. This can take away from research that may be particularly relevant to a national or regional context (Kehm, 2014; Teferra, 2017; Tilak, 2016).

In this section of the book, Marion Lloyd and Imanol Ordorika's chapter focuses on the particularities of Latin America, whereas the second chapter by Creso M. Sá, Nadiia Kachynska, Emma Sabzalieva, and Magdalena Martinez analyses the contrasting dynamics broadly in Central Asia, Central and Eastern Europe, and Latin America. The former provides readers the opportunity to zoom in and focus on one region, while the latter allows readers to zoom out and look at Latin America in comparison to other regions which are also under-represented in much of the literature on rankings. These comparisons are consistent with the aim of the book to avoid reified conceptualizations of rankings and their dynamics, as if they play out the same way everywhere. They simply do not.

Lloyd and Ordorika's chapter engages key issues of who comes to be seen as a knowledge producer and what comes to count as legitimate knowledge to publish. They expand the theoretical debate around rankings by pointing to broader struggles at play for cultural hegemony that require Latin America and other regions in the Global South to play a game designed by the Global North to maintain the latter's privileged position in global markets and politics. They point to how rankings influence government and institutional policies in Europe, Asia, and Latin America and through doing so play a role in amplifying inequity and exclusion.

Sá, Kachynska, Sabzalieva, and Martinez provide a much-needed comparative analysis of rankings with a focus on institutions in Central Asia, Central and Eastern Europe, and Latin America. They point to the marginal position of these regions in the creation of global rankings; however, national rankings are growing in these regions. Their chapter examines the similarities, differences, and trends across jurisdictions within these areas.

In chapter 3, Riyad A. Shahjahan, Annabelle Estera, and Vivek Vellanki remind us that rankings play out visually and spatially. They point to the centrality of rankers' websites as key spaces of representation that reinforce how different regions of the world are perceived. In their analysis of these websites, they found that Global North countries were visually promoted as the most desirable.

Theme 2: Costs of Knowledge, Rankings, and Journal Impact Factors

Global university rankings purport to offer a measure of research productivity, which is measured predominantly by the number of research articles produced by university members and captured largely by one of two citation indexes: Elsevier's Scopus databases and the Clarivate-owned Web of Science (WoS) (Robertson & Olds, 2016). Vernon et al.'s (2018) study analysed thirteen rankings including indicators related to research. It found that for nine of the rankings an average of 33.8 per cent was based on peer-reviewed publications included in the Scopus database (owned by Elsevier) or the WoS Core collection database. Recently, several countries and universities have pulled out of contracts with Elsevier, and academics have signed a petition in regard to Elsevier's monopolistic business practices. Larivière et al. (2015) analysed 45 million documents indexed in the WoS from 1973 to 2013. They document a dramatic increase in the influence of five publishers that they point to as forming an oligopoly of academic publishing. In particular, they demonstrate the power of Elsevier, Springer Nature, and Wiley-Blackwell, who together own 47 per cent of academic papers, with Elsevier owning 25 per cent of the academic publishing marketplace.

Elsevier also benefits from owning the Scopus citation index and CiteScore, which is used to measure impact. When CiteScore is used, instead of Clarivate's impact factor, Elsevier's biggest competitor (Springer Nature) goes down by 25–40 per cent; Elsevier journals go up in impact by 10–12 per cent (Tennant, 2018). The other database used by rankers is WoS, owned by Clarivate (previously Thomson Reuters). Gingras and Khelfaoui (2018) demonstrate that US citations are overrepresented in WoS based on how this information is collected (e.g., only collecting data in English). In sum, counting articles to determine research productivity may appear a straight-ahead indicator; however, the process is skewed. For example, Elsevier privileges journals it publishes within its own citation index (Scopus), which is then used by rankers to determine the research productivity of a university.

Nobel Prize winner Randy Schekman argues journal impact factors are doing to academia what a bonus culture did to banking (Schekman, 2013). A focus on journal IF encourages citation bartering, in which researchers within a friendship network agree to cite each other. Work that is most likely to be published in these top-ranked journals often reinforces the status quo and citation network. What is lost is replication and less newsworthy scholarship (Gruber, 2014).

Higher education rankings draw on one of two citation databases – Scopus and WoS, which have reinforced a citation monopoly. The result is that journal IF and university rankings reinforce the power of monopolies to determine what and who counts in higher education (Hall & Page, 2015).

Impact factors and university rankings have led to comparing diverse institutions based on the same scale and ranked accordingly. Paradoxically, rankings and impact factors also "(over) differentiate entities by assigning a unique position or ordinal value" (Bouchard, 2017, p. 958), even when differences are statistically insignificant.

The academic publishing industry has gone through numerous mergers and acquisitions (Kivinen & Hedman, 2008; Kivinen et al., 2017; Peters, 2019). Morrison (2015) notes the impact that rankings, mergers, and acquisitions have on the cost of knowledge and sharing knowledge with people who do not have access to university libraries. Several authors have also pointed to how the conflation of wealth with the quality of education has led to greater inequity and narrowing of knowledge (Gonzales & Waugaman, 2016). Smyth (2017) maintains that relationships and policies are being transformed "based on a league table derived through some system of opaque bibliometrics" (p. 110). In the same vein, Gingras (2016) argues,

It is astonishing that so many university presidents and managers lose all critical sense and seem to take rankings at face value. Only a psychosociological analysis of managers and administrators would explain the appeal of a grading system that has no scientific basis. (p. 79)

Gingras's comprehensive work interconnecting rankings and impact factors demonstrates the need to see rankings as part of larger societal forces at play, including the push to increase revenue through market-driven internationalization. How rankings impact faculty members' labour conditions has remained relatively marginalized. Some have argued that the pressure to publish in top-ranked journals and the financial incentives offered to faculty to do so is a factor in increasing incidents of plagiarism (Douglass, 2016). Zhang and Grieneisen (2013) point to a dramatic increase in retractions that involve misconduct allegations, from 55.8 per cent to 71.9 per cent over the period of 2007–10. Guraya et al. (2016) argue that

> an involuntary obsession to publish with the primary intention to obtain promotions, high scientific rankings, and improved job security. This compelling pressure to publish results in widespread publication of non-significant research with a high index of plagiarism that eventually leads to an increased frequency of retractions. (p. 1562)

However, impact factors would not have the power they do without the acceptance of them by academics who are editors or who sit on hiring and tenure committees (Casadevall & Fang, 2017).

Clearly, there are many factors at play, including that software tools have made it easier to catch plagiarism online; however, concerns over the growing demand for "fast" scholarship is a matter of concern. Still, some researchers point to how rankings privilege the natural sciences and marginalize the social sciences and humanities, which impacts the type of scholarship valued and funded at institutional levels (Mustajoki, 2013; Zhou, 2014). Disciplines that see books as the dominant form of scholarship (e.g., music) are at a disadvantage because rankers privilege journal articles captured by Scopus or WoS citation databases over books. Fast scholarship also encourages "me too" scholarship and discourages new approaches that may require years of development with few or no publications during this time (Alberts, 2013).

A fundamental assumption underpinning rankings is that their algorithms are accurate and comprehensive. Rankings influence what knowledge is seen as worthy of funding and what knowledge is cast as lacking in economic usefulness (Rieder et al., 2018). Ishikawa's (2009) extensive scholarship on rankings points to the colonial focus on English-language publications that excludes the vast majority of the world's scholarship. Boussebaa and Tienari (2019) argue that this "Englishization" of scholarship homogenizes knowledge and reinforces hierarchies of knowledge based on colonial geopolitics. The illusion of capturing knowledge from everywhere is interconnected with the increasing role played by international organizations in educational policymaking. Regulative structures including trade agreements play a central role in not only governance but, as Zapp and Ramirez (2019) explain, also the "cognitive processes in shaping the order of the global higher education field and the behaviour of its actors" (p. 477).

In this section of the book, Chuing Prudence Chou expands on her work concerning the role of the rankings in pushing Taiwanese academics to publish in English. She analyses the impact of rankings on two departments – ethnology and education – at the National Chengchi University. She demonstrates how rankings privilege journal articles over books, which were traditionally more prized in Taiwan. What is left out of rankings can threaten the "epistemic viability" of knowledge from local and national contexts. She points to the impact of ranking metrics that privilege fast scholarship, decrease access to research for local audiences, and entrench gender disparity.

Heather Morrison connects impact factors with university rankings and provides an analysis of academic resistance to these metrics. She analyses the Leiden Manifesto approach to providing a critique of impact factors and a way forward that allows for the diversity of knowledge production and dissemination. As Morrison points out, the norm for historians is to write books; therefore, they can seem like a slovenly lot if one looks just at the number of articles published. A physicist might have a low h-index (includes a scholar's most-cited papers and how many times they are cited in the published work of others) but score high on Google Scholar. She argues that the issue is not only the collection of data about research productivity but also how the data are analysed.

Ralf St. Clair is a dean of education at the University of Victoria in British Columbia. He contends that rankings privilege the Anglosphere. St. Clair examines data around which institutions make it to the top and the impact of universities in the Global South attempting to get into the rankings. He points to the lack of attention to the values at play in determining who is world class. Community and local concerns are absent, and the process of playing the ranking game can further marginalize the already marginalized.

Theme 3: Influence of Rankings on Institutional and Individual Well-Being

Cathy O'Neil (2017), in her book *Weapons of Math Destruction*, focuses on the *U.S. News & World Report* rankings to demonstrate the problem of a few proxy indicators (e.g., the ratio of faculty to students as a proxy for teaching quality) becoming the standard for ranking universities. The result, she argues, is a "reputational arms race": rising tuition fees and often less funding for the students who need it most. She points to how the proxy indicators developed by journalists tell us more about the modeller than about higher education. Modellers for rankings such as *U.S. News* assume that Harvard, Stanford, Princeton, and Yale are the best and then look at what makes them best – money and students with high SAT scores. Other issues such as equity, affordability, and ethics do not play a role in this model of excellence. Instead, O'Neil argues, "As colleges position themselves to move up the *U.S. News* charts, they manage their student populations almost like an investment portfolio" (p. 61). A student might have high grades but be poor; another might be an excellent athlete and rich but have poor grades. In each case, the student brings assets and liabilities. Rankings are mainly based on non-transparent, corporate proprietary algorithms for which there is currently no regulation in terms of their creation, dissemination, or use. Kauppi (2018) argues, "Companies like Google, Thomson Reuters, Elsevier and Clarivate Analytics produce the raw material for the global governance of higher education and research" (p. 1753).

The concept of rankings is not new. In seventeenth- and eighteenth-century Harvard, the president ranked students based on the capital of their fathers, and these rankings determined where students ate dinner and who lived where (Pierce, 2010). At Oxford, the wealthiest were provided better places to live and their own dining hall. They did not face a heavy workload or discipline of any sort for bad behaviour (Wells, 2015). There was no attempt to create an illusion that this ranking was based on academic merit.

Today, rankings appear more objective or rigorous. Highly ranked universities continue to be among the wealthiest HEIs, and their students are overwhelmingly middle and upper class (Kivinen et al., 2017). Children who have parents in the top 1 per cent of income earners are 77 per cent more likely to attend an Ivy League university as compared to students in the bottom-income quintile (Chetty et al., 2017). Top-ranked institutions increasingly reinforce each other by stating in postings for faculty that applicants should be from a top globally ranked, world-class institution or implicitly making the assumption that applicants from top-ranked institutions are the most qualified (Smyth, 2017).

Education at a top-ranked institution does not provide a level playing field to graduates. Those who come in with high levels of capital maintain their advantage over those who come in with less (Bourdieu & Passeron, 1977). Today university leaders frequently recognize the limitations of rankings while often believing they have no choice but to participate (Athavale et al., 2017). Since the late twentieth century, much of the higher education world dealt with significant cuts in public funding and enrolment increases; these were paired with government demands for universities to partner with industry to serve the knowledge economy (Gopaul et al., 2016). Within this context, Mennicken et al. (2018) argue that rankings make efforts to increase socio-economic and racial diversity less critical than achievement in ranking metrics.

The Big Three privilege research over teaching, and therefore academics who are seen as research productive garner incentives that those who excel in teaching or other forms of community engagement do not, which can entrench gender disparities. Kwiek (2019), for example, found that young female academics spend 8.1 more hours on teaching per week than do men. Men garner more research grants early in their career, which sets them up for more grants. Due to structural discrimination (e.g., expectation of higher service and teaching loads), females are less likely to garner this initial research grant success, and this will affect them throughout their career.

Miguel Lim (2017) shows how higher education rankers become seen as experts through events including the Times Higher Education Summit, where university leaders have opportunities to learn how to improve their rankings. Rankers frame problems in higher education and market their branding and software products as solutions aimed at giving universities the information they need to improve their rankings, including metrics to evaluate faculty based on publication in high-impact English-speaking journals, industry funding, and enhancing reputation through branding. Lim (2018) points to the different business models used by rankers to sell products to different audiences. Already prestigious institutions receive external legitimacy through rankings (Stensaker et al., 2019).

Espeland et al. (2016) argue that "governing by numbers" has turned universities into "engines of anxiety" that impact organizational structures, those selected to attend certain law schools, and professional opportunities. Locke (2014) maintains that a focus on rankings can divert attention away from improving education and towards an emphasis on spending time and money on building reputations. Highly ranked universities hire based on research abilities, not teaching (Altbach, 2012), which can result in teaching and learning being devalued (Moosa, 2018). The focus on performative metrics such as the h-index and rankings can lead to a focus on identity management that impacts the academic's sense of self, research questions, and relationships with peers (Clarke & Knights, 2015; Gruber, 2014).

Esposito and Stark (2019) point to the need to move beyond arguing about the objectivity of rankings to understanding that what makes them powerful is not whether they are correct but whether they are seen as credible by readers and their social networks (p. 10).

There are global trends, but it is important to remember differences within and across contexts as well. Musselin (2009), for example, points to the different roles of government in France, Germany, and the US. In Germany academics are federal civil servants and pay for the most part is set by government. In France professors are paid based on a national salary grid. Conversely, the US is market driven and professors are paid "market price" based on what departments see as similar pay. Compared to jurisdictions such as Germany, the US and China are highly vertically stratified, and resources flow more freely to those institutions at the top (Finkelstein & Jones, 2019). In this part of the book, Mayumi Ishikawa expands on her pioneering scholarship concerning rankings. In her chapter, she provides an analysis of the power of university rankings not just on higher education but on government policy and job prospects for Japanese graduates as well. She explains that until recently faculty at Japanese universities were trained in Japan, but there are new pressures for graduate students to become part of the global elite structure of education to be competitive with those who graduate from highly ranked universities. Graduates from "branded universities" can enjoy privileges over locally educated elites in increasingly globalized labour markets.

Gary R.S. Barron points to the ways that universities change how they come to know themselves by aligning the data they collect to that used by rankers, but this is not all-encompassing. He shows how a university may collect data aligned to become part of the "global ranking assemblage" but also maintain data collection and analysis focused on local actors.

Nathan C. Hall explores an area in which there is a dearth of research – rankings and mental health. He points to the extensive literature on the psychology of university recruitment concerning rankings but a lack of empirical studies looking at rankings pertaining to the mental health of students and faculty. He proposes, based on his pilot data, that the well-being of staff and students is related to the rankings of their respective universities. He argues that assessing a university should include the quality of life, motivation, and emotional well-being of faculty and graduate students.

Rankings permeate society. The question is who decides what to measure and what do these decisions mean for how we deal with the "wicked problems" (Rittel & Webber, 1973) of today and educate the next generations of leaders, builders, health care professionals, researchers, artists, scholars, educators, and scientists of tomorrow. The aim of this book is to facilitate public conversations about the role of the rankings industry in framing what a good education is and to imagine alternatives.

REFERENCES

Alberts, B. (2013, May). Impact factor distortions. *Science, 340,* 787. https://doi.org/10.1126/science.1240319. https://science.sciencemag.org/content/340/6134/787/tab-pdf

Altbach, P.G. (2012). The globalization of college and university rankings. *Change: The Magazine of Higher Learning, 44*(1), 31. https://doi.org/10.1080/00091383.2012.636001

Athavale, M., Bott, J., Myring, M., & Richardson, L. (2017). Deans' perceptions of published rankings of business programs. *Journal of Education for Business, 92*(2), 81–8. https://doi.org/10.1080/08832323.2017.1289885

Badat, S. (2010). Global rankings of universities: A perverse and present burden. In E. Unterhalter & V. Carpentier (Eds.), *Global inequalities and higher education: Whose interests are we serving?* (pp. 117–41). Palgrave Macmillan.

Barnard, B. (2018, 28 September). End college rankings: An open letter to the owners and editors of U.S. News and World Report. *Forbes*. https://www.forbes.com/sites /brennanbarnard/2018/09/28/end-college-rankings-an-open-letter-to-the-owners -and-editors-of-u-s-news-and-world-report

Bhattacharjee, Y. (2011). Saudi universities offer cash in exchange for academic prestige. *Science, 334*(6061), 1344–5. https://doi.org/10.1126/science.334.6061.1344. Medline: 22158799

Bouchard, J. (2017). Academic media ranking and the configurations of values in higher education: A sociotechnical history of a co-production in France between the media, state and higher education (1976–1989). *Higher Education; Dordrecht, 73*(6), 947–62. https://doi.org/10.1007/s10734-017-0121-5

Bourdieu, P., & Passeron, J.C. (1977). *Reproduction in education, society and culture.* Sage.

Boussebaa, M., & Tienari, J. (2019, 6 March). Englishization and the politics of knowledge production in management studies. *Journal of Management Inquiry*. https://doi.org/10.1177/1056492619835314

Bowman, N.A., & Bastedo, M.N. (2011). Anchoring effects in world university rankings: Exploring biases in reputation scores. *Higher Education, 61*(4), 431–44. https://doi.org/10.1007/s10734-010-9339-1

Cantwell, B. (2016). The geopolitics of the education market. In E. Hazelkorn (Ed.), *Global rankings and the geopolitics of higher education* (ch. 18). Routledge. https:// doi.org/10.4324/9781315738550

Cantwell, B. (2018). High participation systems of higher education. In B. Cantwell, S. Marginson, & A. Smolenteseva (Eds.), *High participation systems of higher education* (pp. 3–38). Oxford University Press.

Casadevall, A., & Fang, F.C. (2017). Reply to Argüelles and Argüelles-Prieto, "Are the editors responsible for our obsession with the impact factor?" *MBio, 8*(6). https:// doi.org/10.1128/mBio.02079-17

Challenge Success. (2018). A "fit" over rankings: Why college engagement matters more than selectivity. Stanford Graduate School of Education. https://ed.stanford .edu/sites/default/files/challenge_success_white_paper_on_college_admissions _10.1.2018-reduced.pdf

Chetty, R., Friedman, J., Saez, E., Turner, N., & Yagan, D. (2017). Mobility report cards: The role of colleges in intergenerational mobility. National Bureau of Economic Research working paper 23618. https://doi.org/10.3386/w23618

Clarke, C.A., & Knights, D. (2015). Careering through academia: Securing identities or engaging ethical subjectivities? *Human Relations, 68*(12), 1865–88. https://doi .org/10.1177/0018726715570978

Douglass, J.A. (2016). How rankings came to determine world class. In J.A. Douglass (Ed.), *The New Flagship University* (pp. 9–29). Palgrave Macmillan. https://doi .org/10.1057/9781137500496_1

Espeland, W.N., Sauder, M., & Espeland, W. (2016). *Engines of anxiety: Academic rankings, reputation, and accountability*. Russell Sage Foundation.

Esposito, E., & Stark, D. (2019). What's observed in a rating? Rankings as orientation in the face of uncertainty. *Theory, Culture & Society, 36*(4), 3–26. https://doi.org/10.1177/0263276419826276

Evans, C. (2019, 21 June). A year after rankings scandal, Fox dean pushes for transparency and stability. *Temple News*. https://temple-news.com/a-year-after-rankings-scandal-fox-dean-pushes-for-transparency-and-stability

Finkelstein, M.J., & Jones, G.A. (2019). *Professorial pathways: Academic careers in a global perspective*. Johns Hopkins University Press.

Fowles, J., Frederickson, H.G., & Koppell, J.G.S. (2016). University rankings: Evidence and a conceptual framework. *Public Administration Review, 76*(5), 790–803. https://doi.org/10.1111/puar.12610

Gallup-Purdue. (2014). The 2015 Gallup-Purdue Index.

Gingras, Y. (2016). *Bibliometrics and research evaluation*. MIT Press.

Gingras, Y., & Khelfaoui, M. (2018). Assessing the effect of the United States' "citation advantage" on other countries' scientific impact as measured in the Web of Science (WoS) database. *Scientometrics, 114*(2), 517–32. https://doi.org/10.1007/s11192-017-2593-6

Gonzales, L.D., & Waugaman, C. (2016). Embedded colonial power: How global ranking systems set parameters for the recognition of knowers, knowledge, and the production of knowledge. In K. Downing & F.A. Ganotice Jr. (Eds.), *World university rankings and the future of higher education* (pp. 302–27). IGI Global. https://doi.org/10.4018/978-1-5225-0819-9.ch016

Gopaul, B., Jones, G.A., Weinrib, J., Metcalfe, A., Fisher, D., Gingras, Y., & Rubenson, K. (2016). The academic profession in Canada: Perceptions of Canadian university faculty about research and teaching. *Canadian Journal of Higher Education, 46*(2), 55–77. http://search.proquest.com/docview/1824508712/abstract/894CAADE8A47 4BB4PQ/1

Gruber, T. (2014). Academic sell-out: How an obsession with metrics and rankings is damaging academia. *Journal of Marketing for Higher Education, 24*(2), 165–77. https://doi.org/10.1080/08841241.2014.970248

Guraya, S.Y., Norman, R.I., Khoshhal, K.I., Guraya, S.S., & Forgione, A. (2016). Publish or perish mantra in the medical field: A systematic review of the reasons, consequences and remedies. *Pakistan Journal of Medical Sciences, 32*(6), 1562–7. https://doi.org/10.12669/pjms.326.10490. Medline:28083065

Hall, C.M., & Page, S.J. (2015). Following the impact factor: Utilitarianism or academic compliance? *Tourism Management, 51*, 309–12. https://doi.org/10.1016/j.tourman.2015.05.013

Hazelkorn, E. (2015, January). The obsession with rankings in tertiary education: Implications for public policy [Conference paper]. World Bank, Washington, DC.

Holon IQ. (2018, 3 June). *$10 trillion global education market in 2030*. HolonIQ. https://www.holoniq.com/2030/10-trillion-global-education-market

Hosier, M., & Hoolash, B.K.A. (2017). The effect of methodological variations on university rankings and associated decision-making and policy. *Studies in Higher Education, 44*(1), 201–14. https://doi.org/10.1080/03075079.2017.1356282

Ishikawa, M. (2009). University rankings, global models, and emerging hegemony critical analysis from Japan. *Journal of Studies in International Education, 13*(2), 159–73. https://doi.org/10.1177/1028315308330853

Jaschik, S. (2018, 10 July). Lies, damn lies and rankings. *Inside Higher Ed.* https://www.insidehighered.com/news/2018/07/10/temple-ousts-business-dean-after-report-finds-online-mba-program-years-submitted

Kauppi, N. (2018). The global ranking game: Narrowing academic excellence through numerical objectification. *Studies in Higher Education, 43*(10), 1750–62. https://doi.org/10.1080/03075079.2018.1520416

Kehm, B.M. (2014). Global university rankings – impacts and unintended side effects. *European Journal of Education, 49*(1), 102–12. https://doi.org/10.1111/ejed.12064

Kivinen, O., & Hedman, J. (2008). World-wide university rankings: A Scandinavian approach. *Scientometrics, 74*(3), 391–408. https://doi.org/10.1007/s11192-007-1820-y

Kivinen, O., Hedman, J., & Artukka, K. (2017). Scientific publishing and global university rankings: How well are top publishing universities recognized? *Scientometrics,* 1–17. Retrieved from http://link.springer.com.ezproxy.library.ubc.ca/article/10.1007/s11192-017-2403-1

Kwiek, M. (2019). *Changing European academics: A comparative study of social stratification, work patterns and research productivity*. Routledge.

Larivière, V., Haustein, S., & Mongeon, P. (2015). The oligopoly of academic publishers in the digital era. *PLOS ONE, 10*(6), e0127502. https://doi.org/10.1371/journal.pone.0127502. Medline:26061978

Lim, M.A. (2017). The building of weak expertise: The work of global university rankers. *Higher Education, 75*(3), 415–30. https://doi.org/10.1007/s10734-017-0147-8

Lim, M.A. (2018, 28 September). University rankings: How do they compare and what do they mean for students? *The Conversation.* http://theconversation.com/university-rankings-how-do-they-compare-and-what-do-they-mean-for-students-104011

Locke, W. (2014). The intensification of rankings logic in an increasingly marketised higher education environment. *European Journal of Education, 49*(1), 77–90. https://doi.org/10.1111/ejed.12060

Lynch, K. (2014). New managerialism, neoliberalism and ranking. *Ethics in Science and Environmental Politics, 13*(2), 141–53. https://doi.org/10.3354/esep00137

Marginson, S. (2014). University rankings and social science. *European Journal of Education, 49*(1), 45–59. https://doi.org/10.1111/ejed.12061

Mennicken, A., Musselin, C., & Fourcade, M. (2018). Wendy Espeland and Michael Sauder, *Engines of anxiety: Academic rankings, reputation, and accountability*. New York, NY, Russell Sage Foundation, 2016. *Socio-Economic Review, 16*(1), 207–18. https://doi.org/10.1093/ser/mwx044

Merton, R.K. (1968). The Matthew effect in science: The reward and communication systems of science are considered. *Science, 159*(3810), 56–63. https://doi.org /10.1126/science.159.3810.56

Mittelman, J.H. (2017). *Implausible dream*. Princeton University Press.

Moosa, R. (2018). World university rankings: Reflections on teaching and learning as the Cinderella function in the South African higher education system. *African Journal of Business Ethics, 12*(1), 38–59. https://doi.org/10.15249/12-1-165

Morrison, H. (2015). Open access to scholarly knowledge: The new commons. In P.W. Elliott & D.H. Hepting (Eds.), *Free knowledge: Confronting the commodification of human discovery* (pp. 256–66). University of Regina Press.

Morse, R., Mason, M., & Brooks, E. (2018, 22 August). Updates to 8 schools' 2018 best colleges rankings data. *US News & World Report*. https://www.usnews.com /education/blogs/college-rankings-blog/articles/2018-08-22/updates-to-8-schools -2018-best-colleges-rankings-data

Muller, S.M. (2017). Academics as rent seekers: Distorted incentives in higher education, with reference to the South African case. *International Journal of Educational Development, 52*, 58–67. https://doi.org/10.1016/j.ijedudev.2016.11.004

Musselin, C. (2009). *The market for academics*. Routledge. https://doi.org/10.4324 /9780203863060

Mustajoki, A. (2013). Measuring excellence in social sciences and humanities: Limitations and opportunities. In T. Erkkilä (Ed.), *Global university rankings: Challenges for European higher education* (pp. 147–65). Palgrave Macmillan. https:// doi.org/10.1057/9781137296870_9

Nguyen, V.T. (2019, 19 March). Perspective: College admissions are corrupt because universities are. Here's how to fix them. *Washington Post*. https://www.washingtonpost .com/outlook/2019/03/19/college-admissions-are-corrupt-because-universities-are -heres-how-fix-them

Olcay, G.A., & Bulu, M. (2017). Is measuring the knowledge creation of universities possible? A review of university rankings. *Technological Forecasting and Social Change, 123*, 153–60. https://doi.org/10.1016/j.techfore.2016.03.029

O'Neil, C. (2017). *Weapons of math destruction: How big data increases inequality and threatens democracy*. Broadway Books.

Ordorika, I., & Lloyd, M. (2013). A decade of international university rankings: A critical perspective from Latin America. In P.T.M. Marope, P.J. Wells, & E. Hazelkorn (Eds.), *Rankings and accountability in higher education: Uses and misuses* (pp. 209–31). Be Press.

Paradeise, C., & Thoenig, J.-C. (2013). Academic institutions in search of quality: Local orders and global standards. *Organization Studies, 34*(2), 189–218. https://doi .org/10.1177/0170840612473550

Peters, M.A. (2019). Global university rankings: Metrics, performance, governance. *Educational Philosophy and Theory, 51*(1), 5–13. https://doi.org/10.1080/00131857 .2017.1381472

Pierce, B. (2010). *A history of Harvard University: From its foundation, in the year 1636, to the period of the American Revolution.* Kessinge Publishing.

Pusser, B., & Marginson, S. (2013). University rankings in critical perspective. *Journal of Higher Education, 84*(4), 544–68. https://doi.org/10.1353/jhe.2013.0022

Richards, D.A.R., Awokoya, J.T., Bridges, B.K., & Clark, C. (2018). One size does not fit all: A critical race theory perspective on college rankings. *Review of Higher Education, 42*(1), 269–312. https://doi.org/10.1353/rhe.2018.0030

Rieder, B., Matamoros-Fernández, A., & Coromina, Ò. (2018). From ranking algorithms to "ranking cultures": Investigating the modulation of visibility in YouTube search results. *Convergence, 24*(1), 50–68. https://doi.org/10.1177 /1354856517736982

Rittel, H.W.J., & Webber, M.M. (1973). Dilemmas in a general theory of planning. *Policy Sciences, 4,* 155–69.

Robertson, S.L., & Olds, K. (2016, 18 November). Rankings as global (monetising) scopic systems. In E. Hazelkorn (Ed.), *Global rankings and the geopolitics of higher education* (ch. 3). Routledge. https://doi.org/10.4324/9781315738550

Sadlak, J. (2014). University rankings: The manifestation and driver of competition for excellence within the new higher-education landscape. In P. Mattei (Ed.), *University adaptation in difficult economic times* (ch. 8). https://doi.org/10.1093/acprof:oso /9780199989393.003.0008

Schekman, R. (2013, 9 December). How journals like *Nature, Cell* and *Science* are damaging science. *Guardian.* https://www.theguardian.com/commentisfree/2013 /dec/09/how-journals-nature-science-cell-damage-science

Scholars at Risk. (2019a, 13 December). SAR's response to the US executive order titled "Combating Anti-Semitism." Scholars at Risk. https://www.scholarsatrisk .org/2019/12/sars-response-to-the-us-executive-order-titled-combating-anti -semitism

Scholars at Risk. (2019b). Free to think 2019. Scholars at Risk.

Schultz, M., Mouritsen, J., & Gorm, G. (2001). Sticky reputation: Analyzing a ranking system. *Corporate Reputation Review, 4*(1), 24–41. https://doi.org/10.1057/palgrave .crr.1540130

Smyth, J. (2017). *The toxic university: Zombie leadership. academic rock stars, and neoliberal ideology.* Palgrave Macmillan. https://doi.org/10.1057/978-1-137 -54968-6

Stack, M. (2016). *Global university rankings and the mediatization of higher education.* Palgrave Macmillan. https://doi.org/10.1057/9781137475954

Stack, M. (2019). Academic stars and university rankings in higher education: Impacts on policy and practice. *Policy Reviews in Higher Education, 4*(1), 4–24. https://doi.org /10.1080/23322969.2019.1667859

Stensaker, B., Lee, J.J., Rhoades, G., Ghosh, S., Castiello-Gutiérrez, S., Vance, H., …
Peel, C. (2019). Stratified university strategies: The shaping of institutional
legitimacy in a global perspective. *Journal of Higher Education, 90*(4), 539–62.
https://doi.org/10.1080/00221546.2018.1513306

Taylor, M., Perakakis, P., Trachana, V., & Gialis, S. (2014). Rankings are the sorcerer's
new apprentice. *Ethics in Science and Environmental Politics, 13*(2), 73–99. https://
doi.org/10.3354/esep00146

Teferra, D. (Ed.). (2017). *Flagship universities in Africa*. Palgrave Macmillan. http://
www.palgrave.com/de/book/9783319494029

Tennant, J. (2018). Democratising knowledge: A report on the scholarly publisher,
Elsevier. *Education International*. https://issuu.com/educationinternational/docs
/2018_eiresearch_elsevier_final_en

Tilak, J.B.G. (2016). Global rankings, world-class universities and dilemmas in higher
education policy in India. *Higher Education for the Future, 3*(2), 126–43. https://doi
.org/10.1177/2347631116648515

Usher, A. (2015, 25 September). University rankings and the eugenics movement.
HESA. http://higheredstrategy.com/university-rankings-and-the-eugenics-movement

Verger, A., Steiner-Khamsi, G., & Lubienski, C. (2017). The emerging global education
industry: Analysing market-making in education through market sociology.
Globalisation, Societies and Education, 15(3), 325–40. https://doi.org/10.1080/14767
724.2017.1330141

Vernon, M.M., Balas, E.A., & Momani, S. (2018). Are university rankings useful to
improve research? A systematic review. *PLOS ONE, 13*(3), e0193762. https://doi
.org/10.1371/journal.pone.0193762. Medline:29513762

Wells, R. (2015). "Those that have most money must have least learning":
Undergraduate education at the University of Oxford in the eighteenth and early
nineteenth centuries. In A. Simões, M.P. Diogo, & K. Gavroglu (Eds.), *Sciences in
the universities of Europe, nineteenth and twentieth centuries: Academic landscapes*
(pp. 11–29). https://doi.org/10.1007/978-94-017-9636-1_2

Wilder, C. (2013). *Ebony and ivy: Race, slavery, and the troubled history of America's
universities*. Bloomsbury Academic.

Yeung, R., Gigliotti, P., & Nguyen-Hoang, P. (2019). The impact of U.S. News College
Rankings on the compensation of college and university presidents. *Research in
Higher Education, 60*(1), 1–17. https://doi.org/10.1007/s11162-018-9501-7

Zapp, M., & Ramirez, F. (2019). Beyond internationalisation and isomorphism – the
construction of a global higher education regime. *Comparative Education, 55*(4),
473–93. https://doi.org/10.1080/03050068.2019.1638103

Zhang, M., & Grieneisen, M.L. (2013). The impact of misconduct on the published
medical and non-medical literature, and the news media. *Scientometrics*, 96, 573–87.
https://doi.org/10.1007/s11192-012-0920-5

Zhou, Z. (2014). The SSCI syndrome in higher education: A local or global
phenomenon. http://public.eblib.com/choice/publicfullrecord.aspx?p=1697612

THEME 1

Geopolitics, Rankings, and Journal Impact Factors

The chapters in this section point to the ways in which global university rankings interact with media, government rankings, and regional geopolitics. The authors demonstrate the need to understand rankings as a global phenomenon that requires a nuanced analysis regarding how rankings operate in different locations. Marion Lloyd and Imanol Ordorika, for example, point to differences within Latin America. The former president of Chile focused plans on providing free education at the higher education level and a more equitable system. Conversely, the Ecuadoran government focused on funding a relatively small number of students to attend top-fifty globally ranked universities. Creso M. Sá, Nadiia Kachynska, Emma Sabzalieva, and Magdalena Martinez show how the accepted symbol of rankings was used to implement an anti-corruption index of higher education institutions in Kazakhstan with the intention of being seen as a "world education space." Riyad A. Shahjahan, Annabelle Estera, and Vivek Vellanki argue that rankings come to be normalized in different contexts not merely through printed text but also through visuals that reinforce a colonial geopolitics of knowledge. All three chapters address regions that are under-represented in critical literature on rankings. Studies therefore show that rankings do not stand on their own but are part of wider policy and politics agendas, and as such, they seek to shape higher education in different directions.

1 International University Rankings as Cultural Imperialism: Implications for the Global South

MARION LLOYD AND IMANOL ORDORIKA

Introduction

When researchers in Shanghai unveiled the first international university ranking in 2003, the news was met with little fanfare. Few could have foreseen that, virtually overnight, the model would become a global phenomenon, shaping higher education policy everywhere from Beijing to Budapest to Brasilia (Marginson, 2007; Ordorika & Lloyd, 2013). Fifteen years later, however, the rankings are as influential as they are ubiquitous. At once mirroring and propagating broader hegemonic trends, they have generated an enormous – and, we argue in this chapter, highly problematic – impact on individual institutions and on national higher education systems as a whole.

In developing the pioneering Academic Ranking of World Universities (ARWU), researchers at Shanghai Jiao Tong University pursued primarily domestic goals (Liu & Cheng, 2005). In 1998, then president Jiang Zemin announced Project 985, which sought to create a system of "world-class" universities in China. As part of those efforts, the government set out to determine how Chinese universities stacked up against the global standard-bearers, particularly those in the United States and Europe. The resulting ranking formed part of a broader strategy to bolster scientific research and fuel economic growth in the country. However, the model would soon be replicated far beyond national borders, with major implications for institutions throughout the world.

In 2004, the *Times Higher Education* magazine supplement (THE) created its own international ranking in conjunction with the British firm Quacquarelli Symonds (QS). Then, in 2009, the two companies parted ways and began producing rival rankings. Today, there are some twenty international league tables – evidence of the growing demand for the systems in an increasingly globalized and competitive higher education market (*The Economist*, 2018).

While national or regional tables have existed for several decades in the English-speaking world (Turner, 2005; Webster, 1986), the impact of the international rankings – and ARWU, THE, and QS, in particular – has become particularly significant in influencing policymakers in many countries. Despite the considerable variations in their methodologies and results (both among rankings and from year to year), the systems are portrayed as objective measures of the overall quality of universities (Lloyd et al., 2011; Marginson, 2012; Ordorika & Lloyd, 2013). In practice, however, the rankings serve as *Harvardo-meters*, measuring how closely institutions adhere to a sole model of higher education – that of the elite, Anglo-Saxon research university, of which Harvard is the premier example (Ordorika, 2011).

The rankings phenomenon has prompted a large body of research, a majority of which focuses on the systems' impact on policy (Ehrenberg, 2004; Dill, 2006; Ordorika & Lloyd, 2013, 2015) and their methodological limitations and short-comings (Florian, 2007; Ishikawa, 2009; Jaienski, 2009; Ordorika & Rodríguez, 2010; Van Raan, 2005; Ying & Jingao, 2009). There is also a growing literature that analyses the rankings from a critical theoretical perspective; such studies tend to focus on the role of the classification systems in replicating and further-ing neo-liberal policy agendas within higher education (Hazelkorn, 2007, 2008; Marginson 2012; Marginson & Ordorika, 2011; Pusser & Marginson, 2012).

In this chapter, we contribute to the theoretical debate over the international university rankings by employing critical perspectives that view higher educa-tion as a *field of power* (Bourdieu, 2008) and *conflict* (Ordorika, 2003). We dem-onstrate how the hierarchical systems play a role in assigning value, in effect endorsing certain aspects of universities (scientific production and prestige) over others (their role in promoting more equitable and democratic societies). The process, we argue, is a form of what Bourdieu and Wacquant (1999) have termed "cultural imperialism," in which particularisms resulting from a specific national context are presented and imposed as universal standards.

Secondly, by providing examples from regions as disparate as Europe, Asia, and Latin America, we show how the classification systems' influence extends far beyond educational policy arenas and across a wide range of cultural and political contexts. Instead, we view the rankings as fundamental agents in the broader contest for cultural hegemony on a global scale. The implications of that struggle for hegemony are particularly significant for Latin America and other parts of the so-called Global South, where institutions are forced to compete on an uneven playing field while adhering to rules determined in the Global North.

We begin by outlining our theoretical frame, which posits the rankings as key tools in furthering the hegemony of the US-based model of higher education. We then discuss the logic of the rankings, as both products of the new market-driven, managerial culture in higher education and actors in its propagation throughout the world. Next, we analyse the ways in which the systems foment social exclusion and inequality and exacerbate North-South dichotomies through the imposition of an arbitrary set of norms (Bourdieu & Passeron, 1981), to the detriment of local and national priorities. Finally, we review the impact of the rankings paradigm on government and institutional policies in Europe, Asia, and Latin America.

By encouraging countries to emulate a sole, hegemonic model of institution, the rankings ignore national and regional traditions in higher education while undercutting local development priorities. In Latin America, for instance, the systems do not account for institutions' broader contributions to society as "state-building universities," a regional tradition that has no equivalent in the English-speaking world (Ordorika & Pusser, 2007). Institutions that adhere to this model are characterized by "autonomy, democracy and co-government, the development of science and knowledge, academic freedom, and, above all, the assumption on the part of the university of political responsibility for nation-building and the defense of democracy" (Ordorika, 2018). With the exception of research production, none of those attributes are measured by the rankings.

Nor is the process value-neutral. The rankings promote a neo-liberal, market-oriented logic, which views higher education as a competitive sphere (Marginson & Ordorika, 2011). Institutions must vie for access to funding (both public and private) and students (who are increasingly seen as customers) in order to survive in an increasingly fierce global market. Furthermore, in relying almost exclusively on easily quantifiable data, the rankings assign greater value to certain areas of university activities; for instance, they prioritize research over teaching and the hard sciences over the humanities – hierarchies which are largely arbitrary in nature.

Much more is at stake than national or institutional pride. In establishing a single, hegemonic gold standard for higher education, the rankings have fuelled a global "academic arms race" (Ehrenberg, 2004; Dill, 2006) among institutions and nations. Countries as diverse as China, France, and Brazil (Huang, 2017; Lloyd, 2017; Ordorika & Lloyd, 2013) have invested billions of dollars in remaking their higher education systems, in a largely fruitless bid to catch up to the global standard-bearers. In doing so, they have adopted, often uncritically, a single notion of "excellence" (Readings, 1996); this concept, in turn, is deeply infused with a specific set of cultural norms and priorities.

The process is a manifestation of what Bourdieu and Wacquant (1999) have termed US-based "cultural imperialism," which "rests on the power to universalize particularisms linked to a singular historical tradition by causing them to be misrecognized as such" (1999, p. 41). In this way, "numerous topics directly issuing from the intellectual confrontations relating to the social particularity of American society and of its universities have been imposed, in apparently de-historicized form, upon the whole planet" (Bourdieu & Wacquant, 1999, p. 41). Examples range from the now-ubiquitous merit-pay systems for university professors and researchers to the push to create "world-class universities" in some of the world's poorest regions.

An apparent irony of this process is the fact that the most influential international rankings are produced outside the United States, in effect inadvertently propagating US cultural hegemony throughout the world. Meanwhile, in the US context, domestic rankings carry far more sway; in recent years, more than a dozen universities have acknowledged inflating the data they provide to the highly influential *U.S. News & World Report* ranking to improve their standing in the competitive US market (Jaschek, 2018). Nonetheless, the influence of the American model on the methodologies of the international rankings is undeniable. The systems privilege indicators that are characteristic of or even unique to the US context – for example, the number of publications in English-language journals or the level of patent production by universities.

Still, the rankings paradigm is facing significant resistance in many parts of the world. Critics from Johannesburg to Mexico City are questioning the neutrality of the systems and their outsized role in dictating policy in areas ranging from higher education to immigration (Ambrus, 2012). In the process, they are challenging dominant cultural dogma, defined by Bourdieu and Wacquant (1999) as "these commonplaces, in the Aristotelian sense of notions or theses with which one argues, but about which one does not argue" (p. 42).

The debate reflects dual and often conflicting goals for tertiary education: on the part of the government and industry, of creating a globalized workforce that can compete in the knowledge economy, and social demands for more equitable and mass access to higher education as a mechanism for upward mobility (Labaree, 1997). The outcome of that contest is likely to have far-reaching consequences in shaping the dominant cultural and economic paradigms of the twenty-first century.

The Ideological Debate

More than three decades ago, Altbach (1987) identified five elements that contribute to the competitive advantages of universities in the United States and Europe (and Great Britain, in particular) vis-à-vis their counterparts in the Global South. These are: the modern university as a Western tradition; the dominance of the English language; the uneven distribution of research capacities; the control over knowledge dissemination; and the "brain drain." That model is even more relevant today in the context of globalization and the "knowledge society." In both cases, universities are seen as playing a critical role and thus are subjected to unprecedented scrutiny. However, as the dominance of the US institutions in the international rankings reveals, the playing field is far from even.

By projecting the Anglo-Saxon model of the elite research institution as the ideal to follow, the rankings effectively reward those institutions that most closely adhere to a set of essentially arbitrary norms (Bourdieu & Passeron, 1981). An example is the preference given to publishing in English-language journals, which favours not only English speakers but also researchers in the hard sciences, given the greater number of journals (and thus citations) in those fields. For instance, in Scopus, the database consulted by most of the main rankings, 49 per cent of citations are of publications in the life sciences and medicine, followed by the natural sciences (27 per cent) and engineering and technology (17 per cent); meanwhile, the social sciences and humanities represent just 6 per cent and 1 per cent of citations, respectively (QS, 2015). In 2015, the QS ranking introduced a weighting system to correct for some of those imbalances among research fields, but science-heavy institutions continue to have a competitive advantage (the top-ranked institution in 2020 was the Massachusetts Institute of Technology, MIT) (QS, 2020).

As a result, many governments have prioritized programs in the STEM fields (science, technology, engineering, and math), whose scientific output is more visible on a global scale. A key example is Brazil's Scientific Mobility Program, which spent $3.5 billion to send more than 100,000 STEM students to study at top-ranked universities – a majority of them in the United States – between 2012 and 2017 (Caldeira, 2017).

Meanwhile, disciplines deemed less "profitable" in the global economy are suffering from neglect. In 2015, twenty-six national universities in Japan announced plans to close or scale back their humanities and social science faculties in order to "serve areas that better meet society's needs" (Grove, 2015). The move affected programs in nearly half the sixty national universities offering such courses.

Furthermore, the rankings have both highlighted and exacerbated the inequalities among institutions and national systems (Marginson, 2016). For instance, highly placed institutions are more likely to attract international scholars and students, an indicator that in turn increases their standing in the QS and THE rankings. The same is true in the case of government funding strategies. As we will show further on in this chapter, many governments divert scarce funding towards their most highly ranked institutions, in a bid to improve their standing, in turn bolstering the prestige of the country's higher education system on a regional or global level. The result is a manifestation of the "Matthew effect," in which the rules of the game tend to favour past winners, further increasingly their power and prestige.

The competitive logic of the rankings is in turn a reflection of broader neo-liberal policies, first championed by the United States and Britain in the 1980s and later adopted by governments throughout the world. These include major reductions in government funding and the decline of the public sphere in general (Boggs, 1997; Pusser, 2012), which has been replaced by notions of individual responsibility and what Slaughter and Leslie (1999) have termed "academic capitalism." Other changes include the new "audit culture" (Apple, 2007), flexibility and quality control, diminished institutional autonomy, and increased emphasis on knowledge production and industry collaboration. The emphasis on accountability has fuelled societal demands for access to information in both the public and private spheres. As a result, universities have faced growing pressure to develop instruments to measure, classify, and track their performance in academic and administrative areas (Bolseguí & Fuguet, 2006; Elliott, 2002; Power, 1997).

The new administrative logic has also weakened traditional academic hierarchies and communities, while undermining collegial bodies and practices. Other changes in recent decades include the massification of enrolments, the indiscriminate dissemination of knowledge via the internet, and the incorporation of non-university institutions, particularly those operating for profit, into broader higher education systems (Ordorika & Rodríguez, 2010). In that context, rankings have introduced new, external measures of academic hierarchy. The shift has profound implications, including a loss of autonomy for individual institutions and higher education systems and a tendency towards the homogenization of priorities and goals, at the expense of locally determined agendas.

Proponents of the rankings argue that this shift is both necessary and desirable. In their view, it is in the interest of higher education institutions, governments, publishers, scientific communities, and other relevant actors to agree on classification criteria that are based on common ideals and academic values in order to compete in the global knowledge economy (Ordorika & Rodríguez, 2010). In reality, however, the ranking methodologies are steeped in the norms and values of the dominant cultures. Central to those values is the cult of "meritocracy," in which outcomes are confused with intrinsic worth (whether on an individual or institutional level), at the expense of equality and equity (Marginson, 2016).

Critics of the rankings, meanwhile, argue the need for culturally sensitive approaches to evaluating the quality of institutions, ones that consider regional and national higher education traditions. In Latin America, where scholars and university rectors have criticized the influence of the rankings in shaping government policies (*Final Declaration*, 2012), there is a long tradition of "state-building universities" (Ordorika & Pusser, 2007). While such institutions have played a key role in designing government institutions, training government workers, and tackling national problems, their contributions are not considered in the rankings. An alternative in the US context is the *Washington Monthly* ranking, which rates universities based on "what they do for the country"; indicators include the percentage of low-income students and those enrolled in military training programs, as well as graduation rates for federal grant recipients (*Washington Monthly*, 2018).

The main international rankings also fuel the privatizing trend in higher education worldwide, by rewarding attributes that are characteristic of the top private institutions in the United States: high tuition and large endowments; highly competitive selection processes, for both students and faculty; and a heavy emphasis on research, ideally leading to industrial patents and other profit-making ventures (Ordorika & Lloyd, 2013). It is no coincidence that only one public institution – the University of California–Los Angeles – made it into the top twenty spots in the 2021 edition of *U.S. News & World Report*'s National University Rankings, the grandfather of the national league tables (*U.S. News*, 2020). The same can be said for the majority of the international rankings; almost without exception, they are dominated by private institutions or public ones that charge far higher tuitions than their private counterparts in the developing world. For example, tuition (not counting room and board) at Berkeley ($14,300) and Oxford ($12,100) is more than twice that of the most expensive private universities in Mexico (University of California, Berkeley, 2020; Oxford University, 2020; *Universia*, 2020).

In some cases, the rankings have adopted an explicit stance in favour of private higher education. When analysing the outcome of their 2012 ranking of Latin American universities, the producers of QS cited the increasing presence of private universities among the top spots as the key to Brazil's dominance in the line-up. According to the company's analysis:

> Private investment in education seems to be the most reasonable way of increasing the proportion of overall national income invested in education. Likewise, collaborations between the private sector and higher education institutions, as well as the strengthening of connections between curriculum design and employers' requirements, should be perceived as important tools for improving productivity and creating more opportunities for enrolment in good quality tertiary education. (QS, 2012)

It is a ringing – and largely misleading – endorsement of the market's role in higher education. QS overlooks the fact that two-thirds of enrolment in Brazil is already concentrated in the private sector, much of it in poor-quality, for-profit institutions, while the bulk of research continues to be conducted in the public sector (Lloyd, 2013a). Furthermore, the company does not explain the discrepancy between its results and those of the Brazilian government or the other international rankings, in which the country's public institutions consistently occupy the top spots. For example, of the 179 graduate programs that earned a top score in the government rating system in 2017, only 14 were located at private universities (*O Globo*, 2017).

By recommending still greater private investment in the country's higher education system, the ranking company is staking its ground in one of the most critical debates facing the sector today: whether higher education constitutes a public or a private good. The implications of that policy trend extend far beyond higher education, encompassing the role of government and the state in promoting collective societal goals.

The rankings' methodologies also reflect an ideological shift within the United States in the post-Fordist period, with the demise of the welfare state and the introduction of individualistic and market-driven policies (Tauss, 2012). John Dewey's once-prevalent view of education as serving to promote upward mobility, democratic values, and social cohesion has been replaced by a new "neoliberal common sense in education" (Torres, 2013), whose main role is to fuel economic development by producing workers and technology for the new knowledge economy. As a result, universities are encouraged to prioritize research above other missions, such as teaching and outreach – a focus that is in turn rewarded by the rankings.

In that context, many states and institutions face pressure to conform to the US model, pushing them into conflict with their national and local priorities (Pusser, 2012). Those governments that aspire to see their universities appear among the top 100 in the international rankings must consider the economic and social implications. Almost without exception, the most highly ranked institutions are those with annual budgets exceeding $1 billion (Hazelkorn, 2008) and which derive at least part of their funding from private sources.

However, there is heated debate among academics and policymakers as to the pertinence and cost of attempting to transform institutions in the Global South into "world-class universities," a term favoured by the Shanghai Ranking and the World Bank (Salmi, 2009). As Altbach argued in 2003,

> A realistic and objective perspective is needed when thinking about world-class institutions of higher learning. For most countries, even large and relatively wealthy ones, only one or two world-class universities are possible or even desirable. For many countries, a world-class university is beyond the ability of the nation to support. Research universities are at the pinnacle of a differentiated academic system in a country – the rest of the system is just as important as its top. (p. 7)

Those arguments are even more relevant today, as a growing number of countries have set explicit goals for establishing world-class universities. Examples include economic powerhouses like Germany and France, the emerging BRICS countries (Brazil, Russia, India, China, and South Africa), East Asian countries such as Singapore, South Korea, and Taiwan, and even poorer countries such as Vietnam, Ghana, and Nigeria (Andoh, 2017; *The Economist*, 2018). In justifying channelling an ever-larger share of funding to a few leading institutions, many governments have cited their countries' poor showing in the international rankings – as if the classification tables were a goal unto themselves.

There are some exceptions, however. In Brazil, for instance, the left-leaning governments of Luiz Inácio Lula da Silva (2003–10) and Dilma Rousseff (2011–16) invested billions of dollars in a bid to increase both quality and equity across the entire higher education system (Lloyd, 2017). While not the explicit goal, those efforts helped cement the dominance of Brazilian institutions in the regional rankings; Brazilian institutions occupied seven of the top ten spots in the most recent *Times Higher Education* ranking for Latin America (*Times Higher Education* [THE], 2020).

Cultural Imperialism and Hegemony

At the root of the rankings' influence are their claims of objectivity. As previously mentioned, a majority relies heavily on internationally recognized measures of research production, such as the number of scholarly articles included in the Web of Science or Elsevier's Scopus databases. However, even those measures, which are clearly biased towards English-language publications, reflect the hegemony of the US higher education model – and of its elite institutions in particular. As Young (1990) argues in her defence of the "politics of difference," such "claims to impartiality feed cultural imperialism by allowing the particular experience and perspective of privileged groups to parade as universal" (p. 10).

In addition to political clout, cultural imperialism yields considerable economic rewards. By establishing themselves as the global standard-bearers, the institutions benefit from increasing numbers of foreign students and researchers; that trend, which has continued despite the Trump administration's anti-immigrant policies, in turn augments American institutions' prestige internationally. During the 2018–19 academic year, the number of foreign students attending US universities surpassed 1.1 million (Institute for International Education, 2019). Of those, more than half came from China (33.7 per cent) and India (18.4 per cent), emerging economies that have pumped billions of dollars into revamping their higher education systems, in part through training future academics and professionals in the world's top-ranked institutions.

In the case of China, the strategy is starting to pay off in terms of the increasing flow of international students to the country; between 2011 and 2016, the number of international students nearly doubled, from 292,000 to 443,000, and the number of long-term students more than quadrupled, from 75,000 to 333,000, according to official government statistics (China Power, 2018). Yet the US economy remains the biggest winner in the internationalization market; foreign students contributed an estimated $41 billion to the US economy in 2018–19 (National Association for Student Affairs Professionals, 2019).

However, it would be a mistake to interpret the adoption of the ranking paradigm as an intentional strategy or imposition on the part of policymakers in Washington or London. The process by which the systems have been normalized and replicated throughout the world is actually much subtler and thus harder to counteract. We argue that the hegemony of the rankings paradigm derives primarily from its incorporation into the dominant discourses within each society, through its adoption by government and university policymakers, the media, and the public at large.

While some countries have adopted alternative institutional paradigms, such as the Indigenous or intercultural universities created over the past two decades in Canada, Mexico, Bolivia, Ecuador, and elsewhere, such institutions remain the exception and face considerable hurdles. In Ecuador, for instance, the government closed down the Amawtay Wasi Intercultural University for Indigenous Peoples and Nations in 2013, arguing that it did not comply with minimum accreditation standards. The university reopened in 2018 after changing its status from a private to a public institution, bringing it under greater government control and scrutiny (Confederación de Nacionalidades Indígenas de Ecuador, 2018).

In higher education, hegemony is established through the construction of dominant views, as well as the framing of the field and its accepted discourses and notions. This occurs in a complex interaction between formal and cultural political processes and government and economic relations, both within institutions and in broader national and international contexts.

> Institutions in the strongest countries exercise power by forming widespread understandings of the nature and role of higher education, acceptable outcomes and processes, and the prevailing standards and norms. They frame the field itself, determining the conditions of interaction and the terms of competition. (Marginson & Ordorika, 2011 p. 82)

To the degree to which rankings inform government decisions about higher education, they "serve as a key source of power and legitimacy in broader state contests" (Pusser & Marginson, 2012, p. 98). At the same time, the rankings adopt a "disciplinary role" towards institutions that fall outside the established guidelines. This occurs through

> encouraging institutions in those nations – despite differences in resources, stage of development, national histories, traditions, languages, and cultures – to adopt the template of the globally dominant universities that lead rankings: comprehensive research-intensive institutions with selective admissions, emphasizing science and technology and elite professional schools. (Pusser & Marginson, 2012, p. 106)

The choice of indicators, in turn, reflects the dominant values systems that guide the US political and economic models. Bourdieu and Wacquant (1999) describe the process by which US values are projected as global standard-bearers:

> Thanks to a symbolic inversion based on the naturalization of the schemata of neo-liberal thought, whose dominance has been imposed for some 20 years by the relentless sniping of conservative think tanks and their allies in the political and journalistic fields ... the refashioning of social relations and cultural practices in advanced societies after the US pattern – founded on the pauperization of the state, the commodification of public goods and the generalization of social insecurity – is nowadays accepted with resignation as the inevitable outcome of the evolution of nations, when it is not celebrated with a sheepish enthusiasm. (p. 42)

By adopting the criteria and results of the rankings, higher education institutions and government policymakers are affording them legitimacy, in turn paving the way for their wider adoption by society at large. At the same time, they are legitimizing their own value systems, in which certain aspects of a university's function – namely research production – are more highly prized than others.

We further argue that the naturalization of the rankings discourse is an example of *symbolic violence*, by which "the dominant apply to the relations of domination categories constructed from the point of view of the dominators, in that way making them appear natural" (Bourdieu, 2001, p. 50). Like hegemony, the concept of symbolic violence points to the role of peripheral nations in adopting the rankings' logic. Under that perspective, rather than helpless victims of the "rankings game," national policymakers are active participants in accepting and reinforcing the US model of higher education. While government and institutional policymakers in the Global South have expressed frustration over the hegemonic influence of the rankings in international forums (Ambrus, 2012), higher education policies in most of those countries continue to reflect the influence of the rankings' paradigm. Examples include merit-pay systems for faculty and institutional funding mechanisms linked to scientific output, which have been adopted by many Latin American countries in recent years; such systems reward scientific output above teaching, in keeping with the rankings' methodologies (Lloyd, 2018c).

The motivation behind the Academic Ranking of World Universities serves to illustrate this argument. While the ranking emerged in China, far from the centre of US economic and political influence, its creators were inspired by a desire to emulate the leading American universities. The campaign, which had the backing of the Chinese government, reflects the increasing global competition for students and professors, as well as the growing importance of higher education as an engine for economic development in the knowledge economy

(Marginson & Ordorika, 2011). As we will see in the following section, the new quest to create "world-class" universities, which in turn place highly in the rankings, has important implications for national policies in many countries, particularly those in the Global South.

Rankings and National Higher Education Policies

One key area in which the rankings have become contentious elements in the struggle for cultural hegemony is in government policymaking. Countries such as China, France, Russia, Brazil, Ecuador, and Peru are using the results of the rankings as justification for implementing sweeping reforms to their higher education systems, or to justify reforms that are already under way. In most cases, the changes follow neo-liberal policy trends in the United States, including a reduction in state funding for universities, and the adoption of accreditation systems and incentives linked to research production. Many governments are also using the results to condition access to study-abroad scholarships and work visas – policies which have generated a backlash in some countries.

The Policy Debate in Europe

The rankings race has also had a major impact in regions with well-established higher education systems, such as Europe. In France, a country with one of the world's oldest university traditions, the hierarchical systems have fuelled highly controversial reforms. In February 2018, the French Parliament approved changes to admissions policies for the country's seventy public universities, introducing an element of selection for the first time in more than 100 years. Previously, all high school graduates who sat for the university entrance exam, known as the *baccalauréat*, were guaranteed access to public higher education. The policy is the most visible symbol of the country's commitment to "education for all," which in turn represents one of the most important gains of the French Revolution. However, the government has justified the changes, citing dropout rates of 60 per cent, overcrowding, and the institutions' poor showing in the international rankings (Lloyd, 2018a). The new Law for Student Orientation and Success sparked massive student protests starting in early 2018, with dozens of universities or faculties partially blocked or occupied as of May that year (*The Local*, 2018). Critics accuse the government of abandoning hard-fought social gains in favour of pro-market policies (Lloyd, 2018a).

A key element driving the government decision was the fact that only one French university finished in the top 100 in the 2018 THE ranking: Paris Science and Letters was ranked seventy-second (THE, 2018). The university was founded in 2010 by combining nine existing research centres and professional schools in Paris. The move formed part of a government campaign dating back at least a decade to create world-class research universities by melding existing institutions into larger entities and channelling millions of dollars into funding graduate research programs. Those efforts seemed to pay off, with three French universities finishing in the top 100 in the 2020 THE ranking, while Paris Science and Letters moved up to the forty-fifth spot, followed by the Sorbonne University (eightieth) and the École Polytechnique (ninety-third) (THE, 2020b).

Similarly, in Russia, the government of President Vladimir Putin embarked on an ambitious reform of the country's higher education system starting in 2012, including through the merging of existing institutions and the closure of others, in a bid to improve the system's international reputation. Officials announced plans to condition where students awarded study-abroad grants could attend university, based on a list of 210 qualifying institutions. Other strategies include investing in a select group of Russian universities and recruiting top talent, in hopes of improving the institutions' standing in the rankings (Nemtsova, 2012).

Russia has also devised its own national and international university rankings to counteract the influence of the international tables. The international ranking, which was first conducted in 2017, does not take into account reputational indicators, which Russian officials deem biased in favour of the most well-known institutions (namely those in the United States and Britain). It also assigns greater weight to teaching and student performance (as opposed to research) and attempts to measure universities' interaction with society. Another key difference: the ranking gives priority to institutions in Japan, China, Brazil, India, Iran, Turkey, and members of the Commonwealth of Independent States, a confederation of ten post-Soviet republics (IREG Observatory on Academic Ranking and Excellence, 2017; *SI News*, 2016).

In justifying the move in 2012, the Russian education minister, Andrei Fursenko, argued that the rankings are an "instrument of competitive battle and influence" and thus should not be monopolized (Kishkovsky, 2012). A total of thirteen Russian universities appeared in the top 200 of the inaugural Moscow International University Ranking in 2017, compared with just one in the ARWU ranking and none in the THE ranking (Academic Ranking of World Universities, 2017; THE, 2017). However, the top five institutions were still the traditional standard-bearers: Harvard, Massachusetts Institute of Technology, Stanford, Yale, and Cambridge, in that order (IREG Observatory on Academic Ranking and Excellence, 2017).

The new internationalization push, in particular, has sparked heated criticism from within Russian academe, with faculty arguing that the country would be better served by investing in its native talent. By 2016, the government was forced to scale back the scope of the reforms due to resistance from affected institutions. At the centre of the debate is lingering mistrust within the Russian establishment of Western – and in particular US – cultural dominance in the post–Cold War era.

The rankings have also fuelled policy changes in other key areas, such as immigration. In Denmark, the government evaluates candidates for work visas depending on whether they attended a highly ranked university. Applicants whose alma mater was in the top 100 of the QS ranking receive 20 points (out of a total of 130 points assigned to educational qualifications) – up from 15 points in 2012 (Rauhvargers, 2013; Workpermit.com, 2018). Meanwhile, those who attended lower-ranked institutions receive fewer points, on a sliding scale. The Netherlands uses a similar system in awarding special "orientation year" permits, which allow holders of undergraduate or graduate degrees from top-ranked universities to temporarily reside in the country while looking for work (Expatica.com, 2020; Rauhvargers, 2013). Beneficiaries must have attended a university ranked in the top 200 in any of the three main rankings or an accredited Dutch institution.

The "World-Class" Movement in Asia

Another region where the rankings are shaping higher education policy is East and Southeast Asia. In recent years, the governments of China, Japan, India, Taiwan, Malaysia, Singapore, and Vietnam, among others, have announced campaigns to create "world-class" universities, in a clear nod to the rankings paradigm. In some cases, such as Malaysia, government officials have made explicit references to the systems in justifying diverting an ever-greater share of government funding to a select group of institutions. What Marginson (2011) has termed the Confucian model of higher education in East Asia – heavy (sometimes authoritarian) state control and highly competitive admissions processes based on a unified national test – has enabled governments in the region to enact sweeping reforms with little resistance from the academic community.

Within this group, the Chinese campaign is by far the most ambitious in terms of scope and investment. In 2017, Beijing officials announced the goal of establishing ten "world-class" universities by 2020 and sixteen top institutions by 2030. Already, some eleven provincial universities have raised close to $6.4 billion towards the project (*People's Daily Online*, 2017).

The country first announced the goal of developing "world-class" universities in 1995, through its 211 Project involving the top 100 universities. The number of targeted universities was reduced to forty in 1995 under Project 985. Since then, the country's higher education system has both expanded and become increasingly stratified along regional and socio-economic lines (Morgan & Wu, 2014). This is partly due to the increasing cost of attending the leading universities. Tuition fees, which were nonexistent prior to the 1980s, have more than doubled since 2000, from around $800 per year to between $2,000 and $4,000 in 2014 (Morgan & Wu, 2014). However, government efforts to address inequality by establishing quotas for poor, rural students starting in 2016 have met with fierce resistance from families in urban centres (Huifeng, 2016).

The Dispute in Latin America

The rankings have had an even more polarizing impact in Latin America, due to the region's long tradition of free, public higher education and resistance to US imperialism (political, economic, and military, as well as cultural) (Ordorika, 2018). The conflict has played out in the rankings' explicit or implicit preference for private universities, which has in turn fuelled calls for increasing private investment in the sector in countries such as Mexico and Colombia. Although initially the top-ranked universities in Latin America were virtually all public, private universities have fared well in the new regional rankings; in the 2020 THE Latin America ranking, the private Pontifical Catholic University of Chile topped the list, while the private Monterrey Institute for Technology and Higher Education in Mexico (ranked fourth) surpassed the National Autonomous University of Mexico (seventeenth), which for years was the region's top-ranked institution (THE, 2020a). The shift reflects the growing weight within the rankings' methodologies of reputational surveys and the degree of internationalization – indicators that favour well-endowed private institutions.

Meanwhile, the rankings do not measure the institutions' role as "state-building" institutions (Ordorika & Pusser, 2007) – a contribution that is difficult, if not impossible, to quantify. In Latin America, public universities, in particular, have played a key role in the economic and social development of their respective nations: by training a majority of the professional workforce, designing state institutions, tackling pressing development problems, and providing a wide array of community service and cultural programs (Ordorika & Pusser, 2007). That model took root a century ago, as a result of the 1918 Córdoba Reform movement in Argentina, triggering similar student-led movements as far north as Mexico. The result was a distinctive Latina American model of higher education, infused with the principles of autonomy, democracy, and "an active institutional compromise [sic] with social progress" (Arocena & Sutz, 2005, p. 581).

However, the "state-building" tradition has come under increasing attack in recent years. Governments throughout Latin America have seized on the region's relatively poor showing in the international tables – with just half a dozen universities listed in the top 500 – to justify implementing or accelerating neo-liberal reforms to their higher education systems. This is true even in the case of self-declared leftist governments, such as those in place in Ecuador and

Peru during the second decade of the twenty-first century; both countries have recently pushed through controversial higher education laws, arguing the need to make their institutions more competitive on a global level.

In the case of Ecuador, legislation passed in 2010 required all university professors to hold PhDs within a decade, despite the fact that at the time only one university in the country offered doctoral degrees (Lloyd, 2010). The law also created a new academic accrediting agency and increased federal control over the university system. Critics accused then president Rafael Correa, who holds a PhD in economics from the University of Illinois, of uncritically mimicking US policies while failing to take into account local realities and priorities (Lloyd, 2010).

Similarly, in 2013, the Peruvian Congress approved a controversial set of reforms to the higher education law, including mandatory accreditation of all universities and programs, the creation of a new federal agency to oversee higher education, and a moratorium on the creation of new universities until new quality controls were in place (Lloyd, 2013b). Opponents, including the National Rectors Assembly and the Federation of Peruvian Students, accused the government of seeking to undermine hard-fought university autonomy under the guise of quality assurance.

Governments in many Latin American countries are also using the rankings to determine where students can study abroad on government grants. Those policies are particularly significant in the case of Brazil, Chile, and Ecuador, which have sent record numbers of students overseas over the past decade in a bid to increase their countries' research capacity. However, critics note that by restricting students to the top-ranked institutions – a majority of which are in the United States – governments are unnecessarily raising the costs of such programs. For example, the Ecuadoran government announced plans in 2012 to spend up to $250,000 per student for the first 2,000 applicants admitted to universities ranked among the top 50 (Associated Press, 2012), far more than the cost of a comparable degree in Europe. In Brazil, meanwhile, a financial and political crisis prompted the government to end the Science Mobility Program in 2017. The program had already come under fire for its exorbitant costs, which included millions of dollars spent on English-language courses at foreign universities, to prepare students to undergo studies in the United States and Britain. Like such exchange programs in many countries, Brazil had also conditioned which universities students could attend based on their standing in the main international rankings.

Resistance to the Rankings

The role of the rankings in dictating government policies has not gone uncontested. In May 2012, dozens of university rectors from throughout Latin America, higher education experts, and representatives from the ranking institutions convened in Mexico City for the conference "Latin American Universities and the International Rankings: Impact, Scope, and Limits." Many of the conference participants voiced concerns over the systems' outsized influence in determining government policies.

Many of their arguments were outlined in the conference's Final Declaration,[1] a ten-page critical analysis of the ranking paradigm and its impact on Latin America:

> The bias toward the Anglo-Saxon research university model does not permit universities in the region to compete on an even footing with their counterparts in more economically developed nations ... The result is a bias against the universities in Latin America and their scientific publications. Finally, there are enormous differences in the amount of investment in higher education and scientific research in different countries, which is the single most important element in determining the presence of institutions in the rankings. (*Final Declaration* 2012, p. 4)

The document reiterated concerns voiced at previous international forums, in which Latin America has occupied a central role. They include the IV Meeting of University Networks and Councils of Chancellors in Buenos Aires, Argentina, in April 2011, which was sponsored by IESALC, UNESCO's higher education institute for Latin America; and the UNESCO Global Forum on Rankings and Accountability in Higher Education: Uses and Misuses, held in Paris, which drew together more than 250 delegates from sixty-eight countries.

There are examples of a counter trend in Latin America, where governments are seeking to expand access to higher education for underprivileged groups. In 2015, then Chilean president Michelle Bachelet announced plans to provide free higher education for the poorest 40 per cent of students, ending decades in which the country had among the most expensive higher education systems in the world. Bachelet was responding to massive demonstrations from 2011 to 2014, which finally brought down her predecessor, the conservative Sebastián Piñera (Lloyd, 2018b).

Similarly, over the past seventeen years, Brazil has implemented the most sweeping affirmative action policies in the Western hemisphere for Afro-Brazilian and low-income students. Those efforts culminated with the federal Quota Law passed in 2012, requiring the country's sixty-three federal universities – which tend to be among the country's top institutions of higher education – to reserve half of all their spots for graduates of public high schools and Afro-Brazilians by 2017. The law sparked widespread opposition, with critics warning that it would negatively impact the academic level of the institutions, not to mention their place in the rankings. The policies reflect competing views of the role of higher education institutions in the twenty-first century, particularly within the Global South.

Final Considerations

After just a decade, or several in the US context, the rankings have established themselves as a new sort of gatekeeper of higher education, a form of bureaucratic certification that has become the norm in both the private and public sectors (Post et al., 2013). This widespread adoption of international rankings has occurred through a complex process of consensual and, at the same time, reluctant acquiescence. So entrenched is the paradigm that governments from around the world, and across the political spectrum, have seized on their universities' relatively weak showing in the rankings to justify bold higher education reforms. These include such upcoming economic powerhouses as Brazil, Russia, India, and China, which, despite challenging US hegemony, have internalized many of the dominant cultural messages implicit in the US-led neoliberal project. Those envision higher education as a competitive marketplace, with a sole dominant model to which all institutions should aspire.

There is also considerable opposition to the ranking paradigm in virtually every region of the world. In Africa, a case not discussed in this chapter, critics are questioning the logic of pursuing the "world-class" university model, given serious material and human resources constraints. However, those critiques often fall on unresponsive ears amid the persistent drumbeat of the hegemonic discourse.

In this chapter, we have analysed the debate over rankings as a reflection of the underlying power dynamics in higher education, which we view as a highly contested and competitive field. We have also shown how the hierarchical systems serve as agents of what Bourdieu and Wacquant (1999) call US-based "cultural imperialism." Legitimized and propagated by international policymakers and the media, the rankings impose a set of largely arbitrary norms, conceived in a specific cultural context, as universal standards to be adopted on a global scale. The process is a form of *symbolic violence*, in which the subordinate actors adopt and internalize the world view of the dominant players (in this case, the neo-liberal policy agenda) as natural and unavoidable (Bourdieu & Wacquant, 1999).

As we have shown, the internalization of this neo-liberal logic has far-reaching consequences for institutions and governments, particularly in Latin America and other developing regions. By encouraging governments and institutions to divert funding to a select group of institutions, in a bid to compete in the "rankings race," the model further exacerbates inequalities in developing nations and the world at large. Marginson (2016) sums up the impact of the competitive logic ingrained in the US-led model of higher education:

The shape of higher education systems is being "stretched" vertically – the university hierarchy is getting steeper. Worldwide there is the ever-growing emphasis on "world-class universities." Every nation, it seems, now wants its own version of the American science multiversity, the kind of institution that figures in global rankings, but is less concerned with achieving Nordic quality in broadly accessible forms of higher education.

Such trends form part of broader changes under way on an international scale. Decades of neo-liberal reforms coupled with the forces of globalization have led to greater levels of inequality in most countries (Picketty, 2014). Meanwhile, in higher education, the neo-liberal logic can be viewed in the erosion of the Nordic commitment to social equality and the demise of the concepts of "education for all" in France and the "state-building" universities in Latin America.

The emergence of the international rankings nearly two decades ago has accelerated those trends by reinforcing the "meritocratic" discourse in higher education, at the expense of the goals of equity and social justice. Finally, the hegemonic logic behind the rankings has perhaps the greatest impact on the countries who can afford it the least.

NOTE

1 The English version of the Final Declaration is available online at http://www .encuentro-rankings.unam.mx/Documentos/Final-declaration-english.pdf.

REFERENCES

Academic Ranking of World Universities (2017). Retrieved from http://www .shanghairanking.com/ARWU2017.html

Altbach, P.G. (1987). *Higher education in the third world: Themes and variations.* Radiant Publishers.

Altbach, P.G. (2003). The costs and benefits of world-class universities. *International Higher Education, 33*, 5–8. https://doi.org/10.6017/ihe.2003.33.7381

Ambrus, S. (2012, 20 May). Educators debate negative effects of international rankings on Latin American universities. *Chronicle of Higher Education.* https://www .chronicle.com/article/educators-debate-negative-effects-of-international-rankings -on-latin-american-universities

Andoh, H. (2017, 24 September). Relevance of the world-class university debate for African universities. *Inside Higher Ed.* https://www.insidehighered.com/blogs /world-view/relevance-world-class-university-debate-african-universities

Apple, M.W. (2007). Education, markets and an audit culture. *International Journal of Educational Policies, 1*(1), 4–19.

Arocena, R., & Sutz, J. (2005). Latin American universities: From an original revolution to an uncertain transition. *Higher Education, 50*, 573–92. https://doi .org/10.1007/s10734-004-6367-8

Associated Press. (2012, 13 July). Ecuador tries a gambit to get smarter people. *Business Insider.* https://www.businessinsider.com/ecuador-tries-a-gambit-to-get-smarter -people-2012-7

Boggs, C. (1997). The great retreat: Decline of the public sphere in late twentieth-century America. *Theory and Society, 26*(6), 741–80. https://doi.org/10.1023 /a:1006849114681

Bolseguí, M., & Fuguet Smith, A. (2006). Cultura de evaluación: Una aproximación conceptual [Evaluation culture: A conceptual approximation]. *Investigación y Postgrado, 21*(1), 77–98.

Bourdieu, P. (2001). *Masculine domination.* Stanford University Press.

Bourdieu, P. (2008). *Homo academicus.* Siglo XXI Editores.

Bourdieu, P., & Passeron, J.C. (1981). *La reproducción: Elementos para una teoría del sistema de enseñanza* [Reproduction: Elements for a theory of a system of teaching]. Editorial Laia.

Bourdieu, P., & Wacquant, L. (1999). On the cunning of imperialist reason. *Theory, Culture and Society, 16*(1), 41–58. https://doi.org/10.1177/026327699016001003

Caldeira, J.P. (2017, 20 June). O fim do Ciência sem Fronteiras depois de R$13 bilhões investidos em bolsas no exterior [The end of Science without Borders after an investment of 13 billion reals]. *Jornal GGN.* https://jornalggn.com.br/noticia/o-fim -do-ciencia-sem-fronteiras-depois-de-r-13-bilhoes-investidos-em-bolsas-no-exterior

China Power. (2018). Is China both a source and hub for international students? https://chinapower.csis.org/china-international-students

Confederación de Nacionalidades Indígenas de Ecuador. (2018, 18 May). Universidad indígena cambia sue status de privada a pública [Indigenous university changes its status from private to public]. https://conaie.org/2018/05/18/universidad-indigena -cambia-estatus-privada-publica

Dill, D.D. (2006, 9 September). *Convergence and diversity: The role and influence of university rankings.* Keynote address at the Consortium of Higher Education Researchers (CHER) 19th Annual Research Conference, University of Kassel, Germany.

The Economist (2018, May 19). How global university rankings are changing higher education. https://www.economist.com/international/2018/05/19/how-global -university-rankings-are-changing-higher-education

Ehrenberg, R.G. (2004). Econometric studies of higher education. *Journal of Econometrics, 121,* 19–37. https://doi.org/10.1016/j.jeconom.2003.10.008

Elliott, J. (2002). La reforma educativa en el estado evaluador [The education reform and the evaluation state]. *Perspectivas, 32*(3), 1–20.

Expatica.com. (2020). Dutch residence permit for bachelor's, master's and PhD degree graduates. https://www.expatica.com/nl/visas-and-permits/Dutch-residence -permit-for-Masters-degree-and-PhD-graduates_108427.html

Final Declaration. (2012, 17–18 May). Latin American universities and the international rankings: Impact, scope and limits, Mexico City, Mexico.

Florian, R.V. (2007). Irreproducibility of the results of the Shanghai Academic Ranking of World Universities. *Scientometrics, 72*(1), 25–32. https://doi.org/10.1007/s11192 -007-1712-1

Grove, J. (2015, 14 September). Universities to scale back liberal arts and social science courses. *Times Higher Education.* https://www.timeshighereducation.com/news /social-sciences-and-humanities-faculties-close-japan-after-ministerial-intervention

Hazelkorn, E. (2007). Impact and influence of league tables and ranking systems on higher education decision-making. *Higher Education Management and Policy, 19*(2), 87–110. https://doi.org/10.1787/hemp-v19-art12-en

Hazelkorn, E. (2008). Learning to live with league tables and ranking: The experience of institutional leaders. *Higher Education Policy, 21*(2), 193–215. https://doi.org /10.1057/hep.2008.1

Huang, F. (2017, 29 September). Double world-class project has more ambitious aims. *University World News, 476.*

Huifeng, H. (2016, 15 May). Thousands of Chinese parents take to the streets to protest university admission quotas. *South China Morning Post.* http://www.scmp.com/news /china/policies-politics/article/1945104/thousands-chinese-parents-take-streets -protest

Institute for International Education. (2018). *Open doors: 2019 fast facts.* https:// opendoorsdata.org/fast_facts/fast-facts-2019

IREG Observatory on Academic Ranking and Excellence. (2017). *Moscow International Ranking "The Three University Missions" released.* http://ireg-observatory.org/en _old/760-moscow-international-ranking-the-three-university-missions-released

Ishikawa, M. (2009). University rankings, global models, and emerging hegemony: Critical analysis from Japan. *Journal of Studies in International Education, 13*(2), 159–73. https://doi.org/10.1177/1028315308330853

Jaienski, M. (2009). Garfield's demon and "surprising" or "unexpected" results in science. *Scientometrics, 78*(2), 347–53. https://doi.org/10.1007/s11192-007-1979-2

Jaschek, S. (2018, 27 August). 8 more colleges submitted incorrect data for rankings. *Inside Higher Ed.* https://www.insidehighered.com/admissions/article/2018/08/27 /eight-more-colleges-identified-submitting-incorrect-data-us-news

Kishkovsky, S. (2012, 26 March). Russia moves to improve its university rankings. *New York Times.* https://www.nytimes.com/2012/03/26/world/europe/russia-moves-to -improve-its-university-rankings.html

Labaree, D.F. (1997). Public goods, private goods: The American struggle over educational goals. *American Educational Research Journal, 34,* 39–81. https://doi .org/10.3102/00028312034001039

Liu, N.C., & Cheng, Y. (2005). The Academic Ranking of World Universities. *Higher Education in Europe, 30*(2), 127–36. https://doi.org/10.1080/03797720500260116

Lloyd, M. (2010, 4 August). Ecuador approves higher-education law with some concessions to universities. *Chronicle of Higher Education.* https://www.chronicle .com/article/Ecuador-Approves/123770

Lloyd, M. (2013a). *Las políticas de fomento a la ciencia y tecnología en México y Brasil: Un estudio de caso de la Universidad Autónoma Nacional de Méxicoy la Universidad de São Paulo* [Science and technology policies in Mexico and Brazil: A case study of the Universidad Autónoma Nacional de México and the Universidad de São Paulo]. Master's thesis in Latin American Studies, National Autonomous University of Mexico.

Lloyd, M. (2013b, 15 August). Reforma universitaria enfrenta a gobierno, estudiantesy academia en Perú [University reform confronts government, students and academe in Peru]. *Campus Milenio, 522.*

Lloyd, M. (2017). "Equidad versus mérito en la universidad: Las políticas de acción afirmativa en Brasil" [Equity versus merit in the university: The politics of affirmative action in Brazil]. PhD diss., National Autonomous University of Mexico.

Lloyd, M. (2018a, 11 April). ¿Otro 1968 en Francia? [Another 1968 in France?] *Campus Milenio, 749,* 8–9.

Lloyd, M. (2018b, 26 April). Déjà vu en Chile por protestas estudiantiles [Déjà vu in Chile due to student protests]. *Campus Milenio, 750,* 8–9.

Lloyd, M. (2018c). El sector de la investigación en México: Entre privilegios, tensiones y jerarquías [The Mexican research sector: Privileges, tensions and hierarchies]. *Perfiles Educativos, 47*(185), 1–31. https://doi.org/10.36857/resu.2018.185.64

Lloyd, M.W., Ordorika Sacristán, I., & Rodríguez Gómez-Guerra, R. (2011). Los rankings internacionales de universidades: Su impacto, metodología y evolución [The international university rankings: Their impact, methods and evaluation]. DGEI-UNAM.

The Local. (2018, 14 May). French university exams halted for hundreds as student protests persist. https://www.thelocal.fr/20180514/french-university-exams-halted -for-hundreds-as-student-protests-persist

Marginson, S. (2007). Global university rankings: Implications in general and for Australia. *Journal of Higher Education Policy and Management, 29*(2), 131–42. https://doi.org/10.1080/13600800701351660

Marginson, S. (2011). Higher education in East Asia and Singapore: Rise of the Confucian model. *Higher Education, 61*(5), 587–611. https://doi.org/10.1007 /s10734-010-9384-9

Marginson, S. (2012, 17–18 May). *Global university rankings: The strategic issues* [Keynote speech]. Latin American Universities and the International Rankings: Impact, Scope and Limits, Mexico City, Mexico.

Marginson, S. (2016, January). Higher education and growing inequality. *Academic Matters.* https://academicmatters.ca/2016/01/higher-education-and-growing-inequality

Marginson, S., & Ordorika, I. (2011). El central volumen de la fuerza: Global hegemony in higher education and research. In D. Rhoten & C. Calhoun (Eds.), *Knowledge matters: The public mission of the research university* (pp. 67–129). Columbia University Press.

Morgan, W.J., & Wu, B. (2014, 15 December). The Chinese dream for higher education and the dilemma it presents. *The Conversation*. http://theconversation.com/the-chinese-dream-for-higher-education-and-the-dilemma-it-presents-35065

National Association for Student Affairs Professionals. (2019). NAFSA International Student Economic Value Tool. https://www.nafsa.org/sites/default/files/media/document/isev-2019.pdf

Nemtsova, A. (2012, 20 June). Russia will recognize degrees from top-ranked foreign universities. *Chronicle of Higher Education*. https://www.chronicle.com/article/Russia-to-Recognize-Degrees/132427

O Globo. (2017, 20 September). 4% dos cursos de mestrado e doutorado obtêm nota máxima e outros 3% podem ser descredenciados pela Capes. https://g1.globo.com/educacao/noticia/4-dos-cursos-de-mestrado-e-doutorado-obtem-nota-maxima-e-outros-3-podem-ser-descredenciados-pela-capes.ghtml

Ordorika, I. (2003). *Power and politics in university governance: Organization and change at the Universidad Nacional Autónoma de Mexico*. Routledge Falmer.

Ordorika, I. (2011, 4 November). *Pertinencia de los rankings en la misión de las universidades* [Pertinence of the rankings in universities' missions] [PowerPoint presentation]. National University of Colombia.

Ordorika, I. (2018). Repolitizar la casa: Las universidades de América Latina a cien años de la Reforma de Córdoba [Repoliticize the house: Latin America universities one hundred years after the Córdoba Reforms]. In R. Guarga (Ed.), *A cien años de la Reforma Universitaria de Córdoba: Hacia un nuevo Manifiesto de la Educación Superior Latinoamericana* [A hundred years since the Córdoba university reforms: Toward a new declaration of Latin American higher education] (pp. 115–29). UNESCO-IESALC/Universidad Nacional de Córdoba.

Ordorika, I., & Lloyd, M. (2013). A decade of international university rankings: A critical perspective from Latin America. In P.T.M. Marope, P.J. Wells, & E. Hazelkorn (Eds.), *Rankings and accountability in higher education: Uses and misuses* (pp. 209–34). UNESCO.

Ordorika, I., & Lloyd, M. (2015). International rankings and the contest for university hegemony. *Journal of Education Policy, 30*(3), 385–405. https://doi.org/10.1080/02680939.2014.979247

Ordorika, I., & Pusser, B. (2007). La máxima casa de estudios: Universidad Nacional Autónoma de México as a state-building university. In P.G. Altbach & J. Balán (Eds.), *World class worldwide: Transforming research universities in Asia and America* (pp. 189–215). Johns Hopkins University Press.

Ordorika, I., & Rodríguez, R. (2010). El ranking Times en el mercado del prestigio universitario [The *Times* ranking in the university prestige market]. *Perfiles Educativos, 32*(129).

Oxford University. (2020). Course fees for 2021-entry. https://www.ox.ac.uk/admissions/undergraduate/fees-and-funding/course-fees

People's Daily Online. (2017, 18 January). China vows to establish 16 world-class universities by 2030. http://www.chinadaily.com.cn/china/2017-01/18 /content_27986238.htm

Picketty, T. (2014). *Capital in the twenty-first century.* Harvard University Press.

Post, D., Stambach, A., Ginsburg, M., Hannum, E., Benavot, A., & Bjork, C. (2013). Los rankings académicos [Academic rankings]. *Archivos Analíticos de Políticas Educativas, 21*(19), 1–19. https://doi.org/10.14507/epaa.v21n19.2013

Power, M. (1997). *The audit society.* Oxford University Press.

Pusser, B. (2012). Power and authority in the creation of a public sphere through higher education. In B. Pusser, S. Marginson, I. Ordorika, & K. Kempner (Eds.), *Universities and the public sphere: Knowledge creation and state building in the era of globalization* (pp. 27–46). Routledge.

Pusser, B., & Marginson, S. (2012). The elephant in the room: Power, global rankings and the study of higher education organization. In M.N. Bastedo (Ed.), *The organization of higher education: Managing colleges for a new era* (pp. 86–117). Johns Hopkins University Press.

QS. (2012, 14 June). *Brazilian higher education in 2012: Background.* Quacquarelli Symonds. http://www.topuniversities.com/where-to-study/south-america/brazil /brazilian-higher-education-2012-background

QS. (2015, 7–9 December). *Methodological refinements for 2015 and beyond* [Presentation]. Reimagine Education Conference, Philadelphia, Pennsylvania. http://www.shanghairanking.com/wcu/wcu6/16.pdf

QS. (2021). *QS World University Rankings. Who rules?* https://www.topuniversities .com/university-rankings/world-university-rankings/2021

Rauhvargers, A. (2013). *Global university rankings and their impact. Report II.* European University Association.

Readings, B. (1996). *The university in ruins.* Harvard University Press.

Salmi, J. (2009). *The challenge of establishing world-class universities.* World Bank.

Slaughter, L., & Leslie, L.L. (1999). *Academic capitalism: Politics, policies, and the entrepreneurial university.* Johns Hopkins University Press.

SI News. (2016, November). Russia to launch its own global university rankings next year. https://www.studyinternational.com/news/russia-to-launch-its-own-global -university-rankings-next-year

Tauss, A. (2012). Contextualizing the current crisis: Post-Fordism, neoliberal restructuring, and financialization. *Colombia International, 76*, 51–79. https://doi .org/10.7440/colombiaint76.2012.03

Times Higher Education [THE]. (2017, December). Russian universities excel in Kremlin-backed rankings. https://www.timeshighereducation.com/news/russian -universities-excel-kremlin-backed-rankings

Times Higher Education [THE]. (2018). World University Rankings 2016–2017. https:// www.timeshighereducation.com/world-university-rankings/2017/world-ranking#! /page/0/length/25/locations/RU/sort_by/rank/sort_order/asc/cols/stats

Times Higher Education [THE]. (2020a). Latin America University Rankings 2018. https://www.timeshighereducation.com/student/best-universities/best-universities -latin-america

Times Higher Education [THE] (2020b). World University Rankings 2020. https:// www.timeshighereducation.com/world-university-rankings/2020/world-ranking#! /page/0/length/25/locations/FR/sort_by/rank/sort_order/asc/cols/stats

Torres, C.A. (2013, 4 August). *El neoliberalismo como un nuevo bloque histórico: Un análisis Gramsciano del sentido común neoliberal en educación* [Neoliberalism as a new historic block: A Gramscian analysis of neoliberal common sense in education]. Conference delivered at the National Autonomous University of Mexico upon acceptance of membership in the Mexican Academy of Sciences, Mexico City, Mexico.

Turner, D.R. (2005). Benchmarking in universities: League tables revisited. *Oxford Review of Education, 31*(3), 353–71. https://doi.org/10.1080/03054980500221975

Universia. (2020, 27 January). Cuánto cuesta una carrera universitaria en México [How much does a university degree cost in Mexico] https://www.universia .net/mx/actualidad/orientacion-academica/cuanto-cuesta-carrera-universitaria -mexico-1136727.html

University of California, Berkeley. (2020). Cost of attendance. https://financialaid .berkeley.edu/cost-attendance

U.S. News & World Report. (2020). 2021 best national university rankings. https:// www.usnews.com/best-colleges/rankings/national-universities

Van Raan, A.F.J. (2005). Fatal attraction: Conceptual and methodological problems in the ranking of universities by bibliometric methods. *Scientometrics, 62*(1), 133–43. https://doi.org/10.1007/s11192-005-0008-6

Washington Monthly. (2018). 2018 college guide and rankings. https:// washingtonmonthly.com/2018college-guide

Webster, D.S. (1986). *Academic quality rankings of American colleges and universities*. Charles C. Thomas.

Workpermit.com. (2018). Danish green card points based system. http://workpermit .com/immigration/denmark/danish-green-card-points-based-system

Ying, Y., & Jingao, Z. (2009). An empirical study on credibility of China's university rankings: A case study of three rankings. *Chinese Education and Society, 42*(1), 70–80. https://doi.org/10.2753/ced1061-1932420106

Young, I.M. (1990). *Justice and the politics of difference*. Princeton University Press.

2 Unfolding National Approaches to University Rankings in Central Asia, Central and Eastern Europe, and Latin America

CRESO M. SÁ, NADIIA KACHYNSKA, EMMA SABZALIEVA, AND MAGDALENA MARTINEZ

Introduction

Rankings of universities have become a truly globalized phenomenon and have undeniably become part of the worldwide higher education discourse. Today, many countries have national rankings of one kind or another devised by newspapers and magazines or initiated by ministries of education, grant councils or accreditation agencies, university associations, or other organizations (Salmi & Saroyan, 2007). National university rankings serve many purposes and interests for a range of stakeholders: they provide easily interpretable information on the standing of universities, they are expected to contribute to the definition of quality, they are intended to stimulate competition and encourage change in organizational strategies, and they provide some of the rationale for the allocation of funds (Marginson, 2007; Sadlak et al., 2008; Stolz et al., 2010).

Increasing interest in university rankings has also been reflected in a growing range of academic literature devoted to the topic. University rankings have been examined from methodological, technical, and conceptual perspectives, often from a critical standpoint. Scholars have questioned the shortcomings of rankings, mainly owing to their combination of indicators, the weightings assigned to each indicator, statistical methodology, and stakeholders' interests (Longden, 2011; Lukman et al., 2010). Many studies have criticized rankings for their disproportionate focus on English-language research published in indexed journals. This downplays the wider mission of higher education by overlooking considerations such as teaching quality, student experience, and community relations (Amsler & Bolsmann, 2012; Harvey, 2008; Pusser & Marginson, 2013).

Despite these limitations, some argue that university league tables will likely diffuse further in both national and global contexts (Hazelkorn, 2015; Teichler, 2011). While the emergence of national university rankings can be seen as an irreversible process, diverse local circumstances and approaches to higher education reforms have brought the meaning of university rankings into question across different contexts. Unlike their counterparts in the Anglosphere and East Asia, countries in Central Asia, Central and Eastern Europe, and Latin America have not been central to the constitution of global rankings. Yet the idea of national university rankings is being advanced across these three regions, and the approaches that are unfolding also reflect the countries' historical developments and pre-existing institutional formations and norms. In response, the purpose of this chapter is to examine and compare the emergence of national university rankings in these three regions. The chapter identifies trends across jurisdictions in Central Asia, Central and Eastern Europe, and Latin America and discusses the implications of the unfolding national approaches to university rankings there.

The Uses of Rankings in Higher Education

In many market-oriented higher education systems, university rankings have emerged to define and communicate the relative standing of universities in a more compelling fashion than policy reports or scholarly analyses. National rankings have a long-standing tradition in the United States, where universities have been ranked since the early twentieth century (Geiger, 1993). The establishment of the Carnegie Foundation's classification in 1973 and that of the *U.S. News & World Report* in 1983 laid the foundation for contemporary ranking systems that are now seen not just in the United States but around the world. Their popularity was grounded on their perceived contribution as independent evaluation mechanisms that quantitatively compared university achievements and performance. Visually presented in the simple form of league tables, rankings are easy to understand and quick to recall (Hazelkorn, 2014).

As rankings provide information on the relative performance of universities, they have been used as a policy instrument to change universities' behaviour in terms of quality assurance and research performance (Espeland & Sauder, 2016; Hazelkorn, 2014). However, in practice, universities have been found to engage in dubious behaviour to adapt to ranking metrics and invest in activities affecting their ranking positions rather than improving student learning experiences (Westerheijden et al., 2011). Rankings may be used symbolically by universities to signal their high academic aspirations and the pursuit of international quality standards. Universities may use their position in rankings to legitimize themselves domestically or internationally (Ramirez, 2010).

Rankings have also induced competition among universities, creating competitive behaviour among universities at national, regional, and global levels. This is achieved by combining four operations: a zero-sum comparison of institutional performance, quantification, visualization, and frequent publication (Werron & Ringel, 2017). Thus, world university rankings have been seen as a symbolic tool of constructing the perceived global competition among universities and transmitting academic quality norms into national contexts (Altbach, 2012; Marginson & van der Wende, 2007; Rust & Kim, 2015).

More broadly, rankings serve political agendas within the contexts they originate in. While global rankings are generated by non-state actors, they have a remarkably close relationship to particular states' agendas (Pusser & Marginson, 2013). For instance, the first world university ranking published by the Center for World-Class Universities at Shanghai Jiao Tong University in 2003 was motivated by the threefold national interest of the Chinese government: establishing the position of Chinese universities in the world, measuring the gap with the success of leading research universities in the United States, and identifying strategies to develop Chinese higher education institutions into "world-class" universities (Jöns & Hoyler, 2013).

Regardless of their putative goals, global ranking systems invariably reward and reinforce a particular university model rooted in the Anglo-European tradition. Mapping the locations of the top 500 universities in both Shanghai and THE-QS rankings in 2009, Jöns and Hoyler (2013) identified four major regional clusters of universities that score highly on ranking performance indicators: North America, Western Europe, East Asia, and Australia. They found that other regions have few universities in the rankings or none at all. This includes the thousands of universities located in Central Asia, Central and Eastern Europe, and Latin America, making them effectively invisible on the world ranking map. These findings reflect the uneven representation of different cultural contexts in world university rankings and show a strong association between global economic asymmetries and ranking outcomes (Jöns & Hoyler, 2013, p. 49).

Given the diversity of higher education systems around the world, national rankings might reasonably be expected to reflect the unique purposes and goals of different states. However, many national rankings measure institutional resources, faculty research productivity, and academic reputation in much the same way as global rankings (Hazelkorn, 2014). Below, we examine the uses of national rankings in Central Asia, Central and Eastern Europe, and Latin America, considering both the influence of broad global trends and the contextual features of higher education in each region.

University Rankings in Central Asia

A region that has been under-researched and under-represented in higher education studies, Central Asia – comprising the five states of Kazakhstan (population 18 million), the Kyrgyz Republic (6 million), Tajikistan (9 million), Turkmenistan (6 million), and Uzbekistan (32 million) – is deserving of much greater attention not only for historic and geopolitical reasons, but also as some of the newest countries in the world. Building nations out of the rubble of the collapsed Soviet Union in the 1990s, Central Asian states are grappling with intensely globalized and globalizing ideas about higher education. Higher education in the region has been influenced by what is known in translation from Russian as the "world education space" – sometimes also called the global education space (Avshenyuk, 2014). This concept incorporates seemingly global norms in higher education, including the European Union–led Bologna Process, the idea of an American-style model of research university, and aspirations to be the "next Singapore" (or other recently successful country).

Despite their recent status as independent countries, these states are also well-established, with institutions, values, and bureaucracies brought forward from their recent histories. Their pre-Soviet histories are also re-emerging, being rediscovered and reimagined. The region has rich traditions of education and discovery: nomadic cultures of learning and trade with multiple societies pre-date by some centuries the formalized Islamic education for which parts of the region became renowned as "centres of academic excellence" (Frankopan, 2015, p. 97). Soviet rule saw the construction of the region's first European-style universities from the 1920s (Krasheninnikov & Nechaev, 1990; Reeves, 2005), creating and rapidly expanding a formalized higher education system. By the fall of the Soviet Union in 1991, a total of 129 higher education institutions (HEIs) were operating across the five republics, with participation rates at around 15–20 per cent of the age cohort (Platonova, 2018). While the communist ideology on which the higher education system had rested did not survive, the structural and normative legacies of this period are immense and can still be felt in the region today, nearly thirty years after the five states gained independence.

Given the relative permeability of Central Asia's higher education systems to the idea of the world education space, it is unsurprising to see recent growth in the number of national rankings. Three broad trends can be identified in the way national rankings in Central Asia are unfolding.

The most significant trend is that the rankings tools that currently exist in the region are all state-run and state-financed. Although private higher education has flourished in some parts of Central Asia – 35 per cent of Kyrgyz HEIs and 50 per cent of Kazakh HEIs (Ministry of Education and Science, Republic of Kazakhstan, 2017; National Statistics Committee of the Kyrgyz Republic, n.d.) are privately operated, for example – management and governance of higher education remain primarily the domain of the state. State agencies have been mandated to set up rankings to support the achievement of broader education policy goals, as is seen clearly in the case of Kazakhstan. As the wealthiest state in the region, it is also a pacesetter among Central Asian states for its maximal deployment of rankings, which it uses well beyond higher education. This is indicative of the general thrust of development across all policy spheres in the country as it seeks to find a place alongside the world's top economies

(Nazarbayev, 2014). This includes the goal of uplifting two Kazakh HEIs to "the world's best university rankings" (Ministry of Education and Science of the Republic of Kazakhstan, 2010, p. 48).

In this search for global competitiveness, Kazakhstan has developed national rankings for HEIs over the last decade. Since 2014, rankings have been run by the Independent Agency for Accreditation and Rating (IAAR), created as a non-profit organization (Independent Agency for Accreditation and Rating [IAAR], 2018). While the organizational status may appear to be separate, IAAR began life as part of the Ministry of Education and Science (Kalanova, 2008) and may be viewed in its current iteration as an arm's-length body that receives funding from the government but is officially independent. The IAAR 2018 ranking covers multi-faculty universities as well as smaller specialist HEIs with one of the following profiles: technical, humanities/social sciences, medical, teacher training, and the arts. In the Kazakh national ranking, each HEI was assessed on five criteria: institutional and individual course accreditation,[1] concentration of talented students and faculty (e.g., number of national university teaching awards), academic mobility, graduate employability, and publications (IAAR, 2018). These factors are common in global ranking methodologies and are closely aligned with the methods used by QS in its World University Rankings (Agachi, 2017).

In smaller neighbouring Kyrgyz Republic, where there are around fifty HEIs, a national ranking has to date been compiled directly by the Ministry of Education and Science. In an early iteration in 2016, the ministry issued a ranking of state-funded HEIs that used six different assessment mechanisms: collaboration with employers, research and innovation, international integration, educational activity (e.g., faculty qualification levels, whether programs are accredited by international agencies), resources and communications (e.g., ICT infrastructure), and social/community development (Sputnik, 2016). By 2018, the ministry had developed an alternative method, organizing a seminar for HEIs to inform them about the new opt-in ranking (Ministry of Education and Science, Kyrgyz Republic, 2018). Interestingly, this new ranking has been outsourced to Kazakhstan's IAAR and uses an identical methodology to that described above.

Until recently largely closed off to the outside world, higher education in Uzbekistan is rapidly transforming under the leadership of President Shavkat Mirziyoyev, who took power at the end of 2016. The country's first national HEI rankings were issued in 2018 after initially being announced in 2013 (Sabzalieva, 2018b). They were organized by the State Inspection for Education Quality, which is part of the Cabinet of Ministers and the Ministry of Higher and Vocational Education. As with early rankings in the Kyrgyz Republic, the Uzbek ranking is also limited to the country's state-funded HEIs, of which there were fifty-seven at the time of the ranking. Twenty-three indicators were used to compose the ranking, covering everything from learning outcomes and faculty composition to classroom and ICT resources. The country's international branch campus HEIs[2] were not included in the ranking; additionally, there were no Uzbek-run or Uzbek-owned private HEIs in the country.

However, the nascent rankings scene in Uzbekistan took a blow weeks after they were released when the country's Ministry of Justice demanded that the rankings be annulled (Sabzalieva, 2018c). At the time of writing this chapter, it was not clear whether the rankings would be officially withdrawn or would undergo a review. While the case remains unresolved, it further indicates the importance of rankings as a national policy tool. This is shown not only through the Ministry of Justice's interest in the details of the ranking, but also in its reference to the work of international ranking bodies[3] and international principles on rankings.[4]

While the Kyrgyz Republic and Uzbekistan appear to be at an early stage of developing national higher education rankings, Kazakhstan has applied the principles of ranking to other aspects of higher education. This is a second trend identified in the use of national rankings in Central Asia: the use of policy tools that generate rankable data that go beyond comparing institutional quality. In 2018, for example, the State Service and Anti-Corruption Agency announced that it was developing a national corruption index of HEIs (Sabzalieva, 2018a). This has been trialled at Al-Farabi Kazakh National University, the country's leading university, with the publication of a departmental anti-corruption ranking. The exact methodology for determining the extent of corruption in each department has not been made public, but it has involved surveys of faculty and students on factors such as professional values and transparency.

Corruption is a deeply embedded legacy in former Soviet systems of higher education, and in many countries it has remained widespread since the economic crisis that followed the collapse of the Soviet Union (Oka, 2018). What is striking about the Kazakh anti-corruption ranking is that it confirms that the state recognizes that corruption in higher education is a persistent problem. Even more remarkable is the way that the government is using a ranking-like policy tool not only to combat this issue but as part of the broader push to greater global standing. This new anti-corruption ranking, expected to be rolled out nationally in 2019 and beyond, signals both Kazakhstan's subscription to the rankings norm in the "world education space" and the ways in which these globally approved symbols can be appropriated at a national level for local purposes.

A third approach to national rankings in Central Asia comes from their absence in two of the five states: to date, there has been no action to create official university rankings in either Tajikistan or Turkmenistan. As in the Kyrgyz Republic, a national newspaper in Tajikistan has compiled an informal ranking of HEIs using such indicators as popularity, cost, and size (Asia-Plus, 2016;

Inform.kg, n.d.), but this is not complemented in Tajikistan by a state-sanctioned rating. Both Tajikistan and Turkmenistan have smaller higher education systems than the other three Central Asian states, with thirty-five and twenty-five HEIs respectively, and all HEIs within those systems are state-funded.[5] The relatively small size of these systems combined with the fact that the HEIs within them are subject to close monitoring by the state means that there is possibly no perceived need for a national ranking: instead, other policy tools are employed to attempt to improve quality and induce innovation into HEIs. Another possible reason that national rankings have not (yet) gained traction in these two states is their relative lack of exposure to global norms in higher education as compared to their neighbours. While Tajikistan has begun to align with these practices – for example, aiming to adopt the Bologna Process by 2020 (DeYoung et al., 2018) – it has come to the game somewhat later than its neighbours. Since gaining independence in 1991, Turkmenistan's politics have been directed towards international isolation. A change of leadership in 2007 brought reform to the country, but it is still comparatively closed to the outside world (Peyrouse, 2012).

University Rankings in Central and Eastern Europe (CEE)

The region of Central and Eastern Europe (CEE) represents a group of ten ex-socialist countries: Belarus, Moldova, Russia, and Ukraine belonged to the Soviet Union, while Bulgaria, the Czech Republic, Hungary, Poland, Romania, and Slovakia were members of the Warsaw Pact, a collective treaty of Soviet satellite states. Higher education systems in CEE share common communist-era characteristics that, despite the variety of independent socio-economic and political paths, explain common patterns in higher education reforms (Dobbins, 2011). Under communist regimes, higher education was subject to a high degree of centralization, ideological shaping of the curriculum, and the separation between teaching and research, where the latter was carried out in other research institutes (Kwiek, 2014; Matějů et al., 2007). Following the collapse of communist regimes in 1989 and 1991, higher education underwent numerous reforms, mainly with the objective of bringing back their academics and students to the European community (Kwiek, 2014).

The trajectory of reforms and policy changes in the region has created a massive transformation in these ten neighbouring countries, from command-driven to market-driven economies. The uneven transition from central planning to a free-market economy in the post-communist CEE countries (Hladchenko et al., 2016, p. 115) has been described as "positioning at the edge of 'academic tectonic plates'" (Neave, 2003, p. 18). During and after the transition, foreign influence has been facilitated by a considerable openness level in the region to international assistance and advice (Dakowska & Harmsen, 2015). The intention to catch up with the West after more than forty years of communist regimes (Kwiek, 2014) is seen in higher education in the influence of global rankings in national policy debates, although universities in CEE have been significantly under-represented in these rankings (Jöns & Hoyler, 2013).[6] The influence of rankings has been further embedded with the expansion of global ranking initiatives and the popularity of the knowledge economy discourse, which is associated with the EU Lisbon Strategy.[7]

The first national university rankings in CEE emerged between 2003 and 2009 when the region was influenced by broader neo-liberal reforms (Antonowicz et al., 2017; Dakowska & Harmsen, 2015; Kwiek, 2014), but the unfolding development of national rankings across the ten countries in CEE has not been parallel. Early national rankings were established in Ukraine (2003), Poland (2009), and Russia (2009), but others did not introduce national rankings until much later (e.g., Belarus's first ranking was in 2014 and Romania developed its ranking in 2016).

The CEE countries with the largest higher education systems – Poland, Russia, and Ukraine – have multiple competing annual national rankings. While many national rankings across the CEE countries are managed by nongovernmental organizations such as research institutes or media outlets, a high level of state control in initiating or running the rankings is evident in Belarus, Bulgaria, and Romania. CEE countries with a comparatively smaller number of universities either do not have national rankings at all, as is the case in the Czech Republic, or, in the case of Hungary and Slovakia, have national rankings of individual faculties rather than universities as a whole.

As the largest of the CEE higher education systems with the legacy of "superpower," it is unsurprising that Russia has ambitiously introduced its own global university rankings: Round University Ranking (RUR) in 2010 and the Three University Missions Moscow International University Ranking (MosIUR) in 2017. A national university ranking emerged in Russia in 2009 when the privately run Interfax Information Agency was contracted by the Ministry of Education and Science to develop and run it. The Interfax University Ranking evaluates Russian universities against six parameters: quality of teaching, research productivity, community engagement, innovation and entrepreneurship, internationalization, and reputation (Ministry of Science and Higher Education of the Russian Federation, n.d.-c). The Ministry of Education and Science believes that the introduction of a new evaluation mechanism in the form of a national ranking and the integration of this mechanism into the governance of higher education and research will stimulate the global competitiveness of Russian universities (Ministry of Science and Higher Education of the Russian Federation, n.d.-b).

Since 2013, a very well-known private ranking agency in the financial sector has run a competing national university ranking called Ranking Expert

RA, which is accredited by the IREG Observatory on Academic Ranking and Excellence.[8] The initiators of this ranking believe that it will "boost the prestige of Russian higher education" in the world (Ministry of Science and Higher Education of the Russian Federation, n.d.-d). The idea of having more globally competitive Russian universities was framed at the national policy level in 2013 as the 5-100 Russian Academic Excellence Project, a government plan to have five universities appear in the top 100 of the global rankings (Ministry of Science and Higher Education of the Russian Federation, n.d.-a). Since November 2018, Russian universities ranked in the THE World University Rankings, QS World University Rankings, and the Shanghai Ranking have been automatically exempted from the government's assessments of quality and other accreditation requirements (Vorotnikov, 2018).

In Poland, another CEE country with a large higher education system, national rankings emerged in the middle of the first decade of the twenty-first century following wide debates about the weak performance of Polish universities in global rankings and their perceived descent to mediocrity. At the policy level, it resulted in the *2008 Green Paper*, which referred to the improvement of Polish universities' performance as a major policy priority (Antonowicz et al., 2017). As with Russia and Ukraine, Poland has several national rankings. Among them, the Perspektywy (Outlook) University Ranking system (since 2009), which consists of several rankings, has been considered the most technically sophisticated mainly because its founder organization, the Perspektywy Foundation, acts as the official secretariat to the IREG Observatory. The main ranking in this system – Ranking of Academic Institutions – applies six sets of criteria very similar to those of global rankings, such as prestige, research potential, research effectiveness, innovation, study conditions, and internationalization (Kwiek, 2016). The relatively high weight given to indicators emphasizing research and internationalization seems to align with the broader policy rationale to move more Polish universities up in the global rankings.

Policymaking in Ukraine has also responded to the desire to have flagship universities recognized globally as far back as 1994 (Hladchenko et al., 2016; Oleksiyenko, 2014); however, Ukrainian universities are still mostly invisible in the global rankings. A new funding formula for public universities that at the time of writing was still in the review stage will consider only a university's appearance in any of three global rankings – QS World University Rankings, the Times Higher Education World University Rankings, and Academic Ranking of World Universities (Cabinet of Ministers of Ukraine, 2018). This development in the funding formula echoes a pervasive idea in higher education reforms in CEE to "catch up with the West" and to demonstrate the region's aspirations to contribute to global knowledge production. National university rankings in Ukraine emerged in the early 2000s, all run by non-governmental organizations. For example, EuroOsvita Top-200 Ukrainian Universities was established in 2003 as an initiative of the National Research Institute of Applied Information Technologies "to implement international expertise and principles of university ranking" ("Euro Osvita," n.d.). The methodology includes indices of education quality, research potential, and international recognition. Indicators of international recognition include university participation in EU regional initiatives such as Horizon 2020, Seventh Framework Programme, TEMPUS, and Erasmus+. Another national university ranking run by the news agency Osvita.ua provides the Consolidated University Ranking, which mainly combines results from other national rankings. The emergence of these rankings as well as the scope of applied metrics and assigned purposes demonstrates their compliance with an earlier political turn towards Europeanization and the Bologna Process.

In comparison to Poland and Ukraine, "there is no relevant political discourse (past or present) around differentiation, and the selection of 'flagship,' 'elite,' 'research' universities" in the Czech Republic (Antonowicz et al., 2017, p. 558). There are twenty-six public universities in the Czech Republic. Charles University and Masaryk University remain the most prestigious ones in the national higher education landscape (Antonowicz et al., 2017, p. 558). The fact that public universities maintain their reputation despite a growing private sector may suggest why having a national university ranking in the Czech Republic is irrelevant from both student needs and policymaking perspectives.

While many national university rankings in CEE have been initiated by the media or academic associations, rankings in Belarus, Bulgaria, and Romania were established by their Ministries of Education. All universities in Belarus are publicly owned and closely controlled by the government; their performance in the state-run ranking indicates the level of university compliance to the national recruitment plan, serving an ostensible monitoring function (TUT.BY, 2014). Thus, the Belarus national university ranking (established in 2014) compares universities by the number of admitted students and the average admissions score as a benchmark of academic quality.

In Bulgaria, while gradual marketization of the higher education system has provided universities with wider autonomy (Dobbins, 2011), academic quality has remained within the scope of government control through the National Evaluation and Accreditation Agency (NEAA). Since 2010, the Ministry of Education and Science and the NEAA have produced the Bulgarian University Ranking System "to support education service users in their choice of a university" ("Bulgarian University Ranking System," n.d.). The purpose of national ranking in Bulgaria has thus been to help students navigate national universities, degrees, and programs because of "the high level of structural fragmentation and overspecialization of the Bulgarian system" ("Bulgarian University Ranking System," n.d.).

The national university ranking in Romania, University Metaranking, was initiated in 2016 by the Ministry of National Education and Scientific Research. It combines data on the position of Romanian universities in nine global rankings "with the view of being potentially included in university international rankings" (David et al., 2017, p. 40). While higher education in Romania is still oscillating between post-Soviet legacies and Bologna Process values (Andreescu et al., 2012; Wodak & Fairclough, 2010), the ministry-led university ranking represents a policy tool to push more universities towards a world-class university model (David et al., 2017).

It is notable that the countries in CEE with a comparatively small number of universities (fewer than thirty-five in total, both private and public) do not have national university rankings. However, national faculty, program, or degree rankings have become alternatives in these jurisdictions. For example, in Slovakia, an independent non-governmental organization called the Academic Ranking and Rating Agency (ARRA) was established in September 2004. From the beginning, ARRA decided to rank individual faculties rather than universities because it was seen as impossible to rank fifteen public HEIs and three (at that time) private HEIs covering the whole spectrum of institutions (Šolc et al., 2014). In Hungary, *HGV*, a popular weekly magazine, publishes the UniPress annual rankings of degrees called Diploma ranking. As with ARRA in Slovakia, it ranks faculties and degree programs rather than universities. Its creators believe that the ranking of programs is more relevant for professional recognition and applicants' employment goals than university rankings that emphasize institution-wide prestige (Eduline, 2016).

University Rankings in Latin America

This section observes the emergence of national rankings in Latin America, which consists of countries with a shared history of colonization and independence from Spain and Portugal and are situated in South America, North and Central America, and the Caribbean islands. This section reviews national rankings in Argentina, Brazil, Chile, Colombia, Honduras, Mexico, Peru, and Uruguay. While Spain and Portugal developed higher education in their Latin American colonies differently, both of their systems mainly targeted elite families and responded to state interests. If the Spanish founded over thirty universities to expand their settlements in the region, the Portuguese opposed the development of educational institutions until the royal family was exiled to Brazil in 1808 following Napoleon's invasion of Portugal, when engineering, law, and medical schools were established (Laus & Morosini, 2005; Santos & Cerqueira, 2009). Following independence during the late eighteenth and early nineteenth centuries, most Latin American states maintained the tradition of colonial universities until the early twentieth century, when the university reform movement emerged in Argentina. Influenced by modernization ideas, this movement led other Latin American states to establish institutional autonomy and democratic governance as central pillars of universities (Arocena & Sutz, 2005).

Debates regarding global university rankings have arguably been muted in Latin America compared to other parts of the world, as governments in the region have by and large not sought to "compete" in the global higher education space. Unlike the originators of the Shanghai and the Russian RUR university rankings for instance, academic leaders in the region have, at times, contested the logics and homogenizing effects of global rankings and actively resisted their use (Becerra et al., 2015; Ordorika & Lloyd, 2015). While there are legitimate concerns about how global rankings marginalize Latin American universities and downplay their local missions (Balán, 2012), these reactions are also partly related to policy preferences and interests of sectoral organizations, unions, and student associations. Regional rankings for Latin America, such as those published by SCImago, QS, and the *Times Higher Education*, are examples of the adaptation of the logic of global rankings to the regional context and have been better received by critics of global rankings (Balán, 2012).

While not widespread in the region, national rankings have emerged in Brazil, Chile, Colombia, and Mexico, countries with large higher education systems, increased levels of privatization, and some presence in global rankings. Together with Argentina, these countries are represented in world university rankings; for instance, they all have universities in the top 300 in the QS World Ranking. With the exception of Argentina, national rankings in these settings generally reproduce the criteria of global rankings. An important driver of these national rankings is the large role played by the private sector in higher education. Following the expansion beginning in the 1990s of the private sector, which now accounts for 88 per cent of institutions, the Brazilian post-secondary education system became the largest in Latin America (Laus & Morosini, 2005; PROPHE, n.d.). In Chile, private institutions account for 73 per cent of the higher education system with the continued implementation of neo-liberal policies in the last thirty years (Brunner, 1993; Gregorutti et al., 2016; Larraín & Zurita, 2008). In Mexico, over 70 per cent of higher education institutions are private (PROPHE, n.d.), while more than half of the Colombian higher education system is private (Uribe, 2015). In these countries, governments have implemented measures to assess institutional quality that to a large extent seek to ensure that the private sector meets minimum standards.

Most university rankings in the region are published by media organizations. In Brazil, the Ranking Universitário Folha, published yearly by the *Folha de São Paulo* newspaper since 2012, includes a university ranking and a program ranking. The university ranking uses domestic and global criteria as it emphasizes research (55 per cent) while also considering education quality (20 per cent), market assessment (20 per cent), and innovation (5 per cent) (Çakır et al., 2015). Market assessment is an important component of the ranking methodology and evaluates hiring preferences by Brazilian employers, while the education quality component considers the opinion of professors on the quality of graduate courses. The university ranking also provides a rank to universities on each criterion evaluated. This national ranking is a domestically oriented classification system of all 196 Brazilian universities. The program ranking is aimed at students, evaluating the forty undergraduate programs with higher enrolment in universities (Folha de São Paulo, 2018).

State-run university rankings have also emerged in Brazil. Since 2008, the Brazilian Ministry of Education has developed assessments, later published as rankings, that measure the quality of undergraduate programs, Conceito Preliminar de Curso (CPC), and the quality of higher education institutions, the Índice Geral de Cursos (IGC) (INEP, 2015a, 2015b; Polidori, 2009). The CPC measures student outcomes and educational resources (INEP, 2015a). The IGC measures the quality of institutions by combining the CPC results and government postgraduate quality assurance measures (INEP, 2015b). These measurements have been used in the media to inform students and their families about differences in program quality. Moreover, they are policy tools the ministry uses to ensure compliance with national quality norms. By deciding on the evaluation criteria and methodology, the ministry communicates government expectations through these assessments to the system and the general public.

In Chile, national rankings using domestic and global criteria were created by the Group of Advanced Studies, a group of academics. These rankings, published annually by the *El Mercurio* newspaper since 2012, include the University Ranking, the Quality of Undergraduate Teaching Ranking, and the Career Guide. The rankings' objectives are to provide information to future students and influence public policy (Universitas, 2016). The University Ranking evaluates teaching-focused universities using a different formula than research-based universities, and it publishes four ranking lists by university type, including "Teaching Universities," "Teaching Universities with Future Research Goals," "Research Universities," and "Research Universities in Selective Areas" (Çakır et al., 2015; Universitas, 2016). This ranking evaluates universities (teaching/research) on the number of admitted students (weighted at 15%/15%); the number of professors, PhD-holding faculty, and publications (25%/15%); faculty-student ratio, average degree length, and retention rates (40%/30%); and years of institutional accreditation and expense per student (20%/10%). In addition to these criteria, research universities are evaluated on research (15%) and doctoral programs and internationalization (15%) (Laus & Morosini, 2005; Universitas, 2016). By adopting this framework, the *El Mercurio* ranking recognizes the distinct roles of institutions and differentiation in the Chilean higher education system.

National rankings implemented by media organizations have also emerged in Mexico, such as those published by *Reforma* and *El Universal*, which mainly target students by providing information about program choice and post-study employability. *Reforma*, published since 2008, surveys over 1,700 employers in the Valley of Mexico region on sixteen careers: management, architecture, communication, accounting, law, graphic design, economics, gastronomy, electrical engineering, systems engineering, industrial engineering, mechatronic engineering, chemistry, medicine, marketing, and psychology (Reforma, 2018). Since 2007, *El Universal* has published an annual supplement, Mejores Universidades, which includes a ranking of higher education institutions and a ranking of twenty-five courses to provide a guide to future students applying to an undergraduate program (El Universal, 2015, 2018).

In Colombia, the magazine *Sapiens Research* with the consulting firm Sapiens Research Group has published multiple university rankings since 2011 (Sapiens Research, n.d.). These include the U-Sapiens research ranking; ASC-Sapiens for the social appropriation of knowledge; ART-Sapiens, a publication of scientific articles; DTI-Sapiens, of technology and innovation development; PRE-Sapiens, an undergraduate programs ranking; and POST-Sapiens, a graduate programs ranking. While the Sapiens rankings are diverse in what they evaluate, they do not provide a comprehensive university ranking that attempts to integrate all criteria. For instance, the U-Sapiens research ranking utilizes public data from government agencies to evaluate the number of indexed journals, graduate students, and research groups in each higher education institution (Sapiens Research, n.d.). The distinction of each ranking shows that they target different audiences and attempt to achieve different goals.

Argentina, which has also witnessed the growing privatization of higher education and has many universities in the world rankings, has not followed the national rankings trends seen in Brazil, Chile, Colombia, and Mexico, as it has not yet adopted state-run or privately organized rankings. While in 2009 53 per cent of higher education institutions were private, public institutions continue to be the main providers of higher education, following the concepts of autonomy and autarchy (Mollis, 2015; PROPHE, n.d.). Currently, Argentina's government has an institutional evaluation procedure by the National Commission for University Evaluation and Accreditation (CONEAU) that ensures that universities comply with national law, but it is not used to inform students or provide a ranking (CONEAU, n.d.). This tendency is also visible in other countries in the region with smaller higher education systems, such as Honduras, Peru, and Uruguay.

National Rankings in Comparative Perspective

The review of national university rankings across three quite different world regions in this chapter shows some of the similarities and differences in the way national approaches to rankings are unfolding. Four patterns emerge from our analysis of these ranking systems and their uses.

First, the idea of ranking universities is disseminating in these regions through both formal national rankings and policy tools that generate rankable data on universities for quality assurance, government control, and accountability. In Kazakhstan and Romania, national university rankings with the target of pushing universities towards a "world-class university" model with a global presence have been introduced. Elsewhere in CEE, the Belarusian government uses the national ranking to control the level of university compliance to the national recruitment plan. In Latin America, while most rankings have been created by media organizations, the Brazilian government-run university rankings were established from quality assessment processes to exercise pressure over private institutions to conform to national norms while ensuring public institutions follow government policies. Following privatization of higher education systems in Latin America, other governments have implemented measures to assess institutional quality, with similar goals to those of Brazil. As the idea of rankings becomes more usual, not only in formal national rankings but also in other policy tools, governments normalize a perspective that emphasizes hierarchy and stratification. This has implications for policymaking by conditioning the way problems are framed and the policy alternatives to address them, which become articulated through the assumption of inter-institutional competition.

A second trend identified in the chapter is the use of rankings to reduce information asymmetries between higher education institutions and the public. The marketization of higher education systems across the three regions has created the conditions in which commercially initiated national university rankings have emerged as responses to the needs of students to obtain appropriate information about a range of available higher education options and to signal their relative value. The rapid recent growth of private higher education sectors in some countries in CEE (Hungary, Poland, and Ukraine) and Latin America[9] (Argentina, Brazil, Chile, Colombia, and Mexico) has expanded the demand for information on the wider array of programs and institutions from parents, future students, and employers. As a result, many media organizations have published rankings that directly target these actors in their decision-making processes, using methodologies that emphasize employability. Thus, the purpose of rankings in these jurisdictions has been to provide comparative information in a more easily accessible way to students and their parents. The creation and use of rankings as an information tool targeting the public clearly emerges in response to privatization and differentiation in these contexts. However, whether national rankings influence student choices in these regions remains an open empirical question.

A third finding is that the size of the higher education system may play a role in determining the relevance of national rankings. In some small systems such as Tajikistan and Turkmenistan in Central Asia, the absence of national rankings may be explained by the fact that the sector is wholly state-run. As governments already exert control over the entire higher education system, they do not need to enforce policy reforms. Further, it may be that in these instances, states do not perceive any need to differentiate between the small number of institutions. In CEE, the absence of national rankings in small higher education systems in Hungary and Slovakia may be because the emphasis is alternatively placed instead on department- or program-level rankings. We also found that small systems in Latin America such as Honduras, Peru, and Uruguay do not have government-run national university rankings.

The fourth observation from this cross-national study is that the extent of exposure to outside ideas on higher education appears to influence the development of national rankings. By making it a national policy goal to have two HEIs perform well in a global higher education ranking, Kazakhstan uses national rankings not only to improve the overall quality of the national higher education system but to enhance and legitimize the country's growing global presence as well. The Central Asian and CEE countries that adopted the Bologna Process in the early 2000s have led the way in operationalizing globally diffused policy mechanisms such as university rankings to stimulate quality and performance improvement of national universities, though focusing only on "flagship" universities in many cases. In cases where Bologna principles are still in the implementation stage, such as the Kyrgyz Republic and Uzbekistan in Central Asia, national rankings are at a more nascent phase. In Latin America, systems that have become highly privatized have undergone policy efforts aimed at quality assurance, coupled with policy prescriptions to induce market-like competition, thus leading to the appearance of ranking mechanisms.

Although a number of countries across the three regions examined in this chapter do not have national rankings, we nevertheless argue that national ranking mechanisms will likely expand further and will continue to remain relevant in Central Asia, CEE, and Latin America. The future expansion of national university rankings will likely be linked to unfolding large-scale national higher education reforms. These reforms will seek to raise the quality of national higher education systems while embracing globalized ideas such as privatization, competition, and quality assurance. In some instances, the objective to become more embedded in global higher education processes will lead to the adoption of globally used metrics and indicators of success in the further development of national rankings. In other cases, incremental policy efforts at enhancing academic quality and ensuring institutional compliance to national standards might lead to new ranking mechanisms.

Now that we have identified a number of cross-national connections and divergences in the unfolding of national university rankings at the policy level in Central Asia, CEE, and Latin America through this study, future research might explore the impact of these developments on universities. The advent of national rankings challenges universities to shift their behaviour in how they respond to policy priorities, institutional mandates, and the needs of students. This calls for close empirical scrutiny of the effects of rankings and the extent to which they are achieving their goals.

NOTES

1 The issue of accreditation is a hot-button topic in Kazakhstan as well as the Kyrgyz Republic. It is directly connected to the idea of (good) quality higher education. All HEIs are being required to go through accreditation processes; independent national agencies have been or are being created to manage institutional accreditation. HEIs gain additional prestige for successfully accrediting courses through specialist international accreditation agencies.

2 Despite difficult political circumstances that are only recently beginning to thaw, Uzbekistan has long been home to international branch campuses. These currently represent institutions from Italy, Russia, Singapore, South Korea, and the United Kingdom.

3 The Ministry of Justice cited the IREG Observatory on Academic Ranking and Excellence, http://ireg-observatory.org/en. See also note 8.

4 The Berlin Principles were cited, http://www.ihep.org/research/publications/berlin -principles-ranking-higher-education-institutions. See also note 8.

5 There are three Russian branch campuses in Tajikistan; all are branches of state-funded universities. The University of Central Asia, which opened a campus in Tajikistan in 2017, is a regional university founded by international treaty. It is not considered a "Tajik" university for the purposes of this chapter.

6 There are over 2,500 universities in CEE. Only Russia's Moscow State University has appeared in the top 100 universities in the ARWU, with another seven universities from the region represented in the top 500: four Russian universities, two from Poland, and one from the Czech Republic. In the *Times Higher Education* (THE) World University Ranking 2018, four universities from Russia, one from Hungary, and one from the Czech Republic appeared in the top 500. Polish universities that first appeared in the 2011 edition of this ranking in the 301–400 band were all moved to the 601–800 band in the 2018 edition.

7 The Lisbon Strategy, also known as the Lisbon Agenda or Lisbon Process, was an action and development plan for the economy of the European Union between 2000 and 2010. It was set out by the European Council in Lisbon in March 2000.

The Lisbon Strategy was heavily based on the economic concepts of innovation as the motor for economic change (based on the writings of Joseph Schumpeter), the learning economy, and social and environmental renewal.

8 The IREG Observatory on Academic Ranking and Excellence is an international institutional non-profit association of ranking organizations, universities, and other bodies. Its purpose is to strengthen public awareness and understanding of issues related to university rankings and academic excellence. In 2006, the Berlin Principles on the Ranking of Higher Education Institutions set a framework for the elaboration and dissemination of rankings – whether they are national, regional, or global in scope – that ultimately is a system of continuous improvement and refinement of the methodologies used to conduct these rankings.

9 Although the higher education sectors in Kazakhstan and Kyrgyzstan in Central Asia include a significant mix of private providers, the expansion occurred much earlier, in the 1990s. It is only in CEE and Latin America that recent privatization is connected to this finding.

REFERENCES

Agachi, P.Ş. (2017). Improving performance of universities using university rankings: Case study, Al Farabi Kazakh National University, Kazakhstan. *Journal of Research in Higher Education, 1*(1), 23–36. https://doi.org/10.24193/jrhe.2017.1.3

Altbach, P.G. (2012). The globalization of college and university rankings. *Change: The Magazine of Higher Learning, 44*(1), 26–31. https://doi.org/10.1080/00091383.2012.636001

Amsler, S.S., & Bolsmann, C. (2012). University ranking as social exclusion. *British Journal of Sociology of Education, 33*(2), 283–301. https://doi.org/10.1080/01425692.2011.649835

Andreescu, L., Gheorghiu, R., Proteasa, V., & Curaj, A. (2012). Institutional diversification and homogeneity in Romanian higher education: The larger picture. In A. Curaj, P. Scott, L. Vlasceanu, & L. Wilson (Eds.), *European higher education at the crossroads: Between the Bologna Process and national reforms* (pp. 863–85). Springer Netherlands. https://doi.org/10.1007/978-94-007-3937-6_44

Antonowicz, D., Kohoutek, J., Pinheiro, R., & Hladchenko, M. (2017). The roads of "excellence" in Central and Eastern Europe. *European Educational Research Journal, 16*(5), 547–67. https://doi.org/10.1177/1474904116683186

Arocena, R., & Sutz, J. (2005). Latin American universities: From an original revolution to an uncertain transition. *Higher Education, 50*(4), 573–92. https://doi.org/10.1007/s10734-004-6367-8

Asia-Plus. (2016, 6 October). Vuzy Tajikistana: Kto samiy-samiy? [Tajik HEIs: Who is the best of the best?]. https://news.tj/ru/news/tajikistan/20161006/vuzi-tadzhikistana-kto-samii-samii (link no longer available)

Avshenyuk, N. (2014). The phenomenon of "global education space" as an object of scientific-pedagogical research. *Comparative Professional Pedagogy, 4*(1), 25–31. https://doi.org/10.2478/rpp-2014-0004

Balán, J. (2012). Research universities in Latin America: The challenges of growth and institutional diversity. *Social Research, 79*(3), 741–70.

Becerra, J.I.V., Arellano, C.I.M., & Orozco, J.E.F. (2015). Perspectivas actuales sobre los rankings mundiales de universidades [Current perspectives on global university rankings]. *Revista de La Educación Superior, 44*(175), 41–67. https://doi .org/10.1016/j.resu.2015.09.001

Brunner, J.J. (1993). Chile's higher education: Between market and state. *Higher Education, 25*(1), 35–43. https://doi.org/10.1007/bf01384040

"Bulgarian university ranking system." (n.d.). Retrieved 20 November 2018 from https://rsvu.mon.bg/rsvu4/#/.

Cabinet of Ministers of Ukraine. (2018). Pro zatverdjennya formuly rozpodilu zagal'nogo obsyagu vydatkiv zagal'nogo fondu budgetu mig zakladamy vyschoy osvity [About approving the funding formula for public universities]. Cabinet of Ministers of Ukraine.

Çakır, M.P., Acartürk, C., Alaşehir, O., & Çilingir, C. (2015). A comparative analysis of global and national university ranking systems. *Scientometrics, 103*(3), 813–48. https://doi.org/10.1007/s11192-015-1586-6

CONEAU. (n.d.). Evaluación externa [External evaluation]. https://www.coneau.gob .ar/coneau/evaluacion-institucional/evaluacion-externa

Dakowska, D., & Harmsen, R. (2015). Laboratories of reform? The Europeanization and internationalization of higher education in Central and Eastern Europe. *European Journal of Higher Education, 5*(1), 4–17. https://doi.org/10.1080/21568235 .2014.977318

David, D., Andronesi, O., Buzea, C., Florian, B., Matu, S., & Vlăsceanu, L. (2017). The 2017 university metaranking Romanian University Ranking. *Journal of Research in Higher Education, 1*(2), 31–50. https://doi.org/10.24193/JRHE.2017.2.2

DeYoung, A.J., Kataeva, Z., & Jonbekova, D. (2018). Higher education in Tajikistan: Institutional landscape and key policy developments. In J. Huisman, A. Smolentseva, & I.D. Froumin (Eds.), *25 years of transformations of higher education systems in post-Soviet countries: Reform and continuity* (pp. 363–85). Palgrave Macmillan.

Dobbins, M. (2011). *Higher education policies in Central and Eastern Europe: Convergence towards a common model?* Palgrave Macmillan.

Eduline. (2016, 17 November). These are the best universities and colleges: The HVG 2017 ranking was published. http://eduline.hu/felsooktatas/2016/11/17/HVG _felsooktatasi_rangsor_2017_ZZ697X

El Universal. (2015). Mejores universidades 2015 [Best universities 2015]. http:// ediciondigital.eluniversalmas.com.mx/suplementos/Mejores_Universidades_2015

El Universal. (2018). Mejores universidades 2018 [Best universities 2018]. http:// interactivo.eluniversal.com.mx/2018/mejores-universidades-2018

Espeland, W.N., & Sauder, M. (2016). *Engines of anxiety: Academic rankings, reputation, and accountability.* Russell Sage Foundation.

"Euro Osvita [European education]. (n.d.). "What is ranking?" Retrieved 13 November 2018 from http://www.euroosvita.net/?category=21&id=229

Folha de São Paulo. (2018). RUF: Ranking das universidades do Brasil [Ranking of universities in Brasil]. http://ruf.folha.uol.com.br/2018

Frankopan, P. (2015). *The silk roads: A new history of the world.* Bloomsbury.

Geiger, R.L. (1993). Research, graduate education and the ecology of American universities: An imperative history. In S. Rothblatt & B. Wittrock (Eds.), *The European and American university since 1800* (pp. 234–59). Cambridge University Press.

Gregorutti, G., Espinoza O., González, L.E., & Loyola, J. (2016). What if privatising higher education becomes an issue? The case of Chile and Mexico. *Compare: A Journal of Comparative and International Education, 46*(1), 136–58. https://doi.org/10.1080/03057925.2014.916605

Harvey, L. (2008). Rankings of higher education institutions: A critical review. *Quality in Higher Education, 14*(3), 187–207. https://doi.org/10.1080/13538320802507711

Hazelkorn, E. (2014). Reflections on a decade of global rankings: What we've learned and outstanding issues. *European Journal of Education, 49*(1), 12–28. https://doi.org/10.1111/ejed.12059

Hazelkorn, E. (2015). *Rankings and the reshaping of higher education: The battle for world-class excellence.* Springer.

Hladchenko, M., de Boer, H.F., & Westerheijden, D.F. (2016). Establishing research universities in Ukrainian higher education: The incomplete journey of a structural reform. *Journal of Higher Education Policy and Management, 38*(2), 111–25. https://doi.org/10.1080/1360080X.2016.1150232

Independent Agency for Accreditation and Rating [IAAR]. 2018. Reyting Vuzov 2018 [HEI rankings 2018]. http://www.iaar.kz/ru/rejting/rejting-vuzov-2018

INEP. (2015a). Conceito Preliminar de Curso (CPC) [Preliminary course concept]. http://portal.inep.gov.br/conceito-preliminar-de-curso-cpc-

INEP. (2015b). Índice Geral de Cursos (IGC) [General course index]. http://portal.inep.gov.br/indice-geral-de-cursos-igc-

Jöns, H., & Hoyler, M. (2013, May). Global geographies of higher education: The perspective of world university rankings. *Geoforum, 46*, 45–59. https://doi.org/10.1016/j.geoforum.2012.12.014

Kalanova, S. (2008). The methodology of ranking higher education institutions in Kazakhstan. *Higher Education in Europe, 33*(2–3), 303–10. https://doi.org/10.1080/03797720802254155

Krasheninnikov, A.A., & Nechaev, N.N. (1990). Universities as centres of culture: An historical approach to higher education in Central Asia. *Higher Education in Europe, 15*(3), 54–60. https://doi.org/10.1080/0379772900150308

Kwiek, M. (2014). Changing higher education and welfare states in postcommunist Central Europe: New contexts leading to new typologies? *Human Affairs, 24*(1), 48–67. https://doi.org/10.2478/s13374-014-0205-1

Kwiek, M. (2016). Global university rankings in the Polish context: The University of Warsaw, a case study." In M. Yudkevich, P.G. Altbach, & L.E. Rumbley (Eds.), *The global academic rankings game: Changing institutional policy, practice and academic life* (pp. 1–23). Routledge.

Larraín, C., & Zurita, S. (2008). The new student loan system in Chile's higher education. *Higher Education, 55*(6), 683–702. https://doi.org/10.1007/s10734-007-9083-3

Laus, S.P., & Morosini, M.C. (2005). Internationalization of higher education in Brazil. In H. De Wit, I.C. Jaramillo, J. Gacel-Avila, & J. Knight (Eds.), *Higher education in Latin America: The international dimension* (p. 387). World Bank.

Inform.kg. (n.d.). Reyting "ymnosti" vuziv Kyrgyzstana [Ranking the "intelligence" of HEIs in Kyrgyzstan]. Retrieved 30 October 2020 from http://www.inform.kg/ru /interesnoe/420

Longden, B. (2011). Ranking indicators and weights. In J.C. Shin, R.K. Toutkoushian, & U. Teichler (Eds.), *University rankings: Theoretical basis, methodology and impacts on global higher education* (pp. 73–104). https://doi.org/10.1007/978-94-007-1116-7_5

Lukman, R., Krajnc, D., & Glavič, P. (2010). University ranking using research, educational and environmental indicators. *Journal of Cleaner Production, 18*(7), 619–28. https://doi.org/10.1016/j.jclepro.2009.09.015

Marginson, S. (2007). Global university rankings: Implications in general and for Australia. *Journal of Higher Education Policy and Management, 29*(2), 131–42. https://doi.org/10.1080/13600800701351660

Marginson, S., & van der Wende, M. (2007). To rank or to be ranked: The impact of global rankings in higher education. *Journal of Studies in International Education, 11*(3–4), 306–29. https://doi.org/10.1177/1028315307303544

Matějů, P., Řeháková, B., & Simonová, N. (2007). Structural growth of inequality in access to higher education in the Czech Republic. In Y. Shavit, R. Arum, & A. Gamoran (Eds.), *Stratification in higher education: A comparative study* (pp. 374–99). Stanford University Press.

Ministry of Education and Science, Kyrgyz Republic. (2018, 2 February). Ministerstvo Obrazovaniya i Nauki KR provedyet ranzhirovaniye vuzov respubliki [Kyrgyz Republic Ministry of Education and Science will conduct national HEI ranking]. http://edu.gov.kg/ru/news/ministerstvo-obrazovaniya-i-nauki-kr-provedet -ranzhirovanie-vuzov-respubliki

Ministry of Education and Science of the Republic of Kazakhstan. (2010). State Program of Education Development in the Republic of Kazakhstan for 2011–2020. Decree of the President of the Republic of Kazakhstan 1118. Astana.

Ministry of Education and Science of the Republic of Kazakhstan. (2017, 16 January). List of higher education institutions and description of their legal form. http://edu .gov.kz/ru/deyatelnost/detail.php?ELEMENT_ID=554

Ministry of Science and Higher Education of the Russian Federation. (n.d.-a). *Project Overview*. 5-100 – Russian Academic Excellence Project. Retrieved 13 November 2018 from https://www.5top100.ru/en

Ministry of Science and Higher Education of the Russian Federation. (n.d.-b). *Rankings*. 5-100 – Russian Academic Excellence Project. Retrieved 13 November 2018 from https://5top100.ru/rankings

Ministry of Science and Higher Education of the Russian Federation. (n.d.-c). *Rankings Interfax*. 5-100 – Russian Academic Excellence Project. Retrieved 13 November 2018 from https://5top100.ru/rankings/interfax

Ministry of Science and Higher Education of the Russian Federation. (n.d.-d). "Expert RA." Retrieved 13 November 2018 from https://5top100.ru/rankings/expert-ra

Mollis, M. (2015). A decade of reform in Argentina. *International Higher Education, 30*. https://doi.org/10.6017/ihe.2003.30.7350

National Statistics Committee of the Kyrgyz Republic. (n.d.). *Official statistics: Education and culture*. Retrieved 13 June 2018 from http://www.stat.kg/ru/statistics /obrazovanie.

Nazarbayev, N. (2014, 17 January). Address of the president of the Republic of Kazakhstan N. Nazarbayev to the nation: "Kazakhstan's Way – 2050: Common aim, common interests, common future." http://www.akorda.kz/en/addresses/addresses _of_president/page_215752_

Neave, G. (2003). On the return from Babylon: A long voyage around history, ideology and systems change. In J. File & L. Goedegebuure (Eds.), *Real-time systems: Reflections on higher education in the Czech Republic, Hungary, Poland and Slovenia* (pp. 15–37). CHEPS.

Oka, N. (2018). Grades and degrees for sale: Understanding informal exchanges in Kazakhstan's education sector. *Problems of Post-Communism, 66*(5), 1–13. https:// doi.org/10.1080/10758216.2018.1468269

Oleksiyenko, A. (2014). Socio-economic forces and the rise of the world-class research university in the post-Soviet higher education space: The case of Ukraine. *European Journal of Higher Education, 4*(3), 249–65. https://doi.org/10.1080/21568235.2014.9 16537

Ordorika, I., & Lloyd, M. (2015). International rankings and the contest for university hegemony. *Journal of Education Policy, 30*(3), 385–405. https://doi.org/10.1080/0268 0939.2014.979247

Peyrouse, S. (2012). *Turkmenistan: Strategies of power, dilemmas of development*. M.E. Sharpe.

Platonova, D. (2018). "Appendix." In J. Huisman, A. Smolentseva, & I.D. Froumin (Eds.), *25 years of transformations of higher education systems in post-Soviet countries: Reform and continuity* (pp. 461–82). Palgrave Macmillan.

Polidori, M. (2009). Políticas de avaliação da educação superior Brasileira: Provão, SINAES, IDD, CPC, IGC e ... outros índices [Evaluation policies of Brazilian higher education: Provão, SINAES, IDD, CPC, IGC and ... other indexes]. *Avaliação Revista*

Da Avaliação Da Educação Superior (Campinas), 14(2). https://doi.org/10.1590 /s1414-40772009000200009

PROPHE. (n.d.). *National databases*. Retrieved 23 October 2018 from http://prophe .org/en/data-laws/national-databases

Pusser, B., & Marginson, S. (2013). University rankings in critical perspective. *Journal of Higher Education, 84*(4), 544–68. https://doi.org/10.1080/00221546.2013.11777301

Ramirez, F.O. (2010). Accounting for excellence: Transforming universities into organizational actors. In L.M. Portnoi, V.D. Rust, & S.S. Bagley (Eds.), *Higher education, policy, and the global competition phenomenon* (pp. 43–58). Palgrave Macmillan. https://doi.org/10.1057/9780230106130_4

Reeves, M. (2005). Of credits, kontrakty and critical thinking: Encountering "market reforms" in Kyrgyzstani higher education. *European Educational Research Journal, 4*(1), 5–21. https://doi.org/10.2304/eerj.2005.4.1.4

Reforma. (2018). Las mejores universidades 2018 [The best universities 2018]. https:// www.reforma.com/aplicacioneslibre/galeriamultimedia/default.aspx?id=108646&m d5=ae30076ca39b806be89b0bd287052353&ta=0dfdbac11765226904c16cb9ad1b2efe

Rust, V.D., & Kim, S. (2015). Globalization and global university rankings. In J. Zajda (Ed.), *Second international handbook on globalisation, education and policy research* (pp. 167–80). Springer Netherlands. https://doi.org/10.1007/978-94-017-9493-0_11

Sabzalieva, E. (2018a, 15 June). Ranking corruption in Kazakh universities. *Emma Sabzalieva* (blog). https://emmasabzalieva.com/2018/06/15/ranking-corruption-in -kazakh-universities

Sabzalieva, E. (2018b, 23 July). Uzbekistan releases first university ranking. *Emma Sabzalieva* (blog). https://emmasabzalieva.com/2018/07/22/uzbekistan-releases -first-university-ranking

Sabzalieva, E. (2018c, 27 September). Resit required: Uzbekistan university rankings declared invalid. *Emma Sabzalieva* (blog). https://emmasabzalieva.com/2018/09/27 /resit-required-uzbekistan-university-rankings-declared-invalid

Sadlak, J., Merisotis, J., & Liu, N.C. (2008). University rankings: Seeking prestige, raising visibility and embedding quality – the editors' views. *Higher Education in Europe, 33*(2–3), 195–99. https://doi.org/10.1080/03797720802253645

Salmi, J., & Saroyan, A. (2007). League tables as policy instruments. *Higher Education Management and Policy, 19*(2), 1–38. https://doi.org/10.1787/hemp-v19-art10-en

Santos, A.P., & de Cerqueira, E.A. (2009). Ensino superior: Trajetória histórica e políticas recentes [Higher education: Recent historical and political trajectories]. *IX Colóquio Internacional Sobre Gestão Universitária Na América Do Sul.*

Sapiens Research. (n.d.). Los mejores colegios y universidades [The best colleges, the best universities]. Retrieved 7 October 2020 from https://www.srg.com.co

Šolc, M., Markulik, Š., & Sütőová, A. (2014). "Quality in contemporary university environment." *Procedia: Social and Behavioral Sciences, 143*, 703–7. https://doi .org/10.1016/j.sbspro.2014.07.467

Sputnik, K. (2016, 20 July). Reyting: Lucshie gosudarstvenniye vuzy nazvali v Minobrnauki [Ranking: Ministry of Education and Science names top state HEIs]. https://ru.sputnik.kg/Kyrgyzstan/20160720/1027933783.html

Stolz, I., Hendel, D.D., & Horn, A.S. (2010). Ranking of rankings: Benchmarking twenty-five higher education ranking systems in Europe. *Higher Education, 60*(5), 507–28. https://doi.org/10.1007/s10734-010-9312-z

Teichler, U. (2011). The future of university rankings. In J.C. Shin, R.K. Toutkoushian, & U. Teichler (Eds.), *University rankings: Theoretical basis, methodology and impacts on global higher education* (pp. 259–65). The changing academy – The changing academic profession in international comparative perspective. Springer Netherlands. https://doi.org/10.1007/978-94-007-1116-7_13

TUT.BY. (2014, 1 September). Minobrazovanie razrabotalo reiting vyzov Belarusi [The Ministry of Education has developed a national university ranking in Belarus]. https://news.tut.by/society/381641.html.

Universitas. (2016). Metodología: Ranking universidades [Methodology: University ranking]. http://rankinguniversidades.emol.com/clasificacion-metodologia-2016

Uribe, L. (2015). The decline of Colombian private higher education. *International Higher Education, 16*. https://doi.org/10.6017/ihe.2010.61.8517

Vorotnikov, E. (2018, 26 October). Government moves to raise quality of higher education. *University World News*, 526 edition. http://www.universityworldnews.com/article.php?story=20181020060212753

Werron, T., & Ringel, L. (2017). Rankings in a comparative perspective: Conceptual remarks. *Geschlossene Gesellschaften: Verhandlungen Des, 38*, 1–14.

Westerheijden, D.F., Federkeil, G., Cremonini, L., Kaiser, F., & Beerkens-Soo, M. (2011). Ranking goes international. In M. Rostan & M. Vaira (Eds.), *Questioning excellence in higher education: Policies, experiences and challenges in national and comparative perspective* (pp. 175–93). Higher education research in the 21st century series. Sense Publishers. https://doi.org/10.1007/978-94-6091-642-7_10

Wodak, R., & Fairclough, N. (2010). Recontextualizing European higher education policies: The cases of Austria and Romania. *Critical Discourse Studies, 7*(1), 19–40. https://doi.org/10.1080/17405900903453922

3 Global University Rankings' Visual Media, Cartography, and Geopolitics of Knowledge

RIYAD A. SHAHJAHAN, ANNABELLE ESTERA,
AND VIVEK VELLANKI

Introduction

Few have examined how global university rankings' (GURs) commercial media outlets (e.g., Times Higher Education [THE] and *U.S. News & World Report* [USN]), particularly their websites' visual representations, construct and circulate the meaning of higher education (HE; recent exceptions are Stack, 2013, 2016).[1] This is alarming given that these commercial GURs' websites garner substantial audiences. In their 2016/2017 media pack, THE boasted 24 million unique visitors over the past year, while USN reported a monthly audience of over 20 million unique visitors and 120 million page views. Furthermore, ranking popularity is largely based on media coverage of GURs (Stack, 2013). We thus lack a thorough understanding of the complex ways in which GURs' visual media depict HE (Stack, 2013).

We suggest that the visual media on commercial GURs' websites are significant sites for critical inquiry because they shape HE's public image and "(mis) educate" the general public (Estera & Shahjahan, 2018; Stack, 2016). Building on recent studies on media logics in global HE, GURs' role as global spaces of equivalences, and GURs' colonial ramifications (e.g., Ishikawa, 2009; Shahjahan et al., 2017), we respond to the following question: How do GURs' websites constitute and normalize HE regions of the world through visualization of HE? Building on our previous work examining GURs' student imagery (Estera & Shahjahan, 2018), here we focus on regional/national imagery because these websites offer an entry point to uncovering the global assemblages – underlying configurations through which global forms of knowledge (i.e., GURs) gain significance by de/reterritorializing space, culture, and society (Ong & Collier, 2005). To answer this question, we critically examined publicly available visual media artifacts on the THE and USN websites. Drawing on Walter Mignolo's (2011) notion of geopolitics of knowledge, Stuart Hall's heuristics of representation (Hall, 1997b, 1997c), and pan-semiotic categories (Kress & van Leeuwen,

2006; van Leeuwen, 1996), we demonstrate how THE and USN ranking media constitute meanings about HE regions globally.

We next elaborate on our theoretical and methodological approaches for our analysis. Based on analysis of two GURs websites' visual imagery, we argue that THE and USN GUR media offer a visual cartography of global HE reflecting the geopolitics of knowledge in global HE. As such, GURs imagery privileges and "humanizes" epistemically privileged core HE regions and HE institutions (HEI). By geopolitics of knowledge we are referring to a set of knowledge/power relations that (a) reflects existing hierarchies in global HE and (b) perpetuates a gaze (or representation) of the world that is considered universal and context free. We suggest that GURs rankings media are not simply constructing and informing viewers about the quality and excellence of HE, but simultaneously teaching them how to view university campuses and regions of the world that often reproduce historical geopolitics of knowledge.

Unpacking Representation and GURs Visual Media

We draw foremost upon Mignolo's (2005, 2011) geopolitics of knowledge to frame our analysis. It signifies how all knowledge systems originate in geographic and social contexts and are situated within historically and transnationally constituted power relations. We use geopolitics of knowledge in the HE context in two ways. First, it refers to the *existing hierarchical global* HE system that privileges certain regions of the world (e.g., Anglo-Euro-American contexts) as metropolitan centres of knowledges and learning while allocating others to the periphery. Within the geopolitics of knowledge, those who occupy zones of being – regions of the world whose humanity is taken for granted (and is socially recognized through human/social rights, and whose knowledge counts as "knowledge") – have the epistemic privilege to articulate global designs (Shahjahan & Morgan, 2016). Yet epistemically privileged centres of knowledge do not map neatly onto national containers but comprise privileged institutions within peripheral zones, such as the University of Cape Town in South Africa (Shahjahan & Morgan, 2016).

Second, by geopolitics of knowledge we refer to a set of knowledge/power relations that privileges a certain *gaze* or representation of the world deemed universal, delocalized, and applied unquestioningly. Here, we will demonstrate that GURs visual imagery reflects and perpetuates a geopolitical gaze (i.e., attitudes towards and views of the world) that originates in geographic and social contexts. Yet positionality of the gaze is simultaneously rendered invisible by its worldwide normalization (Mignolo, 2003). Stuart Hall highlights how representations relate to geopolitical gaze: "I think that what we call 'the global' is always composed of varieties of articulated particularities … the global is the self-presentation of the dominant particular" (1997a, p. 67). Considering visual representations, this means that only certain local contexts, always already derivatives of particular historical-material conditions, have the social privilege (i.e., rankers) to shape a HE global imaginary. To illuminate the particularities of the gaze embedded within GUR images, we draw upon van Leeuwen (1996), who articulates various "pan-semiotic" categories (particular effects of representational choices of social actors) through which a gaze is naturalized (p. 34). In our case, we view the social actors as including tourist sites, university architecture, and students.

To elucidate the geopolitics of knowledge, we ground our visual analysis in Hall's (1997b, 1997c) heuristics of representation. Hall (1997b) argues that a represented object (here "regions") has "no fixed meaning, no real meaning in the obvious sense, until it has been represented" (p. 7). Unlike normative notions of representations that suggest representation as the mere act of depicting, distorting, or standing in for the object already there (i.e., true meaning), Hall (1997b) suggests representation is more complicated, entailing the process by which meaning is given to the depicted object. Therefore, representation constitutes meaning. Furthermore, the reader (or viewer) is as important as the writer (or image maker) in producing meaning and may take different meanings (Hall, 1997b). Thus, we focus on our image readings; intentions of the image producers are beyond the scope of our study.

We use five pan-semiotic categories to analyse the imagery. Hall's (1997c) "identification" is the first category that is key to our analysis. Identification refers to the degree to which one can picture oneself within an image (Hall, 1997b). Advertising "works by attempting to win identification" (Hall, 1997c, p. 16). We see these GURs images as a form of GURs advertising promoting the use of their rankings and legitimizing their "weak expertise" (Lim, 2017).

The remaining pan-semiotic categories come from the work of van Leeuwen (1996) in discourse analysis and Kress and van Leeuwen's (2006) work in "visualization," which explores the "grammar of visual design." Van Leeuwen (1996) provides the pan-semiotic category of "personalization vs. impersonalization," or the "human" element within a representation (p. 59). Kress and van Leeuwen's (2006) "social distance" (p. 124), "angle" (p. 133), and "contact" (offer vs. demand) (p. 186) provide a lens to interpret attitudinal meanings and implied relationships of power between image and viewer. "Social distance" is conveyed through the distance between viewer and object. This difference in relationship between viewer and image makes closer shots more desirable to the viewer, making the image more inviting and personalized and providing more opportunity for identification with the image. Angle – if shots are taken from above, below, or at eye level – communicates a particular power differential. Eye level communicates "equality" between the viewer and image, making identification more likely. Finally, "demand" images include participant gaze at the viewer. The "eye contact" of the "demand" image makes it more desirable to the viewer, more

Table 3.1. Pan-semiotic categories of inclusion/exclusion embedded in visual imagery

Identification	Strong identification (viewer can easily project themselves into image)	↔		Weak identification (difficult for viewer to project themselves into image)
Personalization	Personalization (represented as personalized human beings)	↔		Impersonalization (abstract or objectified human)
Social Distance	Close shot (intimate/ personal)	Medium shot (social)		Long shot (impersonal)
Angle	Eye level, frontal angle (equality/involvement)	High angle (viewer power)		Low angle (represented participant power)
Contact	Demand (gaze at the viewer, which demands relationship)			Offer (absence of gaze at the viewer, as if social actors are items of information on display)

Sources: Hall, 1997c; Kress & van Leeuwen, 2006; van Leeuwen, 1996.

readily inviting identification, in contrast to "offer" images. Table 3.1 summarizes the approach to our visual analysis and use of pan-semiotic categories, wherein representations depicted in a manner that aligns more with the left-hand side are more desirable to the viewer of the GUR image. While Hall's heuristic of representation forms the foundation of our visual grounding, Kress and van Leeuwen provide additional tools for interpreting images and how they reflect the geopolitics of knowledge.

Methodology

To begin, we discuss THE and USN rankings websites to provide context for our subsequent analysis.

THE

Times Higher Education (THE) entered the world of global rankings in 2004 as a joint ranking with Quacquarelli Symonds (QS) until 2009. Since then, Times Higher Education World University Rankings (THEWUR) has added to its rankings portfolio, including World Reputation Rankings (2011), Asia university rankings (2013), 150 under 50 rankings (2012), BRICS (Brazil, Russia, India, China, and South Africa) and emerging economies rankings (2014), and Latin American rankings (2016). According to the THE, such rankings have developed in response to demand for "global league tables that reflect regional and economic contexts[,] and an increasing range of institutions want to benchmark themselves against the world's best" (Baty, 1990). Students are one of THE's main audiences, in addition to governments and universities. As described on its World University Rankings page, THE claims itself as "a vital resource for students, helping them choose where to study."

USN

U.S. News & World Report's (USN) Global University Rankings began in October 2014 (*U.S. News & World Report*, 2014). USN's Global University Rankings builds upon the success and reputation of its US undergraduate college rankings, "the pre-eminent marker of educational value and quality among the US public and beyond" (Chang & Osborn 2005, p. 340). USN is the first American-based publisher to enter the global rankings space (Redden, 2014). In addition to the overall Global University Rankings, regional rankings available for Africa, Asia, Australia/New Zealand, Europe, and Latin America highlight the institutions included in the overall global rankings. For instance, sorting the rankings by region shows that the University of Cape Town is both #1 in Africa and #103 in the world in the 2021 rankings. Notably, USN also provides rankings for the "Best Arab Region Universities," which were developed using a different methodology and because "global university rankings typically include very few Arab region schools," as described on the FAQs page. Similar to THE, USN's Global University Rankings focus primarily on a student audience. As stated by a USN editor and chief content officer, "as higher education becomes more global, our new rankings will set standards and allow students to better evaluate all of their options" (*U.S. News & World Report*, 2014).

Data Collection and Analysis

Our analysis draws on THE's and USN's publicly available media visual artifacts, such as the banners and images on their main page and images connected to blog posts. From the THE website, we collected images from or linked to on their "Rankings" and "Student" pages. From the USN website, we drew images from or linked to on the "Best Global Universities" page, including the "Global University Advice for Students and Parents" section. For both websites, images were no more than one click away from the aforementioned pages.[2] We selected GURs visual artifacts salient to our inquiry available during January 2016–December 2017. Thus, of the 196 images we downloaded, our analysis included the 121 images which had an explicit reference to a region or country. These images were a rich source of qualitative visual data for understanding HE representations (Merriam, 1998) and highlighted GURs' intentional commitment to visualization of HE.

To analyse the images, we downloaded them and placed them into a Power-Point file, pasting one image on each slide in chronological order by the date they were downloaded. To uncover various representational tropes and signifying practices, we openly coded visuals related to "regions of the world." We coded different regions/countries based on corresponding article titles and captions (e.g., "Best Universities in Australia 2017") or on visual markers known to the authors (e.g., the Eiffel Tower in France). We also noted instances where titles were broad yet visually marked by particular locations (e.g., "World University Rankings 2016–2017" depicting the University of Oxford). To code them, researchers then put comments and observations about each image within the notes section of the slide, noting what was shown (e.g., buildings, landscape, etc.), elements of "social distance," "angle," and "offer vs. demand" (Kress & van Leeuwen, 2006), and how these may contribute to a sense of "identification" (Hall, 1997b). We then reorganized the visuals to appear geographically so that images representing each continent and country were together, to aid us in ascertaining any visual patterns between and across regional contexts. As suggested by van Leeuwen (1996), representational choices "need not always be rigidly 'either/or' ... In such cases the categories remain nevertheless useful for making explicit how the social actors are represented" (p. 67). Additionally, we indicate discrepancies and outliers in visual patterns throughout our analysis, indicating variation and also the limitations of these variations.

After the preliminary coding, we further contextualized the data within our framework – drawing from Mignolo's geopolitics of knowledge, Hall's heuristics of representation, and Kress and van Leeuwen's visualization – foregrounding the regional nature of visuals displayed in GURs' website images. In essence, we argue that within each pan-semiotic category described in table 3.1, the more desirable representational choice in GURs imagery generally lies along the left side of the table. Patterns in the pan-semiotic categories thus allow us to make claims about the geopolitics of knowledge.[3] These concepts prompt us to ask: How do GURs' websites constitute regional HE through visualization of HE? With whom and what type of HE regions are the images seeking to promote identification? What kinds of mobilities do they legitimize? Whose desires are they seeking to construct, and how?

Having shared our methodology, we want to note some cautionary tales of visual analyses in GURs research. Like any form of mass communication, websites are not static but constantly in flux. Hence, as we analysed these websites' imagery, we noticed how images are added, moved, or replaced all the time. Thus, we had to choose a time frame (January 2016–December 2017). Furthermore, given that these visual media may include stock images, it is hard to discern where they originated, unless the images contain copyrights or captions telling us where they are from (e.g., Getty Images, iStock). The fact that the images are all sourced from outside USN and THE adds another potential layer of inquiry that is outside the scope of this paper.

Based on our analysis of the visual imagery and applying the above frameworks, we identified three major themes around geopolitics of knowledge: (1) tourist gaze, (2) campus architectural gaze, and (3) (de)humanizing students, which we present next.

Tourist Gaze

While both websites appear to feature most regions of the world (THE more so than USN), our visual analysis revealed hierarchies in representations reflecting the existing geopolitics of knowledge in global HE. GURs imagery favoured epistemically privileged HE regions or institutions. Our collection of GURs imagery territorialized and spatialized global HE by featuring a tourist gaze – carefully chosen images featuring a context's uniqueness and drawing on "selected elements of history, heritage, culture, ways of life, and various features of townscape and landscape" (Bajc, 2011, p. 1466). In our case, such imagery is meant to promote a location's attractiveness as a potential site of learning as it is in stark contrast with an audience's everyday lives. Overall, a tourist gaze helps create anticipations in the audience about what they will encounter during their trip and further fuel desire to experience these particular imaginaries (Bajc, 2011). We will demonstrate later how certain regions of the world are spatialized as "global" or "international" sites of learning using a tourist gaze that is more personalized, while others are impersonally represented through more "extraordinary" cultural or nature-oriented artifacts.

The GURs imagery we studied territorialized global HE by depicting various forms of touristy artifacts (i.e., townscape, landmarks, cultural or historical sites). Such imagery privileged Anglo-American or Western European contexts as desirable/ideal locations for sites of learning as they featured not only touristy national or city markers but also students (signifying learning) that were absent in other regional imagery. Particular tourist landmark and townscape tropes recurred across GURs imagery to symbolize "global" education/universities or "overseas" education. These tourist landmarks consisted of, for instance, the Eiffel Tower, for Paris or France; and the Tower Bridge and a red phone booth, for London or the UK. For instance, in USN blog posts on "overseas bachelor's degrees," "global universities," or "Europe" contained images of smiling students with either the Eiffel Tower, Big Ben, or the Tower Bridge in the background. As such, USN's article "Consider a Gap Year as a Prospective International Student" features a close shot of students with stretched arms next to a red telephone booth with the Big Ben clock tower in the background.[4] Given that these landmarks are conflated with an "overseas" credential (bachelor's degree), a region (Europe), or a type of university ("global"), such imagery spatializes the "global" or "international" in certain ways. Furthermore, while they are depicting tourist objects to spatialize, they simultaneously personalize these regions by portraying smiling human beings (i.e., students), thus encoding such regions as global sites of learning. To put it simply, given the student imagery, a viewer could potentially identify with the image as a student who is there for formal or disciplinary learning. Yet these tourist landmarks were often blurred in the background, thus assuming a familiarity among the audience. In short, the visual representation of the "international," overseas, and/or global with exclusively Western European tourist landmarks highlights the symbolic power of these regions as sites of HE learning, reflecting the existing hierarchies within the geopolitics of knowledge. These particular imageries thus naturalize a geopolitical "gaze" that assumes that global or international learning takes place in such Western European regions.

The geopolitics of knowledge informing GURs imagery was also apparent in how peripheral HE nations/regions' imagery featured touristy cultural or historical sites, social events, or a nature-oriented signifier. The latter regions, mostly non-Western regions, featured either long shots or close shots of landscapes consisting of cultural artifacts/events or nature-oriented objects. For instance, imagery of South Korea, China, and Latin America depicted sakura flowers blooming in Busan, the Forbidden City in Beijing, and Chichén Itzá in Yucatán, Mexico, respectively. We did not observe such touristy cultural social events, historical, or nature-oriented landmarks associated with American or European contexts.

GURs imagery also fixed meanings of particular non-Western HE regions by signifying a social/cultural event (or an informal cultural/social gathering). For instance, social events were prominent in depictions of Japan and Singapore. Images of the former depicted a social event involving a large man-made koi (carp fish), while those of the latter showed kites flying in the sky. Furthermore, a THE image from a January 2016 article entitled "Top 15 Universities in the Arab World Announced" featured a man riding a horse against a desert background appearing to be part of a social gathering. The Arab world is here objectified by tropes of the desert and horses, similar to past Orientalist images, signifying a "fixed" culture that is static, underdeveloped, and still tied to nature (see Said, 1979; Shaheen, 2001). These non-Western tourist images highlight how the distinct "Other" is fossilized in nature, culture, or history, signifying such contexts as sites of "extraordinary" cultural, natural, or historical consumption but not sites of "disciplinary" learning. GURs imagery thus naturalizes a Western-modernity gaze towards "Other" regions. Such imagery, although seemingly meant to highlight "touristy" and "cultural" attractions, ends up being impersonal and distant, as no visible marked students are depicted, nor is learning. Unlike in the epistemically privileged regions, a viewer could project themselves onto the image only as a tourist consuming a tourist site. GURs imagery thus reflects how peripheral zones in HE (e.g., Asia or Latin America) are still considered sources of historical or cultural knowledge but not "formal" or "disciplinary" knowledge gained through its educational institutions (Mignolo, 2003).

In short, GURs imagery's underlying visual grammar allocates such regions to the periphery of global HE, thereby perpetuating the geopolitics of knowledge. Such imagery is embedded in visual pan-semiotic categories of personalization and social distance to differentiate regions of global HE. Such imagery also highlights how the GURs' visual "gaze" towards the world is contextual and historical, and located in a Global North geopolitical space (where rankers are situated), but also are normalized across the globe. In summary, the "global" world of HE is visually represented through a tourist gaze embedded in numerous particularities reflecting the attitudes and values of "the dominant particular" (Hall, 1997a) (i.e., US- and UK-based rankings), reflecting the current geopolitics of knowledge in HE.

Campus Architectural Gaze

Beyond a tourist gaze, GURs' visual cartography featured HE architecture consisting of close/medium shots of campus buildings or long shots of campuses. Images of buildings and campuses powerfully symbolize HE institutions' aspirations and functions. They also act as "silent teachers" for aspiring HE students and their families (Edwards, 2014). Yet a visual grammar underlying such architectural imagery reflected the geopolitics of knowledge. Overall, GURs imagery privileged elite institutions in their respective regions (country or city), thereby legitimizing these rankings' "weak expertise" (Lim, 2017). For instance, UK and US imagery throughout the THE and USN websites depicted eye-level medium shots of university campus buildings in broad daylight at elite institutions like Oxford University, Stanford University, and Harvard University. Such elite universities' imagery featured traditional architecture symbolizing their historicity (i.e., buildings that are classical, highlighting "Western architecture" and distinctive features). Rarely did we see such Western elite universities in views of their existing modern campus buildings. Similarly, GURs imagery featured elite institutions for other countries or regions. This included the University of Humboldt for Germany, Indian Institute of Technology for India, and University of Cape Town for Africa, just to name a few. In short, GURs imagery narrates a story of elite institutions as desirable and core sites of learning and knowledge production, thus naturalizing a spatialized gaze towards these institutions as legitimate knowledge producers.

Yet campus shots highlighted rankers' attitudinal ambivalence towards HE "frontiers" (i.e., Australia or Asia) in terms of admiration, aspiration, or highlighting the rising global competition in HE, thereby legitimizing GURs logics. To this end, certain regional/national contexts featured modern buildings, highlighting functionality and instrumental learning. For instance, the THE's post "The Best Universities in Asia 2017" features an eye-level medium shot of a square modern building that has English labels such as "lecture theatre" on one side of the building and "engineering" on the top side. Furthermore, the THE's "Graduate Employability: Top Universities in Australia Ranked by Employers" highlights a curvy postmodern building (with lots of windows and steel) with students walking nearby. The (post)modern features of such Asian or Australian campuses highlighted the technical nature of their institutions. Such THE imagery, in particular, highlights how rankers would like to put competitive pressure on traditional Anglo-American institutions by depicting Asia or Australia as an admirable aggressor in global HE (e.g., increased investment by certain regions in HE or highly technical education orientation of their HE sectors) (Lim, 2017). In short, GURs imagery through its signifying practices demarcates the new frontiers of instrumental knowledge from the core centres of traditional knowledge.

We were particularly struck by how certain universities in peripheral zones of HE (or constructed as such) were associated with long-range shots of campuses, highlighting the colonial geopolitics of knowledge (Shahjahan, 2016). As mentioned above, while the THE signified Europe and the United States largely with eye-level medium-range shots of a university building or parts of university campuses, India and Africa[5] were marked by high-angle long-range shots of whole university campuses embedded in a natural landscape. The nature orientation and impersonal style of such imagery were particularly striking. These markers highlighted how Indian or African campuses were depicted as "far and away" from "modernity" or urban life (Reynolds, 2014), even though they are highly ranked within their countries or continent. For instance, "Best Universities in India" (THE) is marked by a long shot of the Indian Institute of Technology campus surrounded by mountains and a river. Similarly, the "Best Universities in Africa" (THE) is represented by a very-long-range shot of the University of Cape Town building also surrounded by overbearing mountains. Such visual imagery, particularly long shots, conveys an audience's "god-like top view" (Kress & van Leeuwen, 2006, p. 146) that both is impersonal and suggests a colonizing gaze. Viewers will find it difficult to identify with these regions as sites of learning. Furthermore, the aforementioned images of an Indian and an African institution were the only representations of a university in their country and continent, respectively, in our sample, thus fixing meaning about these HE regions as outside the frontiers of knowledge. In short, such visual imagery stifles any Global North-South or Global South-South student mobility aspirations and naturalizes a spatialized gaze of such regions as far and away.

In short, the core sectors/institutions of global HE are visually represented through medium and close-medium shots of traditional architecture, thereby legitimizing their symbolic power in global HE. These imageries, along with the text, thus construct and normalize a spatializing gaze through which the consumption of higher education opportunities is promoted. Such a campus architectural gaze plays a significant role in linking GUR audiences' affect to a certain place or region of the world (i.e., desirability) as higher-quality sites of learning. We have, however, highlighted above how such visual representations are embedded in particular pan-semiotic categories of social distance (i.e., personal vs. impersonal via a range of shots) and angle (eye level vs. high angle). The question of identification with particular HE regions was particularly salient in regional imagery depicting students for some regions, while students remained absent in others. We elaborate on the latter point in more detail next.

(De)Humanizing Students

We build upon the first theme's elaboration of spatializing tourist and architectural gaze and shift our focus towards visual representations of students. Here we ask, In what regional representations are students included? How does GURs imagery depict students in different regions? In this section, we demonstrate how GUR imagery naturalizes a (de)humanizing student gaze based on their regional locations. By (de)humanizing, we mean GUR imagery signifies "differential humanization," in which students in some parts of the world are presented in a more personalized manner, whereas those from other parts of the worlds are depicted in much more stereotypical or dehumanizing manner. We demonstrate that privileged/core epistemic regions' visual imagery humanizes students by depicting them in a range of settings and activities, more often in "demand" (includes participant gaze at the viewer) and close shots. These students are thus personalized, prompting identification. However, in peripheral epistemic contexts, images depicting students are limited; when visible, students are depicted in a narrow range of social/institutional settings and thus are comparatively dehumanized. Furthermore, this gaze of differential humanization reinforces the normalization of the geopolitics of knowledge and pre-established racial categories.

The desirability and social acceptance of the UK and US as privileged/core epistemic regions is bolstered by images highlighting the humanity of students through multiple meanings and contexts of student life. In the Anglo-American context, the imagery invites viewers to imagine their lives as a whole, whether learning, travelling, laughing, or making friends, thereby extending the imagination of what the HE experiences look and feel like in these regions. Within the university setting, a range of images depicts students learning in classrooms, hanging out on campus, banking, partying, or moving into a residence hall.

For example, the USN's "Decide Between a Top U.S., Global MBA Program" shows a white woman in a close, frontal-angle shot holding several books. She is shown smiling in a demand stance. A long-arched corridor is in the background, presumably depicting the institution. The image conveys a mood of the woman transitioning between classes. The image invites viewers to imagine oneself in the future learning and enjoying the process. At the same time, outside-classroom learning was signified by people shown against national/city landmarks while holding objects associated with students. For example, USN's "It's Not Too Late to Apply for a Bachelor's Degree Program in Europe" depicts five racially diverse students sitting on a park bench with the Tower Bridge in the background. This medium-close shot draws the viewer into the moment with the participants, shown laughing together. The eye-level angle positions the viewer and participant as equals, again inviting the viewer to imagine themselves in this setting. Importantly, as we observed in this image and others, students in epistemically privileged regions also have their humanity shown through their emotional expressions, often smiling and laughing. Furthermore, compared with all other countries and regions, students shown in the UK and US were most often looking at the viewer in "demand" and close-up. Thus, these websites represent HE in epistemically privileged regions as spaces for an invigorated and multifaceted student life. The images naturalize these regions as ideal HE spaces by promoting a humanizing student experience that readily invites viewer identification.

While the GURs imagery reifies the narrative of Anglo-American and Western European contexts as core HE regions where students enjoy a vibrant learning and social environment, visual imagery varied between countries/regions in the wider Western context. For instance, multiple images feature a student, or group of students, hanging out and smiling with the Eiffel Tower in the background. Although the Eiffel Tower is a prominent marker, French campuses are not emphasized like campuses in the US and UK. While France and Canada do not have the same numerical visual representation as the UK and US, their imagery foregrounds students in close, frontal-angle shots in demand stances, emphasizing a vibrant environment. For example, the USN's "Canadian Co-op Programs Blend Classroom, Work Experience" shows a young man in a close, frontal-angle shot. He is seen wearing safety goggles and smiling in a demand stance. He is inside a lab with what appears to be sophisticated scientific equipment in the background. Overall, the image invites the viewers to imagine their future lives as students in these settings – replete with resources, opportunities to learn, and chances to explore the future. Still, other Western contexts provide less opportunity for identification. For instance, the THE article "Best Universities in the Netherlands 2017" shows one student walking down a path toward a university building but at a far distance and from the back. There is a picture of Sweden in the THE article "Best Universities in Sweden," but again, no students are shown. Thus, we see certain nations/regions within Western contexts spatialized as core epistemic sites of HE (UK, US, France, and Canada) while others are on the margins (Netherlands, Switzerland, Italy, Spain).

In contrast to Western contexts imagery, as we mentioned earlier, the depictions of non-Western contexts usually were long shots of university campuses, monuments, landmarks, or cultural/social events. In these images, students (or people) are often absent. However, when students are present, they are miniature in scale or shown in an "offer" stance (with an absence of gaze at the viewer). Additionally, very few images show students in groups, in contrast to the images about the UK and the US. This visual difference conveys the message that social life with peers is absent among students in non-Western contexts. Such visual exclusion creates a social distance and constrains opportunities for viewers identifying and imagining their futures in such settings. While Western contexts were shown more close-up and in demand, the THE's "Best Universities in Japan" shows multiple students from the back against a background of a university building and trees. We do not see any students' faces up close, creating a sense of disconnection. Although the image is shown at eye level, little else visually seeks to draw in the viewer and win their identification. Additionally, students in university campuses are shown in all regions except for South Africa and India. The exclusion of students and lack of visual grammar that invites identification visually minimizes, or denies, the full humanity of students in non-Western HE contexts, reproducing the geopolitics of knowledge.

Last, we were particularly struck by Arab visual imagery that included students, which consistently featured visual tropes of particular clothing styles. No other region of the world had such a prominent use of "clothing" as a visual trope to depict the region. Clothing, particularly the headscarf worn by women and dishdashas (robes) worn by men, was used as markers. The clothing represented throughout these images is only from the Arabian Gulf region, rather than that of the diversity of Arab people in North Africa and Asia. Notably, the imagery accompanying the USN's "5 Facts About American-Style Universities in the Arab Region" is the only instance without this stereotypical clothing pattern. In this image, a young man is shown wearing a dress shirt in a library in an offer stance. The visual trope of a Western dress shirt stands in stark contrast to the rest of the images and, when used to distinguish "American-style universities" in the Arab region, reifies and naturalizes colonial difference, marking some students as modern and cosmopolitan while others are positioned as "ethnic" and parochial. Furthermore, HEIs (US-styled institutions) are visually marked as core/privileged HE sites within marginalized regions (Arab HE). The limited visual depictions of students and the use of stereotypical tropes (animals, clothing, and nature) naturalizes the gaze that has for so long haunted marginalized/peripheral regions (Lutz & Collins, 1993). Overall, the contrasts in student imagery between the core/privileged and marginalized/peripheral

Table 3.2. Contrast in visual grammar of GUR images depicting core/privileged HE regions and peripheral HE regions

	Core/privileged HE regions	Peripheral HE regions
Social distance	Tourist gaze	
	Medium- and close-range shots of prominent tourist landmarks, marked with students to indicate learning	Long-range shots of cultural events or regions objectified by cultural tropes (animals, clothing, etc.)
	Architectural gaze	
	Medium-range shots of traditional architecture signifying as core sites of knowledge production	Long-range shots of (post) modern architecture signifying "new" sites of knowledge production
Angle	Students	
	Eye-level images that invite viewers to participate in the visual	Few eye-level or low-angle images; impersonal images creating weak identification for viewers
	Architectural gaze	
	Eye-level images of campus, inviting viewers to enter an "equal" relationship with the image	High-angle, top-view images of campuses, signifying an impersonal and colonizing gaze
Contact	Students	
	Demand-stance images of students in a variety of activities, humanizing them and creating strong identification for viewers	Offer stance, limited identification and disconnect for viewers

regions reify the colonial racialization wherein predominantly white regions (particularly the UK and US) have their humanity affirmed, while those in Asia, Africa, and the Middle East have their humanity denied.

In summary, the difference in the pan-semiotic categories of social distance, angle, and identification in the GUR student imagery (re)produces the geopolitics of knowledge and the colonial gaze. Images of core/privileged contexts deploy a visual grammar that conveys personalization through close-up, frontal, and eye-level shots and students shown in multiple settings. This visual grammar legitimizes student mobility, as the student consumer is drawn to the epistemically privileged contexts where student life is depicted as desirable, dynamic, and offering multifaceted possibilities. On the other hand, images of marginalized/peripheral regions convey impersonalization through long-range shots and students shown in limited settings, if at all. Comparatively, mobility to these regions is constructed as undesirable. Table 3.2 summarizes our thematic analysis of the visual grammar applied to the GURs imagery.

Conclusion

Through comparative visual media analysis of two GURs websites, we demonstrate how these popular rankings websites perpetuate a normalized, Western-modernity gaze of global HE informed by the geopolitics of knowledge. While these websites emphasize various regions and institutions of the world, their visual imagery is encoded in a hierarchy favouring epistemically privileged regions or HE institutions, thereby legitimizing their rankings. GURs websites territorialize global HE by using touristy artifacts, campus architecture, and/or images of students. More specifically, the contrasting representations of core and peripheral regions in HE construct colonial difference in the way that a fuller humanity, symbolized by students, is afforded to core regions and institutions. To put it simply, GURs' websites offer a visual cartography of global HE, reflecting the geopolitics of knowledge in global HE. By analysing the signifying practices embedded in the visual imagery, we illustrate the specific ways in which *meanings* about HE (e.g., university campuses and regions of the world) are made and *how* they are made, illuminating how global actors like GURs media act as "powerful symbolic tools in a mediatized higher educational environment" (Stack, 2013, p. 579). Our analysis suggests that we need a critical view of both GURs and the role their media play in the mediation of geopolitical dynamics in HE.

Our analysis asserts that visual media geared towards global audiences (i.e., GURs websites) play an important public pedagogic role. As a marketing tool, the GUR websites perform an affective role by constructing the desires or aspirations of GUR consumers, such as students, parents, policymakers, and universities, through the aforementioned signifying practices. Such visual imagery produces a "semiotic parade" with the hopes of "attracting new consumers and retaining existing ones" (Stack, 2016, pp. 89–90). While such global sites seldom claim accuracy of cultural traditions and knowledge of regions, their visuals highlight how their imagery seeks identification with global audiences (including the Global North and South). Such imagery can only work by assuming audiences have normalized and internalized the idea that core centres of HE (whether between or within countries or HEIs) are universal, neutral, and desirable. Due to colonial/imperial histories, the Global South is often complicit in such hegemonic representations, as they arouse some form of familiarity. For instance, one can ask why the images of Oxford or Harvard, or landmarks like the Eiffel Tower or Big Ben, might be attractive to students from Asia or Africa. Our analysis of visuals in such websites reflects the Anglo-American hegemony and global power relations within HE tied to the global political economy, whereby student flows across the globe are polarized and uneven (Shields, 2013). Such normalizing encourages the continued use of global rankings, which disproportionately favour epistemically privileged locations and HEIs, benefiting the rankers themselves. Furthermore, rankers continue to play a major role in the geopolitics of knowledge in the ways in which they constitute HE globally, through both their rankings and their visual media.

Our analysis raises important questions about the role of rankings websites as new spaces of representation in the spatialization of higher education. These websites play a significant role in linking GUR audiences' affect to a certain place or region of the world (desirability, pride, etc.). Beyond simply depicting the "rankings" themselves in the forms of tables and charts, they employ visual imagery as cognitive aids, facilitating information seekers to sift more efficiently through, and gain knowledge from, vast amounts of accumulated data about global HE. As such, we need to understand these GUR websites and their visual imagery as part of a wider geopolitics of knowledge, which comes to have an economic impact by marketing certain HE destinations as "global" or "world class" or "international." Furthermore, these websites construct and circulate reputations of places and regions by lending credibility to claims and beliefs, such as the truthfulness of a world-class university (e.g., Harvard), the believability of quality claim (e.g., Oxford), or the trustworthiness of a region of HE as a desirable student destination (e.g., the Global North). These websites mostly draw their own imageries and texts from pre-existing databases, which in turn are based on previously established iconic forms of representation, such as the Eiffel Tower and Big Ben. These pre-existing databases may originate in the field of tourism and leisure. Future research could critically examine these representational "genealogies" of regions of the world and probe further how they operate (i.e., rendered and activated) across fields of practice (tourism, higher education, etc.). We recommend moving beyond the plentiful methodological critiques and impact studies of GURs in the existing literature to critically examine the underlying geopolitics of knowledge informing HE representation and visualization. In short, our analysis raises questions about the interconnections between culture, power, and geopolitics of knowledge in the growing visualization, spatialization, mediatization, and branding of HE (Estera & Shahjahan, 2018; Stack, 2016).

NOTES

1 We focus on these two rankings websites as they provide a comparative analysis of corporate media products that are situated in the UK and US, respectively, and have different histories with global rankings. Unlike the THE, USN is a recent player in global university rankings. The prominence of imagery on these two rankings websites in terms of number, size, and relevance to our themes made them ideal

case studies. Both GURs are interested in the rankings game because it helps garner audience and advertising potential (Stack, 2013).

2 In other words, we collected images that were (a) displayed on the listed pages and (b) displayed after clicking a link on the listed pages. For instance, on the USN homepage section "Global University Advice for Students and Parents," we collected the six images shown on that page. We then clicked the links associated with those six images and found that there were additional "Recommended Articles" listed underneath the image on the new page. We collected these images as well, since they were one click away from the original "Global University Advice for Students and Parents" page. It is important to note that while multiple images of peripheral HE regions are present, we have to dig deep into the websites, so these are not one click away from the main pages.

3 We believe the cumulative and wide-ranging nature of evidence we have identified in the following sections, rather than a singular pattern or numeric representations, supports our argument regarding the geopolitics of knowledge in the GURs imagery. Thus, we intentionally highlight the *breadth* of signifying practices and their manifestations, which to us is still a type of "depth," albeit different than the traditional "linear" depth of numerous examples. We do not include numbers or percentages in our analysis, as our visual analysis draws upon our frameworks wherein representation constitutes meaning (i.e., signifying practices) (Hall, 1997b, c, van Leeuwen, 1996; Kress & van Leeuwen, 2006), rather than positivist forms of representational practices (number of instances) constituting meaning. In essence, we have sought to open up the dialogue on GURs beyond an objectivist paradigm of numbers (which underpins the logic of GURs) by offering a mode of analysis that does not rely on numbers and scores, such as percentages. We view our chapter as joining the growing body of work of visual analysis that is not based on positivist numeric representations (e.g., Bonilla-Silva, 2012; Osei-Kofi & Torres, 2015; Stack, 2013, 2016).

4 We could not include images from the GURs websites in our chapter due to the image copyrights and the high fees for the reproduction of these images (even for academic uses). This may be one of the factors why website visual analysis is rare and why these images continue to escape academic scrutiny.

5 We denote India and Africa not seeking to make an equivalency between a country and continent, but in direct reference to the THE's article titles ("Best Universities in India" and "Best Universities in Africa"). Indeed, we find it concerning that no articles featured individual African countries, perpetuating the colonial idea of Africa as a homogenous continent.

REFERENCES

Bajc, V. (2011). Tourist gaze. In *Encyclopedia of Consumer Culture* (Vol. 3) (pp. 1466–8). SAGE.

Baty, P. (1990, 1 January). Developing narrative. *Times Higher Education World University Rankings*. https://www.timeshighereducation.com/world-university-rankings/2014/brics-and-emerging-economies/analysis/developing-narrative

Bonilla-Silva, E. (2012). The invisible weight of whiteness: The racial grammar of everyday life in contemporary America. *Ethnic and Racial Studies, 35*(2), 173–94. https://doi.org/10.1080/01419870.2011.613997

Chang, G.C., & Osborn, J.R. (2005). Spectacular colleges and spectacular rankings: The "US News" rankings of American "best" colleges. *Journal of Consumer Culture, 5*(3), 338–64. https://doi.org/10.1177/1469540505056794

Edwards, B. (2014). *University architecture*. Routledge.

Estera, A., & Shahjahan, R.A. (2018). Globalizing whiteness? Visually re/presenting students in global university rankings websites. *Discourse: Studies in the Cultural Politics of Education, 40*(6), 930–45. https://doi.org/10.1080/01596306.2018.1453781

Hall, S. (1997a). Old and new identities, old and new ethnicities. In A.D. King (Ed.), *Culture, globalization and the world-system: Contemporary conditions for the representation of identity* (pp. 41–68). University of Minnesota Press.

Hall, S. (1997b). *Representation: Cultural representations and signifying practices*. Sage.

Hall, S. (1997c). *Stuart Hall: Representation and the media – Media Education Foundation transcript*. http://www.mediaed.org/assets/products/409/transcript_409.pdf

Ishikawa, M. (2009). University rankings, global models, and emerging hegemony: Critical analysis from Japan. *Journal of Studies in International Education, 13*(2), 159–73. https://doi.org/10.1177/1028315308330853

Kress, G., & van Leeuwen, T. (2006). *Reading images: The grammar of visual design*. Routledge.

Lim, M.A. (2017). The building of weak expertise: The work of global university rankers. *Higher Education, 75*, 415–30. https://doi.org/10.1007/s10734-017-0147-8

Lutz, C., & Collins, J.L. (1993). *Reading National Geographic*. University of Chicago Press.

Merriam, S.B. (1998). *Qualitative research and case study applications in education*. Jossey-Bass.

Mignolo, W. (2003). Globalization and the geopolitics of knowledge: The role of the humanities in the corporate university. *Nepantla: Views from South, 4*(1), 97–119. https://www.muse.jhu.edu/article/40206

Mignolo, W. (2005). *The idea of Latin America*. Blackwell.

Mignolo, W. (2011). *The darker side of Western modernity: Global futures, decolonial options*. Duke University Press.

Ong, A., & Collier, S.J. (2005). *Global assemblages: Technology, politics, and ethics as anthropological problems*. Blackwell.

Osei-Kofi, N., & Torres, L.E. (2015). College admissions viewbooks and the grammar of gender, race, and STEM. *Cultural Studies of Science Education, 10*(2), 527–44. https://doi.org/10.1007/s11422-014-9656-2

Redden, E. (2014, 10 October). U.S. News to issue new global university rankings. *Inside Higher Education*. https://www.insidehighered.com/quicktakes/2014/10/10/us-news-issue-new-global-university-rankings

Reynolds, P.J. (2014). Representing "U": Popular culture, media, and higher education. *ASHE Higher Education Report, 40*(4), 1–145. https://doi.org/10.1002/aehe.20016

Said, E.W. (1979). *Orientalism*. Random House.

Shaheen, J.G. (2001). *Reel bad Arabs: How Hollywood vilifies a people*. Olive Branch Press.

Shahjahan, R.A. (2016). International organizations (IOs), epistemic tools of influence, and the colonial geopolitics of higher education policy. *Journal of Education Policy, 31*(6), 694–710. https://doi.org/10.1080/02680939.2016.1206623

Shahjahan, R.A., Blanco-Ramirez, G, & Andreotti, V. (2017). Attempting to imagine the unimaginable: A decolonial reading of global university rankings (GURs). *Comparative Education Review, 61*(S1). https://doi.org/10.1086/690457

Shahjahan, R.A., & Morgan, C. (2016) Global competition, coloniality, and the geopolitics of knowledge in higher education. *British Journal of Sociology of Education, 37*(1), 92–109. https://doi.org/10.1080/01425692.2015.1095635

Shields, R. (2013). Globalization and international student mobility: A network analysis. *Comparative Education Review, 57*(4), 609–36. https://doi.org/10.1086/671752

Stack, M. (2013). The Times Higher Education ranking product: Visualising excellence through media. *Globalisation, Societies and Education, 11*(4), 560–82. https://doi.org/10.1080/14767724.2013.856701

Stack, M. (2016). *Global university rankings and the mediatization of higher education*. Palgrave Macmillan.

U.S. News & World Report. (2014, 28 October). U.S. News releases inaugural best global universities rankings. https://www.usnews.com/info/blogs/press-room/2014/10/28/us-news-releases-inaugural-best-global-universities-rankings

van Leeuwen, T. (1996). The representation of social actors. In C.R. Caldas-Coulthard & M. Coulthard (Eds.), *Texts and practices: Readings in critical discourse analysis* (pp. 32–70). Routledge.

THEME 2

Costs of Knowledge, Rankings, and Journal Impact Factors

In this section the authors clearly show how rankings connect to the education industry, in particular in journal impact factors (IF) and a monopoly of academic publishers. Chuing Prudence Chou provides a case study of how the power of impact factors is experienced in Taiwan and what this means for the epistemic viability of regional knowledge, collegial relations, teaching, and community engagement. Heather Morrison demonstrates that university rankings and journal IF are interconnected business interests that have rapidly increased the cost of sharing knowledge and what is considered world-class knowledge. Ralf St. Clair analyses the impact of rankings on a university in Nigeria and a mid-sized university in Canada. In doing so he points to the need for nuance in understanding context but also the pressure on universities to operate with rankings in mind; for example, he shows how "up-voting" occurs. Universities that are mid-ranked can end up sliding down if they don't actively participate in the reputation game; they therefore work to build their reputation by narrowing their associations to institutions that can help them move up in reputation survey.

4 Academic Culture in Transition: Measuring Up for What in Taiwan?

CHUING PRUDENCE CHOU

Prior to 1994, higher education in Taiwan was under extensive state control in order to spur national economic development and maintain political stability (Mok, 2014). An unprecedented expansion in Taiwan's higher education occurred in the mid-1990s as a response to increased global competition, domestic political elections, demands from civil society, and significant social change. As a result, Taiwan reached the world's second-highest enrolment rate of 18- to 22-year-olds (Ministry of Education, 2013). Amendments applied to the University Law in 1994 altered the governance of the HE sector and allowed higher education institutions (HEIs) greater autonomy, which granted increased freedom in admissions, staffing, and policies (Chou & Ching, 2012; Mok, 2014).

Since the 1980s, private investment in higher education has grown more prolific as neo-liberal policies became more widely utilized around the world and in Taiwan (Chou, 2008). Increasing private investment resulted in HEIs competing against each other for such investment. Governments have also contributed to this climate by developing policies to enhance their universities' competitiveness in academia, facilitate global competitiveness, and expand their international visibility (Chou et al., 2013).

Globalization and the entrenchment of a neo-liberal economic order have had a profound effect on higher education, particularly in the Asia-Pacific region (Chou, 2008). HEIs have pursued internationalization to strengthen their global competitiveness and sought the achievement of "world-class" status to increase their international clout and access to markets. In addition, the pursuit of "world-class" status facilitated a growing demand for the development of comparable and cross-national indicators of research quality. Within this wider context, rankings and indexes are viewed with such importance that governments have formulated policies to reward HEIs that are successful in moving up the rankings. Across the Asia-Pacific region, some of the Quacquarelli Symonds (QS) highest-ranking HEIs are located in China, Hong Kong, Japan, Singapore,

South Korea, and Taiwan (Quacquarelli Symonds, 2017). This indicates that HEIs in the Asia-Pacific region have enacted successful reforms to internationalize and pursue "world-class" status as defined by rankers. However, the quantifiable and unquantifiable costs to HEIs and governments who seek to achieve this status remain obscured in the media and government records.

In the case of Taiwan, the HEI rankings originate from the Taiwanese governments' shifting of its governance philosophy over HE from "government control" to "government supervision." This came to fruition through the development of quality assurance mechanisms and the promotion of a performance-driven culture. In the early 1990s, Taiwan's Ministry of Education (MOE) commissioned several agencies to conduct evaluations of programs offered by HEIs (Lo, 2014). These early evaluations were conducted on an institutional basis; however, limited resources of these institutions restricted their capability to manage their evaluations. In response, the Taiwanese government implemented a revision to the University Law in 1994 to transfer responsibility of conducting evaluations of HEIs to the MOE (Lo, 2014). Further reforms, such as the establishment of the Higher Education Evaluation and Accreditation Council of Taiwan (HEEACT) in 2005, brought MOE and HEI funding together in maintaining an independent agency to conduct HE evaluation and accreditation. In 2011, the HEEACT's role in the HEI ranking system expanded when it began conducting institution-based evaluations. The aims of such evaluations are to clarify the goals and missions of HEIs, to identify HEIs' strengths and weaknesses, and to provide suggestions for their improvement. In order for departments of HEIs to survive, they must pass their evaluations, as departments who fail for two consecutive years will be requested by the MOE to terminate their enrolment and operations.

Such an evaluation system raised concerns of how institutional autonomy is maintained within HEIs in Taiwan. Despite some HEIs being granted the status of self-accreditation and HEIs having authority to establish their own regulations on evaluation, the University Evaluation Regulation of 2007 stipulates that HEIs are under obligation to be evaluation by the MOE and its agency (HEEACT) (Lo, 2014).

Additionally, the creation of the Taiwan Social Science Citation Index (TSSCI) is considered a breakthrough in the establishment of a research-oriented performance culture in Taiwan's HE system (Lo, 2014). The purpose of the TSSCI was to help HEIs achieve "world-class" status, since "world-class" HEIs are predominantly research-oriented. As a result, the measurement of HEIs' performance in Taiwan placed great emphasis on research output. Citation indices, particularly the SCI (Science Citation Index) and SSCI (Social Sciences Citation Index) from the United States, were considered strong indicators of the research performance of faculty members. However, the local academic community strongly opposed using citation indices based in foreign countries for the purpose of faculty performance evaluation. Since all major citation indices were developed for English-language journals, many academics in Taiwan struggle to publish their research within these journals due to language restrictions and cultural bias. Taiwan academics also question how suitable these journals are for local studies (Lo, 2014).

The issue of HEI rankings in Taiwan has repercussions not only domestically but also within the Asia-Pacific region. As cross-strait issues, China-Taiwan relations are a major focus of geopolitical concern, and HE is also a field of contention between the two sides. Due to Taiwan's rapidly aging society and low birth rate, Taiwanese HEIs face a crisis in enrolment shortages (Hsueh, 2018). Taiwan has an issue of brain drain regarding students and academics. Because of the pressures of rankings and stagnant wages, Taiwanese academics are increasingly seeking opportunities abroad. One particular issue for Taiwan is the recruitment of Taiwanese academics and students to China with generous offers from Chinese HEIs (Cheng, 2018; Hsiao, 2017; Hsueh, 2018). Therefore, this chapter provides an excellent case study to analyse how HEI rankings affect geopolitical issues within the Asia-Pacific region. In this case, China, with its greater financial resources, is capable of attracting HE talent from Taiwan, which would hurt Taiwan's competitiveness within the region and globally.

This chapter compares the change in the academic culture of two departments at National Chengchi University (NCCU). The aim is to examine how faculty research performance has changed since the implementation of initiatives aimed at achieving world-class universities in Taiwan. To be ranked world-class in any of the three major ranking systems (QS, ARWU, and THE) requires that faculty publish in top-ranked journals, namely English-language journals. The result is new pressure on faculty to conduct research and write up results in a manner accepted by English-language editors. NCCU was chosen for this study because its focus is primarily social science and the humanities, fields which have been acutely affected by recent policy changes. NCCU includes nine colleges: Liberal Arts, Law, Commerce, Science, Foreign Languages, Social Sciences, Communication, International Affairs, and Education. There are thirty-four departments and forty-eight postgraduate institutes. NCCU has long been among the top universities in Taiwan and is renowned for its Liberal Arts and Humanities, Social Sciences, Management, Politics, International Affairs, Communication, and Education programs. Consequently, a great number of alumni have worked in the government sector. The two interviewees chosen were selected based on their seniority of more than twenty-five years in each department, their service as former administrators, and their experiences sitting on many university promotion and hiring committees. Both have authority and experience in university policymaking and dealing with academic rewards and publications. As indicated by these interviewees, NCCU's reputation was much more prestigious on a national level before the shift in policy towards achieving "world-class" status, as university scholars have shifted their research interests to more global issues. This change in status has been accompanied by a reduction of public funding, the degradation of social prestige, and a decline in the morale of its faculty (Chou & Yang, 2016).

Two initiatives promoted by Taiwan's MOE inform what research is funded and rewarded by universities and government: the World-Class Research University Project (2003) and the Higher Education for Excellence Plan (also known as the Five-Year-Fifty-Billion Plan). The latter was valued at approximately US$1.6 billion invested in twelve leading Taiwanese HEIs in 2005. Many institutions received a renewal of additional funding in 2011 (Chou & Chan, 2016). Over time, these initiatives have prompted a shift in research away from Mandarin publications and locally relevant topics, towards international, English-language publications with significantly less relevance to Taiwanese interests.

University Quality Assurance

Beginning in the 1990s, many vocational/technical colleges were upgraded to "comprehensive universities," meaning they were no longer singularly focused on technical and vocational training and education (TVET) but shifted some resources to four-year bachelor programs. This direction runs counter to their original purpose of spurring Taiwan's economic development. The broadened focus has negatively affected the quality of higher education in Taiwan, a concern expressed by many since that time (Chou, 2008; Hayhoe, 2002). In response to this concern, the University Law was again revised in 2001, shifting the basis of budget allocation to a system of evaluations. In 2005, a professional evaluation association was commissioned to establish and strengthen quality assurance (QA) systems in Taiwan's HEIs (Hou, 2015). In order to improve Taiwan's international academic visibility and competitiveness, most of the QA criteria was meant to be standardized and quantifiable according to the international rankers (Chou & Chan, 2016). The indexes used by the QA systems also derived from journal publications in data sets such as in the SCI, the SSCI, and the TSSCI. All of these evaluation criteria are paper-oriented and quantity-driven, and mostly benefit STEM fields, but they have created an environment wherein quantitative research is highly favoured. Fields which rely more on intensive, longitudinal, qualitative research face a disadvantage under criteria that prefer quick results and frequent publication.

Research Framework

This study compares the change in the academic culture via faculty publication profiles in two departments of Taiwan's NCCU to measure the impact of the recent emphasis on global rankings in Taiwanese higher education. The departments surveyed, the Department of Education and the Department of Ethnology, reacted differently to the changes in recent decades. These departments were chosen as part of an international research project published in *Higher Education Policy*, the quarterly journal of the International Association of Universities (IAU), and funded through the World Universities Network (WUN). They were selected under the assumption that the drive for international research and publication had begun much earlier in science, technology, engineering, and mathematics (STEM) fields, but that research in education and ethnology had traditionally been conducted with strong national rather than global interests in mind, before recent shifts in national and institutional priorities towards global competitiveness (Post & Chou, 2016).

Two instruments were used to account for these changes: in-depth interviews with two senior faculty members (one from each department) and an extensive documentation database of faculty publication over the course of two decades. Each faculty's journal publications were recorded for 1993, 2003, and 2013 to examine how faculty research performance has transformed under the world-class university ranking and global competition. Yearly publications per faculty member were averaged for each of the two departments to illustrate changes in research behaviour. Each publication was tabulated for (1) language of publication (English, Mandarin, Japanese, or other language) and (2) whether the research was ultimately published in a national or an international journal.

In-depth interviews were conducted with senior faculty members from each department to gain further insight into faculty morale, accessibility to the means of career advancement, changes in the character of academic labour within the specified fields, and changes in the goals and direction of knowledge production. The open-ended questions used for these interviews are listed in the appendix.

Short-Term Outcomes of World-Class Policies

Each individual university, along with Taiwan's Ministry of Education, must be compliant with the new QA systems, which monitor publication records of individual faculty members in international and domestic journals. In response, each university in Taiwan established its own strategy to increase international visibility, enhance scholarship, and increase scholarly contributions (Mok, 2014). In terms of quantity of publication, these measures have been remarkably successful. In 1981, only 543 academic papers were published in Taiwan, accounting for 0.12 per cent of global publication that year. By 2012, that number had increased to more than 26,000, 2.07 per cent of global publication (Kuo & Liu, 2014). According to the interviewee from the Department of Ethnology at NCCU, measures taken by the university since 2013 have made the department "more comprehensive," with a "faculty that has more diverse backgrounds and research interests. We have anthropology, education, history, geography, linguistics; we are more like a comprehensive way to observe ethnic culture."

Although these measures have contributed to improved rankings and global exposure in the short term, academic staff in Taiwan's leading universities, especially those in social sciences and humanities, are increasingly experiencing pressure to "publish globally or perish locally" (Hanafi, 2011). The interviewee from the Department of Ethnology explained, "Those who embrace and benefit from this international journal game reinforce it and contribute to the pressure for all to comply if they want to survive." Interviewees indicated that new hires to their departments were hired in large part because of their perceived potential to publish in international journals, indicating a significant shift towards a global perspective for the next generation of faculty.

Owing to various initiatives implemented by the government and HEIs in Taiwan, Taiwan's scholarly publications, international visibility, university rankings, and overall publications in SSCI-recognized journals have risen. In the 2015 QS World University Rankings, National Taiwan University (NTU) ranked seventieth in the world and has been in the top 100 universities since 2009 (Quacquarelli Symonds, 2015). Simultaneously, Taiwan's research publication output in SSCI-recognized journals increased by over 56 per cent, from 2,298 to 3,590, between 2008 and 2013 (World of Science, 2014). Despite its increase in publication output though, Taiwan's academic impact rankings have improved only incrementally, gains which may not justify the cost to nationally focused scholarship and faculty morale. All the while, Western nations such as the United States continue to maintain their dominant position in terms of academic impact. This indicates that, despite Taiwan's ambitious policies towards achieving world-class universities, its research has not improved in terms of international competitiveness based on the criteria of WOS (World of Science), a major "world-class university" citation database (World of Science, 2014).

Three Decades of Publication

Findings suggest that although international visibility has improved over the period in question, overemphasis on rankings and citation indices has strained the morale of academic labour, narrowed the pathway to academic career advancement, and encouraged research that favours global trends over national interests. As shown in table 4.1, the publication rates remained constant in both departments prior to 2003, when policy incentives to publish in English or in international journals had yet to be implemented. After these incentives were introduced, university faculty in the Department of Education published

Table 4.1. Three Decades of Publication in Two Departments

Year	Average number of papers published per faculty member	
	Ethnology	Education
1993	0.78	1.48
2003	0.78	1.67
2013	1.3	4.17

significantly more journal articles. There was also an increase of journal publications among faculty in the Department of Ethnology, but to a much lesser degree.

Examination of the papers published in academic journals supports these conclusions. In the three years examined (1993, 2003, and 2013), eighty-nine published papers were surveyed from the Department of Education (thirty-two in 1993, twenty-five in 2003, and thirty-two in 2013), and twenty-seven papers (seven, seven, and thirteen papers in each respective year) from the Department of Ethnology. In education, articles submitted to Mandarin publications shifted from 90.6 per cent in 1993 to 100 per cent in 2003 and to 65.6 per cent in 2013. In ethnology, only one paper was published in English in the years surveyed.

In the Department of Education, the papers submitted in English in 1993 came from only a handful of faculty members, most of whom were junior faculty who specialized in statistics or quantitative research methodologies. In 2013, however, there was a significant increase in submissions to English-language or international journals, as well as co-authorships from a larger percentage of faculty. This may be due, in part, to the increased pressure to publish in internationally recognized journals, especially considering the institution of a probationary period for newly hired faculty in 2005 that gave strong incentives to publish frequently and globally. However, in ethnology, the publication of journal articles fluctuated in the years surveyed. Only seven publications were noted each in 1993 and in 2003, and although four new faculty members were hired, that number only increased to ten in 2013.

Within the two departments, there was a significant divergence in the source of publishers utilized to publish research articles. In the Department of Ethnology, 28.3 per cent of publications were published through Taiwanese publishers in 1993, while the other 71.7 per cent of articles were published in Mainland China. However, researchers surged to Taiwan in 2003 and 2013, inverting the trend completely. In the Department of Education, faculty members published mostly through Taiwanese publishers before 2003, but shifted their attention to international journals afterwards. As discussed above, the shift to international journals and to higher expectations for frequency of publication has coincided with higher strain on faculty members and a likely divergence from research priorities that are aligned with local and national interests in favour of those of more global significance.

Faculty Voices

Two senior faculty who had been working in their respective department for more than twenty-five years participated in an extensive interview based on the questions indicated above. The interviews suggest that between 1993 and 2013, hiring and faculty promotion became more dependent on English writing ability and journal publication rates. Additionally, interviewees indicated that anxiety and morale have worsened, and the role of the "public intellectual" has diminished in Taiwanese society as expectations for publication in SSCI-recognized journals have risen. Despite the efforts and sacrifices made to achieve the goals of these recent policy changes, those interviewed expressed doubts about the benefits reaped from them.

The interviewee from the Department of Education expressed misgivings about the impact of Taiwanese academics both domestically and internationally, despite the proliferation of international research in recent years. "There is a growing international presence, but what kind of impact is there for the international community? I think that there is no significant growth in the field of education. In academic circles abroad, the academic influence of Chinese scholars is still insufficient. As for domestic academic circles, their English periodicals cannot be read. On the contrary, scholars of the older generation [have] a chance to be accepted by the Taiwanese public because of their publication of a Mandarin book."

The themes of research topics include the term "global" more often as the audience targeted by faculty in Taiwan consists predominantly of international journal editors in the US and UK. This suggests that researchers may be forgoing research on issues that specifically affect Taiwan in favour of more broadly global issues. The interviewee from the Department of Ethnology asserted that "internationalization of journals is not a bad thing, but I think … that Taiwan's politics should be internationalized, and academics should be localized. We are doing it backwards. Localization is not to say that [a researcher] can only do Taiwanese research, but … after you take root [in Taiwan], you can go abroad and present your ideas. It will be more meaningful than it otherwise would have been to the international academic community."

Greater numbers of publications in international journals have also shifted the language used in writing up research in Taiwan. International publications often require academic research to be published in the English language, which makes such research less accessible for Taiwanese audiences. The interviewee from the Department of Education described this, saying, "In the past, the university was not at all interested in English. But now it is swinging to the other extreme: you have to contribute mainly in English. If you submit in English, you will be more prominent." As observed in Taiwan, English-language writing ability now acts as a proxy measure for academic merit despite the fact that it is a non-English-speaking academic community. The same interviewee went on to explain that the emphasis on English-language publication deters researchers from publishing in the way that they had before the globalization trends took hold: with books. "Focusing on English publications, and disregarding special books, means that local people cannot benefit from their research." Overemphasis on international publication also limits the time and energy academics have for social engagement, teaching, and public discourse.

Regarding the language of publication, in 1993 and 2003 all publications from the Department of Education were in Mandarin, and the department was focused on publication of books, rather than papers in academic journals. The professor from that department explained that, "At that time, a lot of books were published, because they could take books to the National Science Council and apply for rewards." In fact, "it would be very strange to use English. Local journals may not even accept submissions in English. However, after 2003, research published by the faculty in Mandarin declined from 100% to 74% and were replaced by papers published in English" (Chou & Chan, 2017). Alternatively, faculty in ethnology continued to publish their research in Mandarin throughout the period and publication rates remained relatively low compared to the rates seen in education (1.3 papers per person in 2013). "We have poor research performance based on the current evaluation criteria but teaching quality is good ... The teachers of the ethnic minority, as a whole, are very good at teaching," explains the ethnology professor. "Our service in terms of social participation and contribution, especially to Minority people and communities, is impressive and typically well received. We serve many leading policy makers on minority studies but lack academic visibility."

Between the two disciplines, there were significant differences in promotions. In the Department of Ethnology, promotions were less common than in the Department of Education. Factors that contribute to this disparity may include a unique culture within the respective departments; different methodologies preferred by the respective fields of study, which may favour or inhibit higher frequency of publication; or even each department's level of morale; but the data and interviews from the two departments indicate that research output in internationally recognized English-language journals contributes to promotion success (Chou & Chan, 2017).

Responses from the interviewees reinforced this correlation. The interviewee from the Department of Ethnology explained their frustration with the lack of recognition for publications that were not in English, saying, "I have three very important papers, all of which I published in journals that yielded zero credit. Qinghai, Ningxia, and Gansu, China, three of the best academic journals." The interviewee from the Department of Education also expressed misgivings: "Because of the publication pressure at NCCU, the newer faculty are driven to publish more journal articles, especially for SSCI credit, so they can get promotions as soon as possible." The interviewee goes on to lament what they believe has been lost in this process, saying, "NCCU used to be proud of producing books, and the faculty wasn't encouraged to publish journal articles before 2003. Although NCCU has expanded the publication of journal articles, books are shrinking to a great extent."

Conclusion

A decade has passed since the 2010 higher education reforms were implemented in Taiwan to improve higher education quality and increase international visibility and competitiveness. Various effects can be observed within Taiwan's HE system, and although international visibility has improved, there are some trends of concern regarding research publication, accessibility of research for local audiences, and the role of teaching in academia. The linkage between these factors also impacts epistemic viability of knowledge produced by Taiwanese universities. As seen in the findings above, journal publications have now become the task of utmost importance for university and college faculty. Promotions and rank are now more dependent on the number of SSCI, SCI, and TSSCI publications an academic has published. This has led to a gradual diminishing and devaluing of the teaching and "public intellectual" role of an HEI faculty member and funnelled academic labour into a mentality of publication for the sake of career advancement rather than for epistemological advancement or national interests (Chou & Chan, 2017).

A "winner takes all" environment amongst colleagues has emerged in Taiwan's HEIs. As a result, in certain departments, promotions are dependent on a narrow set of criteria, and many faculty members lack opportunities for such promotions. Due to promotions being overly dependent on the publications of faculty member and whether they are published in SSCI-, SCI-, or TSSCI-relevant journals, such output is produced by a small number of faculty. In the case of the Department of Education, faculty members published significantly more articles than they did prior to the enactment of higher education reforms. Further research could clarify the implications of this trend, which may suggest that research topics are being geared to appeal to journal editors despite not being locally relevant. In the case of the Department of Ethnology, its low publication rate and predominantly Mandarin-language medium indicates that certain disciplines are less vulnerable to institutional pressure to meet standards deemed necessary for institutions to become "world-class universities." As suggested above, this may be due to a number of factors, including the academic culture within the Department of Ethnology and the different methods of ethnological research.

The Taiwanese government's response to the pressures of competitive university rankings has been to introduce a series of reform policies that emphasize quantitative research and a new probation and self-evaluation system designed to monitor faculty research output. The phenomenon of "publish globally or perish locally" has thus emerged, especially in the humanities and social sciences, which comes at the expense of local policy issues and academic visibility to taxpayers. Although there is evidence that policymakers are responding to the issues discussed in this study (Chou et al., 2013), further reform would be welcome, especially by faculty from institutes of technology, whose practical skills and knowledge have been neglected in the current promotion system. Though the SSCI-focused mentality has been imbedded in all faculty reward and evaluation systems across Taiwan, social concerns and awareness about the preceding issues have been more and more evident and accepted as grounds for change. It is likely that additional multi-channel alternatives will come into effect in future, and it is hoped that the "publish globally and perish locally" phenomenon will be considered along with the inevitable drive for global talents and human resources in forthcoming policy. NCCU, as one of Taiwan's most vulnerable HEIs under the current paper-driven policy, should also take the lead in researching world-class university rankings from postmodern perspectives.

Ultimately, this research highlights the costs that have been incurred as a result of Taiwan's increasing pursuit of "world-class" status for its HEIs. Despite the number of publications increasing overall, the lack of increase in the international academic impact at the expense of local relevancy and academic diversity indicates that publication quantity is being pursued while academic excellence is yet to be achieved. The current world-class university policy is not justifiable and comprehensive enough to convince many academics in Taiwan. It will be of the utmost importance for policymakers in Taiwan to consider how past reforms have placed greater academic strain on faculty members and may be directing research goals away from those aligned with local and national interests towards more global issues. These issues have already caused damage to morale in many academic settings and have the potential to exacerbate the gender disparity in education and direct the valuable academic talent available in Taiwan away from its original goal: the improvement of Taiwanese society. When considering renewing old reforms or enacting new ones, policymakers would significantly benefit from taking the outcomes of past reforms into consideration in order to enhance Taiwan's higher education for the benefit of all in Taiwan.

ACKNOWLEDGMENTS

The author is indebted to Philip Henderson for his editing assistance and input to this chapter.

REFERENCES

Cheng, J. (2018, 28 June). Professor flight? "30 million RMB can't buy democracy and academic freedom." *CommonWealth Magazine*. https://english.cw.com.tw/article/article.action?id=2005

Chou, C.P. (2008). The impact of neo-liberalism on Taiwanese higher education. In D. Baker & A. Wiseman (Eds.), *The worldwide transformation of higher education* (pp. 297–312). JAI.

Chou, C.P., & Chan, C.F. (2016). Trends in publication in the race for world-class university: The case of Taiwan. *Higher Education Policy, 29*(4), 431–49. https://doi.org/10.1057/s41307-016-0016-6

Chou, C.P., & Chan, C.F. (2017). Governance and academic culture in higher education: Under the influence of the SSCI syndrome. *Journal of International and Comparative Education, 6*(2), 63–75. https://jice.um.edu.my/index.php/JICE/article/view/1ChouChan/jice.2017.6.2.63

Chou, C.P., & Ching, G. (2012). *Taiwan education at the crossroads*. Palgrave Macmillan.

Chou, C.P., Lin, H.F., & Chiu, Y.J. (2013). The impact of SSCI and SCI on Taiwan's academy: An outcry for fair play. *Asia Pacific Education Review, 14*, 23–31. http://doi.org/10.1007/s12564-013-9245-1

Chou, C.P., & Yang, Y.F. (2016). How Taiwan's higher education caught in the world-class university rankings: From NCCU's perspective of the Consolidated Curriculum Reform. *Taiwan Educational Review Monthly, 5*(1): 111–18.

Hanafi, S. (2011). University systems in the Arab East: Publish globally and perish locally vs publish locally and perish globally. *Current Sociology, 59*(3), 291–309. https://doi.org/10.1177/0011392111400782

Hayhoe, R. (2002). Teacher education and the university: A comparative analysis with implications for Hong Kong. *Teaching Education, 13*(1), 5–23. https://doi.org/10.1080/1047210120128555

Hou, A.Y.C. (2015). The quality of mass higher education in East Asia: Development and challenges for Asian quality assurance agencies in the glonacal higher education. In J.C. Shin, G.A. Postiglione, & F. Huang (Eds.), *Mass higher education development in East Asia: Strategy, quality, and challenges* (pp. 307–24). Sense.

Hsiao, T.F. (2017, 4 August). "Farewell, Taiwan." *CommonWealth Magazine, 628.* https://english.cw.com.tw/article/article.action?id=1649

Hsueh, C.M. (2018, 5 August). Higher education crisis in Taiwan. *Inside Higher Ed.* https://www.insidehighered.com/blogs/world-view/higher-education-crisis-taiwan

Kuo, H.F., & Liu, H.Y. (2014, 12 September). An analysis of the overall academic publication capacity in Taiwan for the last twenty years. STPI Research Portal. https://portal.stpi.narl.org.tw/index/article/28

Lo, W.Y.W. (2014). *University rankings: Implications for higher education in Taiwan.* Springer Singapore.

Ministry of Education, Republic of China (Taiwan). (2013). Education statistics. MOE. https:// stats.moe.gov.tw

Mok, K.H. (2014). Promoting the global university in Taiwan: University governance reforms and academic reflections. In C.P. Chou (Ed.), *The SSCI Syndrome in higher education: A local or global phenomenon* (pp. 1–23). Sense.

Post, D., & Chou, C.P. (2016). Preface: Measuring up for what cause? *Higher Education Policy, 29*(4), 423–9. https://doi.org/10.1057/s41307-016-0023-7

Quacquarelli Symonds. (2015). QS World University Rankings 2015/16. QS Top Universities. http://www.topuniversities.com/university-rankings/world-university-ran kings/2015#sorting=rank+region=+country=+faculty=+stars=false+search=national

Quacquarelli Symonds. (2017). QS World University Rankings 2018. QS Top Universities. https://www.topuniversities.com/university-rankings/world-university -rankings/2018

World of Science. (2014). *Science Citation Index.* Thomson Reuters.

Appendix

Interview Questions:

1. What has been the research direction of faculty from your department from 1993 to 2013? What are the main forms of publication?
2. What are key factors that have changed your academic publications in terms of topics and languages selected since your first publication? How may these factors be related to the regular appraisal/publication assessment implemented by your university?
3. NCCU has encouraged faculty to publish papers in international academic journals. How has this requirement affected your department?
4. Is there considerable pressure on your department to meet deadlines or quotas for research? Specifically, what are the constraints and expectations on young faculty members?
5. What is the ratio of submissions to domestic and foreign journals in your department? What is the ratio between Chinese and foreign language publications?
6. What changes have you observed in publication topics and languages over the years since 1993 by your colleagues in your own department? Similar or dissimilar, and in what ways?
7. How is the regular appraisal/publication assessment in your university related to the national scheme of research assessment or ranking if there is any?
8. What are the advantages and disadvantages of the research assessments used in your university since the 1980s?
9. What problems have you and the other members of your department's faculty encountered regarding promotion?
10. How have hiring practices changed for your department? What qualifications and experiences does NCCU look for when hiring new faculty?

5 What Counts in Research? Dysfunction in Knowledge Creation and Moving Beyond

HEATHER MORRISON

A Brief History of Journals, Bibliometrics, and Rankings

In 1665, two scholarly entrepreneurs independently seized the potential of the printing press and the postal system and invented the modern scholarly journal. Guédon's (2001) *In Oldenburg's Long Shadow* presents an overview of the history of the scholarly peer-reviewed journal from its inception in 1665 with Oldenburg's *Philosophical Transactions* and de Sallo's *Journal des Sçavans* to the end of the twentieth century. The idea of peer review has evolved over time, but the format of journals has remained largely the same. Odlyzko (1994) predicted the impending demise of scholarly journals. Print and mail are in the process of becoming obsolete as the standard for production and dissemination of scholarly work, as it becomes electronic and web-based. The continuity of the print-based format, with online journals closely resembling print ones, reflects acceptance of the scholarly journal article as the gold standard for publication in many academic disciplines.

The growth of scholarly journals and articles since 1665 has been remarkably constant. This was first documented by Price (1963, p. 17) in *Little Science, Big Science* and updated by Mabe and Amin (2001) and Mabe (2003). There is an average annual scholarly journal and article growth rate of about 3–3.5 per cent per year from the 1600s to the present day. If there were still just two scholarly journals producing a small volume of articles on an annual basis, it would be feasible for every scholar to read every scholarly article. However, as the volume of production grew, journals began to specialize in particular disciplines and sub-disciplines, at rates varying with the growth of the disciplines.

As production continued to increase, specialization was not enough. Guédon (2001) argues that the growing numbers of journals was the inspiration for a tendency to want to define "core journals." The purpose of the "core journal" concept was to address two problems that arose as the number of journals grew. One problem was the "serials crisis" documented by the Association of

Research Libraries (1989), a combination of increasing numbers of journals and average price rises for journals beyond inflation, year after year, leading libraries to cancel subscriptions. A second problem was the increasing difficulty scholars had in keeping up with the growing literature. In that sense, identifying "core journals" would help busy scholars prioritize their readings and publication venues.

Garfield (1955) proposed "a bibliographic system for science literature that can eliminate the uncritical citation of fraudulent, incomplete, or obsolete data by making it possible for the conscientious scholar to be aware of criticisms of earlier papers" (p. 108). Another proposed purpose of this system was to facilitate communication among scientists. It was in this article that Garfield first coined the term "impact factor" (IF), a then-hypothetical measure of the influence of a highly cited article.

Garfield (2006) describes the history of the development of citation indexing and IF. With support from the US National Institutes of Health, IF became the basis for the development of first the Genetics Citation Index and later the Science Citation Index. IF is a metric applied to journals rather than articles. It is based on two elements: a numerator consisting of the number of citations in the current year to items published in a particular journal in the previous two years, and the denominator, the number of substantive reviews and articles published in the same two years. In other words, IF is the average number of citations to an article in a particular journal for the previous two years. IF varies considerably by discipline and sub-discipline, as well as by journal, and is often evaluated on the basis of the status by quartile within a discipline.

The Science Citation Index developed by Garfield and colleagues in 1961 has morphed and grown into Web of Science, including the Science Citation Index, the Social Science Citation Index, the Arts and Humanities Citation Index, the Emerging Sources Citation Index, the Book Citation Index, and the Conference Proceedings Citation Index, in addition to optional specialized collections. Web of Science is one of a suite of interrelated products produced and sold by Clarivate Analytics (until recently published by Thomson Reuters) and is the basis for their Journal Citation Reports, which provides reports of journal IF.

Figure 5.1 illustrates the relationship and evolution of the core products related to research and research metrics offered by Clarivate Analytics. The initial core underlying product is a massive database of citations to journal articles, Web of Science. The research discovery tool called Web of Science is extensively used by researchers at university and research libraries for research discovery. The same underlying metadata is used for the traditional Journal Citation Reports (JCR). This is the tool originally envisioned by Garfield as a means of identifying a set of "core" or most highly cited journals so that researchers could

Figure 5.1. Core Clarivate products

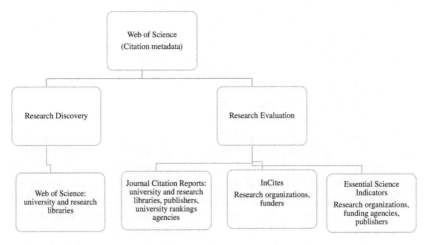

Created by the author

prioritize these for reading and libraries for purchase. JCR is important as a branding tool for publishers. JCR is also used by university rankings agencies. On the right, more recent tools InCites and Essential Science Indicators focus exclusively on metrics for evaluation. These are tools for measuring researchers, not assisting researchers in their work.

At a surface level, information on different pages on the Clarivate website might appear confusing and contradictory. This is because Clarivate offers services to a diverse group of stakeholders with different goals that are not always compatible. On the JCR website, Clarivate claims that JCR "gives you a systematic, objective means to evaluate the world's leading scientific and scholarly journals. By analysing citation references … JCR measures research influence and impact at the journal and category levels, and shows the relationship between citing and cited journals" (Clarivate Analytics, n.d.). JCR includes 11,000 journals from over 230 disciplines. This is about a third of the total active peer-reviewed journals reported by Ware and Mabe (2015) in a recent state-of-the-industry overview report produced for the International Association of Scientific, Technical and Medical Publishers (STM) (28,100 in the English language, 6,450 in languages other than English).

The target markets for JCR, according to the Clarivate website as of October 16, 2018, are librarians, to inform purchase and cancellation decisions; publishers and editors, to assess the effectiveness of journals in the marketplace; researchers, to identify the most influential journals in which to publish; and research managers and information analysts, to "track publication and citation patterns to aid your strategy and policy decisions."

Clarivate Analytics' (n.d.) web advice on the suitability of the use of JCR and other data derived from Web of Science in research assessment is dependent on the target audience of their different products. There is a marked contrast between advice on the JCR website (librarians as the primary target audience) and InCites (research organizations and funding and policy organizations as the primary target audiences).

On the JCR website, Clarivate warns against the use of IF in assessing journal quality, stating that "Clarivate Analytics does not depend on the impact factor alone in assessing the usefulness of a journal, and neither should anyone else ... The impact factor should be used with informed peer review. In the case of academic evaluation for tenure it is sometimes inappropriate to use the impact of the source journal to estimate the expected frequency of a recently published article. Again, the impact factor should be used with informed peer review. Citation frequencies for individual articles are quite varied."

In contrast, the title of the Clarivate website for InCites (like JCR, based on Web of Science data) states that it is "an *objective* analysis of *people*, programs and peers [emphasis added]." Recommended use of InCites data for assessing individual researchers as a primary use is implied for each target audience in their "Who's it for" section. For research organizations, InCites is presented as a means to "identify and manage research activities and their impact," as well as to "identify experts." For funding organizations, uses suggested include to "identify emerging ... researchers and experts" and to "manage funding activity from submissions to progress reports through outcomes." This assumes that emerging researchers and experts can be objectively identified through Web of Science data – i.e., researchers who publish in high-IF journals are presumably "emerging" and "expert." It is also assumed that publication in high-IF journals and high citation counts are objective measures of the quality of research. Publishers are told that InCites provides a means to "identify the best authors and reviewers."

Ware and Mabe (2015) discuss increasing industry criticism of the use of citation data, particularly IF, to judge the quality of individual researchers and departments. Will this industry recognition lead to change, and if so, what form will this change take? Based on major university rankings agencies' descriptions of their methods and Elsevier's (n.d.) description of Scopus, it appears that an evolution from journal-based metrics (IF) to bibliometrics based on individual works (articles, books and book chapters, conference proceedings) has already taken place in a large sector of the market. This shift addresses a major technical critique of IF: using journal IF as a surrogate for article impact. Elsevier's Scopus is the major source of data for the *Times*

Higher Education (THE) and Quacquarelli Symonds (QS) World University Rankings, among others.

Assessment of research and researchers is often conducted by researchers themselves, for example in promotion and tenure decisions and in review of grant applications. While university rankings systems are moving towards article-level metrics, researchers' own practices are deeply ingrained in academic culture and continue to rely primarily on IF. Stephan, Veugelers, & Wang (2017) discuss what they call "back-door bibliometrics," in which researchers and reviewers report and/or use journal IF in assessment even when this is not required. They also discuss the formal use of bibliometric indicators, such as the use of rankings derived from journal IF in Spain in promotion and salary increase decisions, and the payment of bonuses in China according to the prestige of the journal in which a researcher is published. In some regions such as Flanders and Brazil, journal IF is used in allocating resources to universities.

When researchers focus on their own areas of specialization, one might assume that they have the background knowledge to understand commonly used metrics. However, reliance on measures and surrogate measures of journal and article influence is common, although research metrics per se is not a common research specialty. To fully understand university rankings, we need to know who produces the data that feeds into the rankings and how they produce it.

Elsevier's Scopus data is the basis for 38.5 per cent of the ranking for the THE's World University Rankings (WUR) (THE, 2018, pp. 82–3). Citations or research influence account for 30 per cent of the THEWUR. These are based on "almost 62 million citations to more than 12.4 million journal articles, article reviews, conference proceedings and book and book chapters published over 5 years." According to the THE (2018), these data "help to show us how much each university is contributing to the sum of human knowledge ... whose research has stood out ... [and] been picked up and built on by other scholars" (p. 83). THE's "Research Productivity" is a count of the "number of papers published in the academic journals indexed by Elsevier's Scopus per scholar, scaled for institutional size and normalised for subject." Under "Institutional Outlook," "International Collaboration" is a measure of the portion of the university's total research journal publications that have at least one international co-author. The title paper of the THE report states that the work is "in partnership with Elsevier."

QS (2018) World University Rankings uses citations per faculty, a straightforward count of citations to the works of scholars at the university being evaluated, using the Scopus database. Maclean's (Dwyer, 2017) added bibliometrics indicators in 2015, publications per faculty and a field-weighted citation impact factor, drawn from Scopus.

New or Alternative Metrics-Based Approaches

Article metrics is at present in a process of rapid evolution. Several basic trends are observable: a shift from journal- to article-level citation metrics, discussed above; new types of metrics or altmetrics that illustrate different types of indicators of usage, such as views, downloads, and social media usage; and inclusion of metrics and links to downstream citing articles, social media, and so forth on publisher websites. In this section, I present a brief overview illustrating the rapid implementation of diverse approaches, explain in plain terms what researchers and publishers in this area are aiming to accomplish, and argue that while some aspects of these developments are useful for research, there is a problematic lack of critical reflection on the impact of these developments.

In 2012, Haustein published a comprehensive book on the technical details and flaws of scholarly bibliometrics as of that time, concluding with a recommendation for a multidimensional approach to metrics to overcome the flaws evident in any one method. Many other authors, such as Khodiyar, Rowlett, & Lawrence (2014), have similarly discussed the changing nature of assessment of scholarly work.

At present, the state of practice has far outpaced scholarly conceptions of new approaches. As discussed in the previous section, while researchers continue to assume that the journal IF is state of the art in metrics-based evaluation, major university rankings and the world's largest commercial scholarly journal publisher, Elsevier, have already moved to article-level citation metrics using data from Scopus.

Meanwhile, publishing practice already reflects heavy use of new or altmetrics that include and go beyond citations. The state of practice can be easily observed by browsing the websites of scholarly journals.

Box 5.1 illustrates a typical metrics display for a scholarly journal. To see this in action, go to the home page of Elsevier's *Journal of Economic Development*. On the right-hand side of the page is a means for readers to filter articles that includes the

Box 5.1. Typical metrics display for a scholarly journal

2018 Metrics of Journal X
- Impact factor: 3
- 5-year impact factor: 3.5
- CiteScore: 2
- Source Normalized Impact per Paper: 1.8
- SCImago Journal Rank (SJR): 3.2

Box 5.2. Article metrics for imaginary article

Imaginary Education Journal
Article metrics for: Emergency online teaching
Online attention: total altmetric score 3,000

- 2,700 tweets
- 150 blog mentions
- 50 Instagram shares
- On 50 Facebook pages
- Re-posted by 50 news outlets

This Almetric score means that the article is:

- The most shared article of this journal this year
- The tenth most shared article in all education journals published this year

---

options "most downloaded" and "most cited." On the left-hand side of the page is a list of five journal metrics and a link to "view more on journal insights"; this page includes even more metrics. Each metric has an icon "I" for more information; hovering over the icon brings forward the technical explanation for each metric.

Box 5.2 illustrates a typical breakdown of altmetrics by social media site. To see this in action, scroll down the home page of Nature's open access journal *Scientific Reports* to see a section called "Trending," with the word "Altmetric" prominently displayed at the top left-hand corner.

Clicking on the top trending article by altmetric (dinosaur article) reveals more detail about the metrics involved. On February 12, 2019, there were 0 citations from Web of Science. Online Attention indicates tweeting, Facebook, and media attention as illustrated in the following figures. Figure 3 shows total citations, online attention, and the altmetrics score. Figure 4 illustrates further detail that can be found by scrolling down from figure 3, a clickable list of media references, and an option to switch to scientific blogs, as well as a map illustrating Twitter references and a list of tweeting countries in descending order by number of tweets. Further down on the page are explanations of terms and sources.

These Elsevier and Nature journals each report new or altmetrics, but not the same ones. Why? Elsevier uses citation data from its own product, Scopus. Nature Publishing Group uses citation data from Clarivate's Web of Science and CrossRef for *Scientific Reports* rather than Scopus data. Could this be because the two companies are rivals? Nature owns Springer, the world's second-largest commercial scholarly publisher and hence a major competitor for Elsevier. Perhaps Nature prefers not to display Elsevier's Scopus data, or it might be that Elsevier prefers not to provide Nature with a reasonable price for use of Scopus data by a competitor.

Public Library of Science (PLOS, n.d.) provides a detailed explanation of their article-level metrics (ALMs). PLOS defines ALMs as "quantifiable measures that document the many ways in which both scientists and the general public engage with published research." Suggested uses of ALMs for researchers are to communicate impact in general and to funders, to raise a researcher's career profile, and to find collaborators.

Calls for Change in Research Assessment

DORA

The first major call to action is the 2012 San Francisco Declaration on Research Assessment (DORA), initiated by the American Society for Cell Biology. DORA's (2012) recommendations state "the need to *eliminate* the use of journal-based metrics such as Journal Impact Factors in funding, appointment, and promotion considerations" (emphasis added). As of October 2018, DORA has been endorsed by over 600 organizations and 13,000 individuals, myself included.

DORA (2012) does not question the concept of measurement per se, stating, "Funding agencies, institutions that employ scientists, and scientists themselves, all have a desire, and need, to assess the quality and impact of scientific outputs. It is thus imperative that scientific output is measured accurately and evaluated wisely." Implicit in DORA is an assumption that the peer-reviewed journal article will continue to be the most frequent means of dissemination of new knowledge in the foreseeable future. Development of metrics to include new forms of research outputs such as datasets and software is encouraged.

DORA includes general recommendations and specific recommendations for funding agencies, institutions, publishers, organizations that supply metrics, and researchers. Researchers, when involved in committees making decisions such as hiring, promotion, and tenure, are encouraged to make assessments based on scientific content rather than publication metrics. One of the deficiencies of all citation-based metrics noted in DORA is a skew towards review articles, as authors tend to cite review articles rather than the original works that are reviewed. Publishers and researchers are called upon to encourage authors to cite original research. It is recommended that funding agencies and institutions "consider a broad range of impact measures including qualitative indicators of research impact, such as influence on policy and practice" (DORA, 2012). However, publishers are encouraged to "make available a range of article-level metrics" and researchers to "use a range of article metrics and indicators," which suggests a deeper quantitative rather than a qualitative approach. Publishers are asked to "encourage responsible authorship practices and the provision of information about the specific contributions of each author." Qualitative information about author contributions would appear to advance the potential for enhanced qualitative assessment.

Leiden Manifesto

A group of self-described scientometricians, social scientists, and research administrators highlights some of the major issues with journal IF and other metrics and lists ten principles to guide research evaluation, principles crystallized at the nineteenth annual Conference on Science and Technology Conference Indicators, held in Leiden in 2014; hence this list is referred to as the Leiden Manifesto (Hicks et al., 2015). The Leiden Manifesto (http://www .leidenmanifesto.org) has been translated into eighteen languages.

The first principle states, "Quantitative evaluation should support qualitative, expert assessment." The authors cite an "impact factor obsession," stating that "soaring interest in one crude measure – the average citation counts of items published in a journal in the past two years – illustrates the crisis in research evaluation." Critique of metrics is not limited to IF. Simple publication counts can be problematic as well. An example is provided of a relatively low rating of a group of European historians in a national peer-review exercise simply because historians tend to write books rather than journal articles. H-index increases with the researcher's age, even if the researcher does not produce new papers. The h-index is also database-dependent. Computer scientists can have an h-index of 10 in Web of Science but 20–30 in Google Scholar. Precision matters: "a single highly cited publication slightly improves the position of a university in a ranking that is based on percentile indicators, but may propel the university from the middle to the top of a ranking built on citation averages." The authors suggest that relying on a single measure will "invite gaming and goal displacement (in which the measurement becomes the goal)," and one of their proposed solutions is multiple metrics.

Leiden Principle 2 is to "measure performance against the research missions of the institution, group or researcher." There is no single metric that makes sense in every research context. For example, consider an action research project designed to help a community group address an issue of concern to them. Ideally, design of the project's goals and evaluation measures should be undertaken in consultation with, or led by, the community group. The optimal measures of success would probably be real-world indicators of change. Homeless people want homes, not citations to articles about homelessness. Publication of results, written in plain language, in venues that are physically and intellectually accessible to the community, such as the community's own newsletter or blog or a local workshop, may be more effective in meeting the goals of the research than publication in scholarly journals using academic jargon that the group may not have access to or understand, or presentations at scholarly conferences that group members cannot afford to attend. The same principles would apply to academic/industry and academic/government collaborations. This is not to say that traditional academic ideas of excellence do not apply, but rather that measuring excellence by number of publications and citations in prestigious journals is not the optimal way to evaluate every type of research project.

Leiden Principle 3 states, "Protect excellence in locally relevant research." One example of the problem is Spanish law, which states the desirability of Spanish scholars publishing in high-impact journals. In sociology, the highest impact factor journals are published in English in the United States; likely as a result of this, highly cited Spanish sociologists are those who focus on either abstract models or US social problems.

Science Europe's New Vision for More Meaningful Research Assessment

In July 2017, Science Europe (2017a), a non-profit organization based in Brussels representing major research organizations across Europe, issued a position statement "on a new vision for more meaningful research assessment." The preamble contrasts the broad impact of research on society, often gained through a gradual development of new knowledge, with metrics designed to measure the impact of a specific study, and it points out that it is not always possible to connect societal impact with a particular research study. The preamble goes on to discuss the concept of the value of research, a broader notion of research impact that includes societal values. Societal progress draws from both research outputs and other sources; too narrow an emphasis on concrete impact may generate unintended, and not necessarily beneficial, effects on research activity.

The conclusion states, "There is great diversity in the ways in which research brings its immense value to society. Some of these ways are indirect or intangible and cannot easily be measured by strictly defined impact assessment criteria. Others are long-term or unpredictable and may not yet be visible at the time that the research is evaluated ... ultimately, the best way to maximise the value of research to society is by ensuring that the research produced meets the highest standards of quality and excellence." Science Europe's statement emphasizes the importance of trust between researchers and society. This is reflected in Priority 2 of Science Europe's (2017b) *Taillinn Call for Action*, which calls for research organizations and funders to "recognise a broad notion of impact that acknowledges the societal value of research for policy and practice" and asks policymakers, research funders, and academics to "foster the necessary cultural change to embrace the broad notion of impact."

Implementation of change in approaches to research evaluation is in an early stage. In September 2018, the European Commission endorsed Plan S, an ambitious plan to accelerate the transition to open access publishing, and cOAlition S, an organization focused on achieving the goals of Plan S; "the way we evaluate research outputs" is identified as one of the barriers to change (Plan S, n.d.). Science Europe's president Marc Schiltz (2018), in a statement called *Why Plan S*, states, "We commit to fundamentally revise the incentive and reward system of science, using the San Francisco Declaration on Research Assessment (DORA) as a starting point." The basic idea is for all funding agencies, particularly Europe but the aspirations are to inspire change globally, to commit to changing how research is evaluated, from traditional to new or altmetrics. It will be interesting to observe progress towards implementation of this ambitious plan over the next few years.

Discussion

Metrics vs. Quality in Research

Can metric systems capture the essentially qualitative nature of the concept of quality in research? The main goal driving development of citation indexing as described by Garfield in 1955 was so that researchers could track forward from published work to citing works that might point out critique of the original. I argue that the whole idea of using metrics to assess the quality of research and researchers is relatively new and has not received the critical attention that it deserves. This section aims to begin applying scholarly critique to this area.

As DORA notes, there is a skew in citations towards review articles rather than original research. This raises a question: If researchers are citing review articles rather than original research, are they even reading the original research, never mind tracking downstream citations? If we assume that review articles contain all the important information from every reviewed article, capture it accurately, and that the original articles are never critiqued, retracted, or refuted by subsequent research, then reading review articles is not problematic, but then there would be no need for citation linking to uncover critique.

Current approaches to research assessment assume that when it comes to scholarly publishing, more is better. Given the constant increase in the volume of production of scholarly works and the availability of citation indexing to permit more careful checking, shouldn't researchers today be spending relatively more time reading rather than publishing? If they were, wouldn't they be publishing less rather than more? Assessment systems based on the premise that more is better seem likely to risk increasing errors such as invalid results. Research into current practice would be helpful. One might survey researchers on whether they actually read all of the works that they cite, whether they rely on secondary sources such as reviews or go to the originals, and whether they use citation indexes to check downstream citing sources. Or one might analyse written publications to see whether there are errors that might have been caught with more in-depth reading.

Advancing our knowledge requires questioning underlying assumptions in addition to building on existing work. Two assumptions in the area of research assessment that should be challenged are that "impact" itself is necessarily positively correlated with good-quality work and that impact is inherently desirable. The second most highly cited retracted paper according to the *Retraction Watch* (n.d.) blog is the infamous 1998 paper by Wakefield et al. published in the highly prestigious journal *Lancet*, purporting to make a connection between vaccination and autism. This article has been cited over 1,000 times in the list of journals included in Web of Science, with 640 citations before retraction and 468 citations after. Any of the existing or emerging metrics-based approaches to research assessments would find that this study has had a lot of impact. The article was published in a high-IF journal. It is a highly cited article, which would result in high article-level rankings and would boost the h-index of all of the authors. If we consider real-world impact, the influence of this article in the anti-vaccination movement and the subsequent return of diseases such as measles demonstrate an exceptional real-world impact for a single article. This illustrates the danger of assuming that impact is necessarily good. Like almost all qualities of things in the real world, impact is neither good nor bad in and of itself; rather, it must be interpreted in context.

If universities and research funders are relying on university rankings, this provides an additional incentive to focus on traditional forms of publication. For example, the bibliometrics partner of Times Higher Education (2018) in producing the World University Rankings is Elsevier. To measure research productivity, Elsevier counts "the number of papers published in the academic journals indexed by Elsevier's Scopus database per scholar." To calculate citations or research influence, Elsevier "examined … citations to journal articles, article reviews, conference proceedings and books and book chapters." This count of citations to particular types of works is a de facto endorsement of these types of works. It is probably not a coincidence that Elsevier is a highly profitable publisher of exactly these types of works.

My own experience as a scholar confirms this focus on a limited range of formats. My university's online CV system is likely typical in categorizing types of publications – books and book chapters, peer-reviewed journal articles, non-peer-reviewed articles, and so forth. This categorization is understandable for historical reasons; however, the end result is that the majority of my works, and almost all that I consider my most important and leading-edge works, such as the open data discussed above and my scholarly blogs, *Sustaining the Knowledge Commons* and *The Imaginary Journal of Poetic Economics*, are labelled as "other" and would count for little or nothing under existing metrics-based assessment approaches.

Retraction Watch bloggers track and report on published articles that were retracted after publication. Unlike JCR, InCites, or Scopus, *Retraction Watch* addresses the original main goal of citation indexes as proposed by Garfield in 1955, "a bibliographic system for science literature that can eliminate the uncritical citation of fraudulent, incomplete, or obsolete data by making it possible for the conscientious scholar to be aware of criticisms of earlier papers" (p. 108). Most retractions reflect errors discovered after publication but occasionally fraud is uncovered and reported. *Retraction Watch's* (n.d.) top-ten most highly cited retracted papers have been cited more than 550 times in journals indexed in Web of Science (as of January 2018), and this list includes two papers that have been cited more often after retraction than before. The blog also tracks evidence that citation of retracted papers is an ongoing problem.

Retraction Watch demonstrates a fundamental flaw with current approaches to research assessment, which focuses on the *impact* of scholarly work, whether measured indirectly through metrics such as journal IF or directly through article-level metrics, and for the most part neglects the more important question of the *accuracy* of scholarly work.

Bibliometrics and the Economic Sustainability of Scholarly Communication

Increasing market concentration was the subject of investigation by the UK Office of Fair Trading (2002). As described by Morrison (2012), industry concentration and growing profits of a few large commercial scholarly journal publishers were accompanied by a significant decrease in the average number of copies of scholarly monographs produced and sold. Recently, Larivière, Haustein, & Mongeon (2015) reported an increase in concentration in the scholarly publishing market, with the top five publishers accounting for more than 50 per cent of the articles indexed in Web of Science. The Scholarly Publishing and Academic Resources Coalition (SPARC; n.d.) maintains a list of big-deal journal cancellations by university libraries, library groups and state library systems, and national coalitions such as the Consortium on Core Electronic Resources in Taiwan (CONCERT). This is not a healthy system; the high prices and profits of a few commercial scholarly publishers cannot be sustained by academic libraries, and the economic clout behind the big package deals results in little funding left over for publishing scholarly monographs and supporting the journals of smaller publishers, particularly in the humanities and social sciences. My research suggests that the same trend of commercial concentration, involving the same companies, is emerging in open access publishing. As of 2017, the largest open access journal publisher by number of journal titles was Springer Nature (including BioMedCentral), followed by Elsevier (Morrison, 2017).

This development is not an anomaly. Identifying a subset of journals as "core" and therefore more desirable to publish in and more essential to purchase increases their market value. "Core" is in quotes to emphasize that this is an essentialization of the concept for market purposes. The priorities of for-profit publishers are returning profit to shareholders or private owners, not the health of the scholarly publishing ecosystem. Thus, it is logical that journal IF exacerbates the problem of affordability of scholarly publishing and similarly logical to hypothesize that new bibliometrics-based approaches will have a similar effect.

Qualitative Focused Assessment: How, Why, and the University of Ottawa as a Model

There are models for assessing research at the level of evaluation of individual researchers, programs, and institutions that exemplify an understanding of the broader value of research to society and address the complexity of the diversity of research as expressed in the Science Europe vision and the Leiden Manifesto. At my own university, the University of Ottawa, the criteria for evaluating faculty members for promotion and tenure is collaboratively developed by faculty and administration and governed by the Association of University Professors of the University of Ottawa (APUO) *Collective Agreement* (APUO, 2018). The full text of all sections of the collective agreement directly relevant to research assessment can be found in the appendix.

The APUO agreement addresses the question of diverse and evolving forms of scholarly works. Section 23.3.1 (h), regarding the types of material that members may submit for assessment, states, "It is understood that since methods of dissemination may vary among disciplines and individuals, dissemination shall not be limited to publication in refereed journals or any particular form or methods"; one example of other forms is listed in section (a): "in the case of literary or artistic creation, original works and forms of expression." Canada's Social

Sciences and Humanities Research Council recognizes "research-creation" as a valid form of dissemination.

Typically, a new faculty member at the University of Ottawa is hired at the rank of assistant professor and, after six years, applies for the senior rank of associate professor, a promotion that automatically invokes tenure. The criteria for research assessment at this stage are covered under the APUO Collective Agreement section 25.3.2.2 (c). To achieve tenure, a new faculty member must demonstrate production of good-quality scientific, literary, artistic, or professional works that go beyond work done in the completion of the doctorate and that show continuous progress. Evaluation is conducted by three outside evaluators and reviewed by committees at the faculty and university-wide level. A similar process is followed when a faculty member applies for promotion to the rank of full or titular professor. This is a holistic career-level peer-review process.

Ironically, and somewhat mysteriously, in spite of this qualitative and inclusive approach to assessment of research and researchers rather than simplistic metrics, the University of Ottawa does very well in metrics-based rankings. According to the University of Ottawa & Government of Ontario Ministry of Advanced Education and Skills Development's (2017) *Strategic Mandate Agreement 2017–2020*, "Independent national and international rankings (such as Research Infosource, QS World University and the Times Higher Education) consistently place uOttawa among the top three Ontario universities, among Canada's top 10 research universities and among the top two per cent of the world's universities" (p. 17).

Why is this? The answer is not easy to ascertain by reviewing rankings agencies' descriptions of methodology. *Times Higher Education* claims for the 2019 rankings to have the first audited university rankings and appears to be the most transparent. The overall ranking for the University of Ottawa from 2012 to 2019 varied from a high of 171 (2013) to a low of 251–300 in 2017, rising to 201–50 in 2018 and 176 in 2019. The areas where the University of Ottawa appears to score relatively well are citations, industry income, and international outlook. Citations count for 30 per cent of the overall weight and so are likely the major factor. There is no obvious reason from the detailed method description of the THE why the average citations to research published by University of Ottawa faculty would have changed during this time frame. Over this period, the number of full-time faculty members has decreased slightly; one would expect this to decrease the number of citations since less research is being produced. A slight decrease in the faculty complement would account for a slightly higher average citation rate if the faculty complement were factored in; however, the THE methodology does not state that this is the case. Industry income may reflect local economic conditions. The University of Ottawa's central location in the nation's capital (close to downtown, City Hall, Parliament, and national corporate head offices, surrounded by embassies) may be a factor in the university's strengths in industry income and international outlook. However, the wide variation in overall standing over recent years, given a stable university, suggests that changes in how rankings are calculated are a large factor in current standings.

At the University of Ottawa, regular comprehensive assessment processes that include peer assessment of faculty and student research are already in place at the program level. At minimum, each program undergoes a provincially mandated cyclical review every seven years. This is a far more in-depth assessment than counting publications or citations. For example, external reviewers conduct in-person interviews separately with faculty, students, and administrators and have the opportunity to ask questions not just about research outputs but also about institutional support for research in terms of time, facilities, assistance with grant applications, and so forth. In addition, some programs, particularly professional programs, undergo professional accreditation processes that also review research undertaken at the departmental level. For example, the School of Information Studies undergoes a rigorous accreditation process coordinated by the American Library Association.

For a university with these in-depth, holistic research assessment practices already in place, a turn to greater reliance on simplistic metrics based on a limited and backward-looking understanding of formats and what constitutes good-quality scholarly work would be a step backward.

The primary mission of Elsevier is returning profit to shareholders of its parent company, RELX; the primary mission of Clarivate is returning profit to its private owners. The mission of the University of Ottawa (2017–20), with respect to its role as a research-intensive university, is this: "We provide our students with an outstanding education and enrich the intellectual, economic and cultural life of Canada, helping our country play an important and valued role among the nations of the world." The mission of each university will differ slightly but will tend to revolve around the central functions of teaching, research as an activity designed to further our collective knowledge, and service to the academy and to society as a whole. I argue that we should trust scholars and the academy to design and implement assessment mechanisms that reflect and prioritize our goals (missions, vision), not those of outside parties whose primary interests are inherently different from our own.

Conclusion: The Irrational Rationality of Metrics-Based Assessment of Research

It is logical for people to want to measure progress towards the goals that we desire. Many measures are valid and logical. However, when we focus on the measures per se rather than the goals, we can end up with results that do not achieve our goals. This is what I call a superficially rational (mathematical, calculating) approach that is actually irrational in terms of what we are attempting to achieve, or irrational rationality. Current and emerging forms of metrics-based assessment of research and researchers display major problems with irrational rationality, creating incentives that are not compatible with a goal of producing and disseminating quality research. These problems merit urgent attention before our current fixation with metrics further entrenches existing problems and new or altmetrics introduce new ones.

There are valid, logical reasons for use of some metrics in assessing research, researchers, research institutions, and publishers. A university should be able to point to a substantial corps of faculty with a research mandate and a body of research works produced by its faculty to call itself a research university. An individual researcher should be able to point to a collection of published works and/or substantive work-in-progress to be considered a productive researcher. Individual researchers and research teams may find it helpful to develop specific measurable goals that make sense for their own projects. Journals and other publishers can use metrics to assess marketing efforts. Bibliometrics is a useful research method for generating new knowledge. However, just because some metrics are helpful, it does not follow that ubiquitous metrics are helpful. A bit of salt adds flavour to food; excess sodium causes high blood pressure, increasing the risk of heart attack or stroke.

Evaluation based on metrics *looks* scientific, doesn't it? Numbers are objective. Metrics-based evaluation is rational and calculating; scientists often use lots of data. However, the resemblance is superficial. Logic is a powerful tool; but the validity of logical arguments depends on the validity of the underlying assumptions. In order to assess whether we are making progress in science, we need to understand how science works. As discussed above, our current approaches to science are compatible with the production of dangerously erroneous "facts," such as the equation of vaccines with autism and false belief in the safety of drugs; irreproducible research; and a tendency to cite literature reviews that makes one wonder how often the original studies are actually read. If this is the situation in science, what about other branches of knowledge? As Camic, Gross, & Lamont (2011) discuss, while there has been some reflection on practice in the sciences since publication of Kuhn's (1962) *The Structure of Scientific Revolutions* and subsequent development of the field of science and technology studies (STS), parallel study of processes in the area of the social sciences is just beginning. If we do not even know what scholars in the social sciences do, how can we claim to know how to measure whether they are doing it well?

The study of philosophy and practice of science, while more advanced than the study of social sciences, raises more questions than answers about metrics-based approaches. For example, it is logical to assume that the paradigm shifts described by Kuhn (1962) will lead to situations where whether works are cited, and by whom, depends on the phase of development of new ideas. One might hypothesize that works that fit a current paradigm will be cited more than pioneering works, in which case using citations to assess the value of research will tend to incentivize conservatism over innovation.

I argue that Kuhn's work itself illustrates the problem. Thomas Kuhn was a young, white, highly educated male based in the United States who wrote about scientific revolutions in the 1960s. This work was widely read, studied, and cited, within a short time after publication. An earlier work, Fleck's 1930s groundbreaking *Genesis of a Scientific Fact* (Fleck, 1979), did not enjoy this immediate acclaim. In the foreword to Fleck's 1979 edition, Kuhn describes finding this work, written in German, by happenstance while browsing in the stacks of a library. Fleck was a Jewish intellectual lacking formal credentials whose work was published in Germany in the 1930s. Unlike the popular reception of Kuhn's work, only 600 copies were printed of Fleck's work, only 200 were sold, and only 6 were delivered to the United States. Kuhn's philosophy was inspired by this work, but this does not render the work obsolete, as Kuhn's ideas complement rather than supersede those of Fleck. For example, where Kuhn emphasized sudden ruptures in scientific thinking, Fleck emphasized continuity of basic premises in apparently revolutionary advances in knowledge.

What does this have to do with university rankings? I have described a deeply flawed system, with an illusory appearance of scientific basis, that incentivizes quantity of production of research works over quality, convention over innovation, and provides no incentive for the rigorous critique and replication necessary to sound advancement of our collective knowledge. The metrics behind this system feed into university rankings, and the rankings reinforce this trend towards irrational rationality.

The current trend towards new or altmetrics will create even more irrational rationality. It is logical to expect that these new metrics, particularly metrics that do not depend on academic citations, will amplify existing problems with metrics-based evaluation and/or create new ones. I predict that such metrics will reflect pre-existing social biases. The extent to which individual works are cited, downloaded, and shared via social media are likely to correlate with gender and ethnic biases as well as the popularity of topics studied. In addition, metrics that do not depend on academic citations (downloads, tweets, etc.) are far more vulnerable to deliberate manipulation. The fossil fuel industry can afford to hire people to download and tweet evidence of climate change denial, for example. Another factor that should be considered before using such data as a surrogate for quality of research is the impact that usage of such metrics could have on the research itself. For example, if cancer researchers find it helpful to use social media, they can and should do so. But if metrics based on non-academic use were to form the basis of assessment and research in future, this could result in a redirection of efforts from cancer research to social media sharing.

As for the impact of popularity of topics in new metrics, on a cynical note I take comfort in the possibility that someday I may have reason to move forward with a study along the lines of "correlates of perceived attractiveness of juvenile felines on YouTube" (academese for why those kitty cats on YouTube are so darn cute) to prove my worthiness as a researcher. On a serious note, it is my experience as a long-time practitioner of open research that the popularity of my works does not correlate with the importance of its contribution. My groundbreaking book chapter, "The Implications of Usage Statistics as an Economic Factor in Scholarly Communications," begins some of the discussion that continues with this chapter and introduces important but counterintuitive ideas (Morrison, 2005). This work does not enjoy even a small fraction of the social media popularity of my *Dramatic Growth of Open Access* blog series, designed to support the advocacy efforts of a global movement.

The evolution of research metrics described in this chapter captures the irrational rationality of metrics-based research assessment. In the 1950s and 1960s we developed tools to help researchers and libraries cope with the ever-expanding volume of scholarly literature by connecting citing and cited works and identifying highly cited journals to assist libraries with decisions about purchases and cancellations and researchers with decisions about reading and publishing. The resulting metric, IF, became a yardstick for evaluating the worthiness of research and researchers even when it was acknowledged by experts and the producing company that this metric was not at all suitable for this purpose. Attempts to address the technical flaws of IF (connected to journals rather than articles) are adding a new layer of metrics based on citations to individual works that rankings companies are already incorporating into assessment of universities and that are being marketed as a means of assessing researchers. The profit goals of metrics-based companies (scholarly publishers, citation metrics, and rankings services) are overtaking the research missions of universities. We develop tools to help us achieve our goals, then we become slaves to the tools. That is irrational rationality. In the future, if we continue on the current trajectory, we should expect an additional layer of much more illogical metrics-based control of research and researchers in the form of altmetrics based on usage beyond the academy.

If excess reliance on metrics is the problem, what is the remedy? Let's develop and use metrics where they make sense, based on the goals of individual research projects and institutions. But let's do so with a grain of salt and not rely on metrics where such reliance is not scientific and may be counterproductive by creating perverse incentives for quantity and novelty over quality and that favour particular formats, even as they become obsolete. How can we implement this remedy?

We can use approaches that appropriately weight quality and that recognize the diverse forms of research. Instead of translating a research dossier into unscientific metrics, read and review the works. This isn't new, and it shouldn't be hard. This is what we do now when we assess a thesis or peer-review the works of other researchers. At the University of Ottawa, we have a collective agreement that acknowledges the diversity of research and its products; details are in the appendix if readers would like to consider this as one potential model for change.

REFERENCES

APUO. (2016). *Collective agreement between the University of Ottawa and the Association of Professors of the University of Ottawa (APUO) May 1, 2016 to April 30, 2018.* http://www.apuo.ca/wp-content/uploads/2016/10/APUO_CA-2016-2018 _final-2016-09-20.pdf

Association of Research Libraries (ARL). (1989). *Report of the ARL serials prices project: A compilation of reports examining the serials prices problem.* Association of Research Libraries. http://catalog.hathitrust.org/Record/001527850

Camic, C., Gross, N., & Lamont, M. (2011). *Social knowledge in the making.* University of Chicago Press.

Clarivate Analytics. (n.d.). *Products: Journal Citation Reports.* Retrieved 15 January 2018 from https://clarivate.com

Dwyer, M. (2017, 19 October). Measuring excellence: How we rank Canada's universities. *Maclean's.* http://www.macleans.ca/education/measuring-excellence -how-we-rank-canadas-universities

Elsevier. (n.d.). Scopus. Retrieved 23 January 2018 from https://www.elsevier.com /solutions/scopus

Fleck, L. (1979). *Genesis and development of a scientific fact* (T. Trenn & R.K. Merton, Eds.; T. Trenn & F. Bradley, Trans.). Foreword by T.S. Kuhn. University of Chicago Press.

Garfield, E. (1955). Citation indexes to science: A new dimension in documentation through association of ideas. *Science, 122*, 108–11. https://doi.org/10.1126/science .122.3159.108. Medline:14385826

Garfield, E. (2006). The history and meaning of the journal impact factor. *Journal of the American Medical Association, 295*(1), 90–3. https://doi.org/10.1001/jama.295.1.90. Medline:16391221

Guédon, J.C. (2001). *In Oldenburg's long shadow.* Association of Research Libraries.

Haustein, S. (2012). *Multidimensional journal evaluation: Analyzing scientific periodicals beyond the impact factor.* De Gruyter/Saur.

Hicks, D., Wouters, P., Waltman, L., De Rijcke, S., & Rafois, I. (2015, 23 April). Bibliometrics: The Leiden Manifesto for research metrics. *Nature, 520*, 429–31. https://doi.org/10.1038/520429a. Medline:25903611

Khodiyar, V.K., Rowlett, K.A., & Lawrence, R.N. (2014). Altmetrics as a means of assessing scholarly output. *Learned Publishing, 27*, S25–S32. https://doi.org /10.1087/20140505

Kuhn, T. (1962). *The structure of scientific revolutions*. University of Chicago Press.

Larivière, V., Haustein, S., & Mongeon, P. (2015, 15 June). The oligopoly of academic publishers in the digital era. *PLOS ONE, 10*(6), e0127502. https://doi.org/10.1371 /journal.pone.0127502

Mabe, M. (2003). The growth and number of journals. *Serials, 16*(2), 191–7. https:// doi.org/10.1629/16191

Mabe, M., & Amin, M. (2001). Growth dynamics of scholarly and scientific journals. *Scientometrics, 51*(1), 147–62. https://doi.org/10.1023/a:1010520913124

Morrison, H. (2005). The implications of usage statistics as an economic factor in scholarly communications. In D. Fowler (Ed.), *Usage statistics of e-serials* (pp. 173–82). Haworth Press.

Morrison, H. (2012). The commercialization and rationalization of scholarly publication. In H. Morrison, *Freedom for scholarship in the internet age* [Doctoral dissertation, Simon Fraser University]. http://summit.sfu.ca/item/12537

Morrison, H. (2017). Elsevier as an open access publisher. *Charleston Advisor, 18*(3), 53–9. http://www.ingentaconnect.com/content/charleston/chadv/2017/00000018 /00000003/art00014

Morrison, H., Brutus, W., Dumais-Desrosier, M., Laprade, K., Merhi, S., Ouerghi, A., Salhab, J., Volkanova, V., & Wheatley, S. (2017). Open access article processing charges 2016. Scholars Portal Dataverse. https://doi.org/10.5683/SP/KC2NBV

Odlyzko, A.M. (1994). Tragic loss or good riddance? The impending demise of scholarly journals. *Journal of Universal Computer Science, 0*(0), 1–52.

Plan S. (n.d.) What is cOAlition S? Retrieved 21 October 2020 from https://www .coalition-s.org/about

PLOS. (n.d.) Assessment of impact with article-level metrics (ALMs). Retrieved 21 October 2020 from https://plos.org/publish/metrics

Price, D.J. d. S. (1963). *Little science, big science*. Columbia University Press.

QS World University Rankings. (2018). *Methodology*. https://www.topuniversities.com /qs-world-university-rankings/methodology

Retraction Watch. (n.d.). *Top 10 most highly cited retracted papers*. Retrieved 22 January 2018 from http://retractionwatch.com/the-retraction-watch-leaderboard /top-10-most-highly-cited-retracted-papers

DORA. (2012). *San Francisco Declaration on Research Assessment*. https://sfdora.org /read

Schiltz, M. (2018). *Why Plan S?* Coalition S. https://www.coalition-s.org/why-plan-s

Scholarly Publishing and Academic Resources Coalition (SPARC). (n.d.). *Big deal cancellation tracking*. Retrieved 15 January 2018 from https://sparcopen.org/our -work/big-deal-cancellation-tracking

Science Europe. (2017a). *Science Europe position statement: On a new vision for more meaningful research assessment.* https://www.scienceeurope.org/our-resources /position-statement-on-a-new-vision-for-more-meaningful-research-impact -assessment

Science Europe. (2017b). *Taillinn call for action.* https://www.hm.ee/sites/default/files /tallinn_call_for_action_2017.pdf

Stephan, P., Veugelers, R., & Wang, J. (2017, 27 April). Reviewers are blinkered by bibliometrics. *Nature, 544,* 411–12. https://doi.org/10.1038/544411a. Medline:28447652

Times Higher Education. (2018). *World University Rankings 2018.* In partnership with Elsevier. https://www.timeshighereducation.com/world-university-rankings/2018 /world-ranking

UK Office of Fair Trading. (2002). *The market for scientific, medical and technical journals.* No. OFT 396 UK Office of Fair Trade.

University of Ottawa & Government of Ontario Ministry of Advanced Education and Skills Development. (2017). *Strategic mandate agreement 2017–2020.*

Ware, M., & Mabe, M. (2015). *The STM report: An overview of scientific and scholarly journal publishing.* 4th ed. International Association of Medical, Technical and Scientific Publishers (STM). http://www.stm-assoc.org/2015_02_20_STM_Report_2015.pdf

Appendix

The Association of University Professors of the University of Ottawa (APUO) Collective Agreement (2016–2018) section 23.3 (assessment of scholarly activities) states:

> "23.3.1 (a) The member may submit for assessment articles, books or contributions to books, the text of presentations at conferences, reports, portions of works in progress, and, in the case of literary or artistic creation, original works and forms of expression.
> (h) It is understood that since methods of dissemination may vary among disciplines and individuals, dissemination shall not be limited to publication in refereed journals or any particular form or methods."

Typically, a new faculty member is hired at the rank of Assistant Professor and, after six years, applies for the senior rank of Associate Professor, a promotion that automatically invokes tenure. The criteria for research assessment at this stage is covered under the APUO Collective Agreement Section 25.3.2.2 (c) and reads as follows:

> "(c) The Member has produced scientific, literary, artistic, or professional works – or a combination thereof – which are, in accordance with the criteria set forth in 23.3.3.2, deemed of good quality. This assessment shall be made following an overall evaluation of the Member's scholarly works, carried out in accordance with the provisions of section 23.3, during which the opinion of three (3) outside evaluators will have been obtained, in accordance with 23.3.2."

23.3.3 Level of performance of scholarly activities states:

> *23.3.3.1 Whenever this agreement refers to satisfactory performance of scholarly activities by a Faculty Member, it refers to a situation where the Member is regularly engaged in scholarly activities the results of which indicate that her performance, in comparison to a relevant group of peers of comparable rank and experience, is satisfactory.
> *23.3.3.2 The Member's scholarly works shall be considered good if they represent a contribution in addition to that contained in the Member's doctoral thesis or to the work that has been taken to be the equivalent of a doctorate, and if, subsequent to that work:
> (a) in the case of research, they demonstrate continuous progress in the development of the Member's research activities and contribute to the advancement of knowledge in the Member's field of specialization;

(b) in the case of literary or artistic works, they attest to continuous creative activity, well-reputed in the literary or artistic community outside the University of Ottawa;

(c) in the case of professional works, they attest to the practice of a profession above and beyond that which is generally expected of a non-teaching, practicing professional, or they can be considered as a valuable contribution to the advancement of the profession itself.

6 Marginalizing the Marginalized: How Rankings Fail the Global South

RALF ST. CLAIR

University rankings have significant limitations when it comes to recognizing the contributions of universities beyond the Anglosphere, as well as those where the world-class university discourse is not the dominant concern regarding higher education. In this chapter, I explore some of the concrete factors that make it difficult for a university in the Global South to gain traction and improve its position in the rankings. This analysis suggests that the self-referential and mutually reinforcing nature of the ranking metrics minimizes the potential for the established Western universities to face ranking challenges from those outside the existing circle of privilege.

One of the remarkable things about the world university rankings is that they are so unremarkable. In many ways they reinforce our intuitive expectation that Oxford and MIT will do very well indeed and that my university, a medium-sized comprehensive in Western Canada, will be somewhat lower but still in the top 1 per cent of universities in the world. There is something quite troubling about evaluations that produce results that are very similar to what we expect. For example, imagine if the assessment of students made by teachers on the first day of class was highly predictive of the year-end results. We would have a number of questions, ranging from the ethical to the pragmatic, including what exactly the evaluation added to our knowledge. Why not, after all, just use the teacher assessments on day one as our outcomes?

I will not beleaguer this point but just draw out one aspect. If rankings are so reflective of expectations, it raises the question of what actions institutions can take to improve in the rankings. The rationale for rankings as a quality improvement tool is, after all, that institutions will align their activities towards the values encapsulated in the rankings and be rewarded with a better ranking. The power of expectation has the potential to dampen the effects of innovations that would otherwise be rewarded in the rankings. Rankings are controversial in a wide range of other ways, but here I wish to focus on questions around institutions' aspirations to change their ranking position. This is not necessarily a major issue between well-ranked and well-resourced institutions in the West. The question of whether Nottingham overtakes Warwick or not is primarily significant to the denizens of these institutions. Where it does matter, and I would argue that it matters a great deal, is where the message of the rankings aligns with patterns of privilege and marginalization around the world. If the rankings tend to recapitulate colonial understandings of matters such as where the knowledge of the world resides and, by extension, who knows best, it is no longer a local concern for the institutions but a broader question for the political economy of continents (Ishikawa, 2009).

In this analysis I attempt to unpack these issues on a pragmatic level, by analysing the structures of the Times Higher Education World University Rankings (THEWUR) to see what kind of strategies and emphases might be adopted by universities in the Global South (UGS) interested in improving their position in this rankings system. As things stand, rankings suggest that universities in the North are far stronger than those in the South. In 2018, the highest-ranked institution for the South was the Indian Institute of Technology (250–301). The Indian Institute of Technology is seen as the school of choice in computer science and related fields, and computer scientists have commented to me that students applying to the Indian Institute of Technology often mark MIT as their backup choice. It may be that the ranking does not fully capture the status of the institution. The highest-ranked from sub-Saharan Africa, excluding South Africa, was the University of Ibadan (801–1000). These rankings raise a huge number of questions about what is being measured and how, as well as the fundamental legitimacy of the measures. But here I want to keep close to the mechanics and ask what can be done about this disparity. For institutions such as the University of Ibadan, what actions have the potential to affect the ranking positively?

Background

World university rankings matter. Whether we think they should or not, it seems that there is an appetite for them, that they affect a range of decisions in and around universities, and that they hold interest for multiple audiences. University administrators and policymakers appear to pay attention to rankings both as a signal regarding reputation and as one form of institutional accountability (Swail, 2011). It has been argued that one of the positive effects of university rankings has been to anger academics and policymakers enough to engage with the issues of higher education (Hazelkorn, 2014a), a view which I find deeply pessimistic. The idea that negative emotion is the primary motivation for thinking about our universities does not reflect well on our societies. I view the primary question around rankings as very similar to that which bears on other international comparative studies: How can we use the information well and move beyond the crude comparative application of measures to learn positively from the data?

Over the last decade and a half, I have been in administrative positions at universities in the top 50, the top 75, and the top 300 in the *Times Higher Education* (THE) global rankings. While the conversations have varied across these institutions, I have directly observed rankings being brought up more frequently, including in discussions of publications, faculty searches, student recruitment, and selecting the best universities with whom to partner. There is independent evidence to support the importance of rankings to students and their families. A study by the THE in 2017 found that the ranking of the university was the third most frequently cited reason for university choice, following high-quality teaching and availability of financial support (THE, 2017). This finding is supported by Hazelkorn's (2014) slightly older work, which positions reputation as a significant concern for international undergraduate and graduate students and suggests that rankings are a key proxy for reputation. Domestic undergraduate students may use less formal assessments of reputation, particularly in systems where there are relatively small variations in perceived quality (Pizarro Milian & Rizk, 2018), but in situations where informal information is limited, rankings may fill the vacuum. Despite the considerable level of scepticism about the rankings, they are creeping into many corners of academic life.

Two factors strongly influence rankings and tend to help reinforce the perceived dominance of Western universities: language and resources. Quacquarelli Symonds, the company that produces the QS rankings, is un-nuanced in its recommendations regarding language. One of QS's publications suggests "seven ways to improve university rankings in the EECA region"; of these, the second is to "produce papers in English" (QS, 2017). Many of the rankings use automatic indexing systems, which cannot work in every world language (Altbach, 2005). Despite the multilingual claims sometimes put forward, articles in English remain much more likely to be captured and recognized. This point will be explored more fully in the analysis of the THE rankings later in the chapter.

Resources make a difference in a number of ways. It is easier for richer countries in the North to pay high salaries and attract research stars, particularly if these researchers need expensive or specialized equipment. It is hard to imagine a UGS supplying a physics professor with a particle accelerator when the basic municipal power supply is unreliable. More generally, richer institutions tend to be in locations that are more attractive to people able to choose their location. One striking demonstration of this effect is the distribution of Nobel laureates globally (not all of whom need equipment, necessarily). Of the approximately 200 countries in the world, only 75 have ever produced a Nobel Prize winner and, not surprisingly, Northern Europe and the Anglosphere are dominant (World Atlas, 2018). Resources may also allow better student support and greater publicity spending by the institution, though of course this depends on institutional priorities. It is interesting that the GDP of a country and the ranking of its universities are not inextricably linked (Williams & Leahy, 2018), but the absence of countries and institutions with fewer resources – even in a GDP-adjusted list – is striking.

If we assume that intelligence, imagination, and creativity are universal human traits, any regional bias in education is a cause for concern. Entire national systems of universities are being assigned to lower positions on the global scene, to a large extent through the mechanics and unintended consequences of international rankings (cf. Ishikawa, 2009). One possibility is that these systems really are not as good as the British or American systems, but, leaving aside the absurdity of this proposition, it is not clear how this could be known. Rauhvargers's (2013) report suggested,

> An analysis of the procedures through which global rankings select universities for inclusion in rankings indicates that the methodologies used by the main global rankings are not geared to covering large numbers of higher education institutions, and thus cannot provide a sound basis for analysing entire higher education systems. This is reflected in the criteria used for establishing how the sample of universities in each case is selected. (p. 17)

If rankings cannot assess systems, then it follows that rankings of individual institutions must be decontextualized. The question of contextualization – and indeed whether rankings should be contextualized – leads to a question about the nature of universities. More specifically, it leads to reflection on what a good university is. One way to explore this issue, in a somewhat metaphorical fashion, is to consider the meaning of the word "university."

There is a common-sense assumption that the word "university" relates to the idea of "universal." This could be taken to mean either that universities should teach everything or that they should teach the knowledge deemed to be valuable to everybody, emphasizing universal inclusion of knowledge or universal values, respectively. There is a long series of nineteenth-century disputes around these ideas that I will not rehearse here. Current scholarship, however, does not translate the Latin *universitas* as "universal" but instead as a "range of communities or guilds constituted for social purposes" (Alexander & Alexander, 2010, p. 26). The definition makes a difference. The assumption of universality suggests all universities should be doing a similar job and can perhaps be evaluated against universal standards. The second definition, with its emphasis on a community of scholars brought together for a purpose, leads to a much stronger emphasis on the context of the work. In this case, it's far less clear that even attempting to compare institutions on a decontextualized global level is desirable or feasible.

One concept that has emerged alongside the rankings is the notion of the "world-class university," and it is also useful to look at this term. Over fifteen years ago, Altbach (2003) argued that the term was fundamentally meaningless. Since then, it has become, in effect, shorthand for a university that demonstrates the characteristics that lead to a strong placing in global rankings. In fact, the THE defines the term backwards, by pulling out the factors that get a university into the top 200 in their rankings (THE, 2014), an exercise that truly underlines the circularity of the definition. Nonetheless, the concept is having a real-world effect, including pushing towards the "universalization of research science" (Marginson, 2016, p. 299). An acceptable working definition of a world-class university for the purposes of this discussion is one that configures its work, and the representations of that work, in order to be recognized as one of the best institutions in the world. The referent here is not the form of the institution, or indeed what it achieves, but how it represents its actions in a quest for status.

It is important to consider what the current approach means for the universities involved and why rankings are a significant issue. Proponents of the system would argue that global rankings encourage collection of high-quality data on higher education, which in turn leads to quality improvement in institutions and debate on the desirable characteristics of the system. It may also lead to increased interest in university reform, including, perhaps, increased marketization. The less positive outcomes may be the reorientation of the system towards the ranking metrics at the cost of other outcomes, university leaders being held to account for rankings, and a tendency to want to build relationships only "upwards" in the rankings (Rauhvargers, 2013). There is some evidence that one of the broad effects is stratification of higher education on a global scale, with an upper tier having more in common with other similar institutions than with other members of the same system or institutions striving to join this echelon. One clear reward for universities that are successful in this endeavour is that students will compete harder – and pay more – for study spaces in that top tier (Hazelkorn, 2011). It is difficult to know the extent to which rankings have driven global stratification, reflected it, or simply accompanied the trend. Nonetheless, rankings have proven to be a key aspect of the logistics of stratification.

As higher education has globalized more intensively over the last few decades, there have been opportunities for universities in less-developed areas of the world to build capacity by connecting with universities in more-developed settings. The wealthier partner might be involved with faculty development, teaching improvement, or collaborative research in conjunction with the less wealthy. There could be joint programs, for example, with careful planning and design ensuring that both partners benefit deeply from their relationship. When rankings become more influential such partnerships will become more difficult. The less-developed institutions will be looking for higher-ranked part-nerships, and the established institutions may be more cautious about support-ing developing universities. If rankings are the key consideration, one of the few motivations for a higher-ranked institution to partner with a lower-ranked one will be *noblesse oblige*, which is hardly a healthy basis for a relationship.

For a mid-ranked university, it is easy to slide lower in rankings tables without proactive reputational management, meaning in practice that the University of Victoria, for example, encourages partnerships with academics who can "up-vote" UVic in the reputational surveys. This does not mean that universities such as Victoria are entirely driven by such cynical concerns, but it does mean that multiple motivations may lie behind resource investment decisions. When it comes to rankings, the line between cynicism and naïveté can be remarkably thin.

On a broader scale, rankings may reinforce the tendency towards academic neo-colonialism. Given the choice, students may select higher-ranking univer-sities in developed economies by default, both reinforcing "brain drain" and making it hard for the developing institutions to demonstrate their quality. All of these factors suggest that it will be difficult for universities in the Global South to create and develop international connections, and a key strategy for improvement will be lost. If this dynamic were to dominate, developing econo-mies would end up with institutions seen (however unfairly) as second-rate, and the global stratification of higher education would intensify. Indeed, as Ishikawa (2009) argues, both domestic and international stratification increase under the pressure of rankings, as national governments concentrate their resources in the few institutions that can achieve strong positions in the world.

This stratification could be harmful for many reasons. Economically, it would make it yet harder for developing economies to develop and maintain the circumstances that would support humane and appropriate forms of devel-opment. Morally and ethically, the perpetuation of the developed economies as the centre of wealth and knowledge, with all the concomitant implications for the life chances of their citizens, is deeply problematic. The potential of the Global South, its institutions and its peoples, will never be understood until artificial limits to development such as this are set aside. In the next section, I begin to address the questions about whether rankings are fundamentally tilted against UGS and, if so, what can be done.

Analytical Approach

The ranking frameworks have slightly different approaches to the task (which leads to slightly different outcomes). In this discussion I have chosen to focus on the *Times Higher Education* framework. The THE ranking is one of the three systems taken most seriously and viewed as most credible by institutions

(Hazelkorn, 2014a). In 2018 the THE rankings represented 1,000 institutions, or about 3 per cent of the 30,000–35,000 universities in the world (Baty, 2018). It is worth pausing to reflect that currently 97 per cent of all global universities are not participating in the rankings.

The THE is a commercial organization, not a public-interest research body. The final rationale for the rankings exercise is that it makes money for the parent corporation, and this should be borne in mind. The attempts by the authors to address concerns about opacity and explain at least some of the mechanics of the ranking system (cf. THE, 2018) is to be commended, as is their desire to recognize regional variations in support for higher education by providing rankings within regions such as Latin America (albeit with the same criteria). Enough information is available from the THEWUR website to support a reasonable degree of analysis, and the website (which is the primary publication venue for the world rankings) was the source I used in the following discussion. Nonetheless, it should not be forgotten that the primary quality measure for the rankings is whether they generate income for the publisher, not academic values such as validity and reliability, and that the details of the comparisons are proprietary.

The THE has been relatively consistent in its approach over a number of years, and it is possible to use the THE rankings for longitudinal analysis within the period 2012–18. Changes in institutional scores for different elements are available to some degree, although not at the most granular level, and it should be possible to get some idea of which changes make a difference and then apply those insights to the context of a UGS. The thirteen total criteria are grouped into five categories, each of which has a score, and an overall score combines the categories. Each of these scores is ordinal, based on comparison with other institutions, making it infeasible to work backwards to the raw score. For example, there is no way to work out how many more "international publications" would change the rank of an institution. The five categories are not equally weighted, as shown in table 6.1, which lists weights out of one hundred for each (THE, 2018).

It is possible to break down these categories a little more to get a sense of the dynamics. The 30 per cent of the research category includes 18 per cent for reputation, derived from a global survey of academics who are mainly at high-ranking institutions. There are also two components of research income and research productivity, each of which is weighted at 6 per cent and scaled for institution size, purchasing power parity (between national economies), and subject area. Scopus is used to measure productivity. This global index requires English-language abstracts for inclusion and currently has 22 per cent non-English content (Vera-Baceta, 2019). The "citations" category is also based on Scopus and counts citations to Scopus publications in Scopus publications. Altogether 36 per cent of the total score is based on Scopus despite its

Table 6.1. Categories and weights for scoring
in the Times Higher Education rankings

Category	Weighting
Research	30.0
Teaching	30.0
Citations	30.0
Industrial income	2.5
International outlook	7.5

demonstrable, and indeed explicit, failure to capture non-English sources. This is a very significant advantage to the Anglosphere.

THE provides information on changes to its categories and weighting over time, so it is possible to get a sense of those changes and their effects. While this is a relative advantage compared to other ranking systems, the information available to analysts is far from complete. THE changed its approach completely in 2012, making longer-term comparisons impossible, and it is still not clear about its algorithm. For example, though the weighting of different elements is described, any operation performed on the raw scores remains unknown. So while the ordinal value of an institution's citation rate is public knowledge, and therefore its deviation from the mean, the numerical difference between institutions is not public. Once past the surface level the transparency is very limited, and it is challenging to get a sense of the mechanics of the process.

On one hand, this makes it very hard for universities to "cheat" the system, and while there have been examples of institutions changing their behaviours to produce more favourable results, these have been at a relatively crude surface level (see Pérez-Peña & Slotnik, 2012, for an example). Institutions should know that student-teacher ratio matters and be able to consider adjusting it for a better score, which is a different phenomenon from having full knowledge of reputation metrics and covertly influencing colleagues to assign higher marks to an institution. An institution has no idea how many more citations, or what kind of reputational enhancement, will allow it to improve its position, making the system harder to game. On the other hand, the limited knowledge of the algorithm undercuts universities' understanding of why they have been allocated a particular position and what they can do about it. Needless to say, appeals are not possible.

Rankings appear to feature a mix of elements, some of which are straightforward to understand and assess for one's own institution and others which are not clear. A cottage industry of consultants who will come in and advise universities on how to improve their position has sprung up, and with the opacity of the ranking systems, who is to say they are wrong?

THE rankings are not unproblematic. It would be hard to make the case that there is no systemic bias in favour of the wealthy Anglosphere. I will not delve into this too deeply in the current discussion, though there is a great deal more to be said, but instead I acknowledge it as a background feature of the rankings and the possibilities for action available to UGS. The focus of this discussion is empirical analysis of one example of a university that has managed to change its position in the rankings and how it achieved it. Then I will consider the implications of those strategies and whether they are open to UGS.

Findings

There has been a degree of churn at the top end of the rankings, so I was initially optimistic that it would not be too hard to identify strong examples of institutions that had improved their position. It is perhaps worth emphasizing that changes in scores on any of the ranking exercises may – or may not – reflect actual changes on the ground. At best these indicators are loosely coupled to institutional practices and circumstances, and the discussion here is primarily interested in the presentation of the university rather than any claims about fundamental shifts in operations. In identifying cases, I restricted my search to the top one hundred, where there appears to be less noise than in the lower rankings and where institutions are individually ranked rather than being in bands. There proved to be few examples of consistent improvement, and far more where the institution had moved into the top one hundred and out again between 2012 and 2018 – overall twenty-five new universities entered the top one hundred and twelve of those remained in 2018, while the top sixty have been very consistent.

The best example of a rising institution I could find was Nanyang Technological University (NTU) in Singapore. It has some features in common with many UGS, in that it is not an ancient European university, is mid-sized with 33,000 students, and does not have English as a home language (though it is worth noting that English is one of the official languages of Singapore). The available documents, including the institutional website, suggest several years of deliberate strategy to improve the ranking of the institution, resulting in the outcomes shown in table 6.2.

Scores in every one of the five categories show a degree of improvement, but some have really transformed. The teaching score, for example, has only improved slightly, from 41.4 to 49.5, most likely not enough to explain a 117-position rise. Research has come up from 47.8 to 63.0, again significant but not necessarily enough to make the difference, as is true for International Outlook. Industrial Income has come up a lot, but it is not a heavily weighted category. The truly remarkable change is Citations, which moved from 34.5 to 90.7. To put this another way, NTU was less cited than two-thirds of universities

Table 6.2. Times Higher Education rankings results for Nanyang Technological University, 2012–18

Year	Teaching	Research	Citations	Industrial income	International outlook	Overall	Rank
2012	41.4	47.8	34.5	44.4	89.8	45.0	169
2013	45.7	66.9	54.5	99.5	90.9	59.4	86
2014	37.7	54.3	67.5	100.0	91.0	57.2	76
2015	43.9	55.9	75.9	100.0	92.5	62.2	61
2016	48.4	61.3	85.6	99.9	94.6	68.2	55
2017	50.6	60.2	90.7	93.5	95.7	70.0	54
2018	49.5	63.0	90.7	94.0	95.9	70.5	52

in the rankings in 2012 and seven years later was more cited than 90 per cent of them, and it is worth noting that the rise in citations may well have a reputational impact. Taken together these factors have brought about a remarkable change in the position of the institution.

The rise in rankings has not been accidental; NTU has taken deliberate actions to bring it about. The university has increased faculty and staff from 7,307 to 8,311 in the last two years (NTU, 2018a), providing evidence of significant investment in the institution. NTU has implemented the strategy referred to earlier, of building relationships with higher-ranked institutions, which will likely have had an effect on the reputational score.

> NTU actively pursues partnerships with top universities and runs joint and dual PhD degree programmes with well-established universities. Some of its key partners in academia and research include Imperial College London, Technical University of Munich, and University of California, Berkeley. (NTU, 2018c, ¶16)

It is a challenge to fully analyse the Citation scale, the one with the greatest move, even though NTU helpfully provides a citation-per-paper rate. In 2010–14 this was 8.29 and in 2012–16 it was 10.72 (NTU, 2018a). There are three possible explanations when this is placed alongside the remarkable increase on the Citations scale. One is that the scale is so sensitive that a 25 per cent increase in the number of citations per paper brought about the 66-point move. The second is that the quantity of publications increased, and the increasing staff numbers could have helped to bring that about. The third possible explanation is that NTU's strategies to increase citations have been effective. Some such evidence is on the NTU website, such as a library page called "Finding and Improving Your Research Impact" (NTU, 2018b), which features reminders to include a reference to NTU and to spell the name of the institution correctly. The most likely explanation is that all of these changes together (along with

Table 6.3. Times Higher Education rankings results for the University of Ibadan, 2016–18

Year	Teaching	Research	Citations	Industrial income	International outlook	Overall	Rank
2016	22.7	11.1	4.6	29.2	26.1		601–800
2017	27.5	11.3	5.7	40.4	28.8	8.3–18.5	>800
2018	25.9	11.4	7.4	40.3	32.0	15.6–21.4	801–1000

others not so explicit) made NTU into a dominant producer of citations. For example, it is unclear how many citations were generated when access to professors from the partner universities led to high-profile joint publications and easier access to English-language journals. The key points from this discussion are that resources make a difference and that deliberate strategies appear to have a significant influence on outcomes.

The picture is quite different at a university in the Global South. According to the THEWUR, the University of Ibadan is the top-ranked university in sub-Saharan Africa. Like NTU, Ibadan has 33,000 students. The university prides itself on its quality and its historical links to the University of London and sees itself as having contributed enormously to the development of Nigeria and West Africa as a region (Udege & Ekhaguere, 2017). It has appeared in the THE rankings only since 2016, and, as table 6.3 shows, Ibadan has also improved in all five categories over that time. The changes have been a lot smaller than NTU's. Based on the weighting of the categories, for Ibadan to experience the type of climb in the rankings experienced by NTU would require very significant changes in Teaching, Research, and Citations. Ibadan is closer in Teaching than the other two, so Research and Citations would be the areas of focus if the institution were to strategize for greater prominence in the rankings.

Insights and Questions

The most obvious insight is that resources make a huge difference. According to the institution's annual reports, NTU's overall funding has increased a great deal between 2012 and 2017, from US$815 million to US$1.17 billion. Within that, government support went up around 35 per cent, from US$442 million to US$598 million. The University of Ibadan is less transparent about resources, but government support in 2017 was US$36.1 million (Olawoyin, 2016), or around one-sixteenth that of NTU. Given fewer opportunities for industry collaboration, the low level of tuition fees considered affordable in Nigeria (the basic Ibadan tuition for medicine is US$69 per year), and other economic factors, it is likely that the overall income at the University of Ibadan is also proportionally smaller.

It is not fair to reduce university quality to the input of resources; after all, as mentioned earlier, rankings are not reducible to GDP. However, many of the factors considered in the world rankings have a cost to them, which can be considerable in some cases. Some examples are international travel and partnership building, including support for visiting scholarships in both directions. Strong graduate students are often offered considerable scholarships by the wealthier institutions, not to mention the equipment they may need for their work. Even tracking all the activity associated with research can be expensive, requiring both staff and specialized software. The list continues through lab space, with lab-based sciences being an important source of multi-author papers that leverage citations very effectively.

The NTU website shows evidence that the institution's reputation, as well as the more concrete aspects of the operation, has been positively managed. This is a very sensible move given the 36 per cent of the THE ranking derived from recognition and reputation. When I reviewed the website in March 2018, the tagline read, "A university that scores on all points. Where form meets substance: NTU is not just ranked 11th in the world university rankings but also among the most beautiful and sustainable campuses globally." On revisiting the site six months later it was completely redesigned and has a slideshow across the top featuring the ambitions of the university to be a top global institution. It is abundantly clear that this university is focused on increasing its status, and the amount of space given to rankings results suggests that they are a key component of the plan. Many other materials from NTU reiterate the point.

One of the most effective ways to build reputation is to increase awareness and acknowledgment among those who are already reputable and who have the credibility to be taken seriously when they admire an institution. In the case of universities, it seems very difficult to achieve this without significant ability to form partnerships internationally and attract the interest of the top institutions. NTU claims to have "internationalized" its faculty to a great deal, which is an effective way to build international connections. Hiring new PhDs from MIT is a very effective way to make MIT aware of your institution. Reputation is not really a very "clean" measure of institutional quality, being subjective at best, manipulable at worst. Rankings represent a fascinating example of Goodhart's Law (Goodhart, 1981), which can be stated as "when a measure becomes a target, it ceases to be a good measure," as it applies to public services. When a system orients itself to maximize the measure rather than enhance the values represented by a measure, the measure becomes pointless. Reputation, to the extent that it was ever anything other than a circular measure, becomes increasingly less valid as it takes on a more central role in university strategy. Increasing activity to promote the reputation of an institution in the eyes of external parties is hardly a worthwhile outcome of rankings exercises.

The vision statement of the University of Ibadan is "To be a world-class institution for academic excellence geared towards meeting societal needs." A recent history of the university states that "UI has contributed immensely to the development of Nigeria and much of sub-Saharan Africa through its training, research, and community service functions" (Udege & Ekhaguere, 2017, p. 281) and that "the university is engaged in outreach programs to several West African institutions (particularly those recovering from war) to support postgraduate education and staff training" (Udege & Ekhaguere, 2017, p. 327). These statements, and the values they enshrine, bring up the tension mentioned earlier when the meaning of "university" was discussed, around the extent to which a good university sees itself as a community among communities or as a free-floating element on the world stage. The social contract implied by the idea of the world-class university (WCU) is that increased reputation of the institution benefits society more broadly and that this public good justifies the public expenditure and support. If this idea is not accepted, then the value of investment in a university is harder to define.

One public benefit of universities has long been seen as the raised status of the sponsoring state (Clark, 2006). The status of a state is as much a resource in geopolitics as the reputation of a university is in geo-rankings. Investment in a WCU implies that the state wants to consolidate its position as a leader in knowledge production. The focus on "meeting societal needs" at Ibadan implies a different set of concerns and a different conception of the uses of a university, much less to do with status and more to do with the pressing concerns of a developing economy. Ibadan seems not to be as deeply engaged with the notion of the world-class university as NTU, with implications for the ranking process.

The final question I will raise here is how useful a high-ranked WCU would actually be to a country in the Global South. There has been growing interest in the contributions universities make to their regions and cities, including the economic and cultural impact (Drucker & Goldstein, 2007), but no agreement on how this can best be understood. It is currently not clear how the benefits flow from the institution to the community, nor how this flow can be encouraged. For example, one benefit is that universities could prepare well-educated individuals who would go on to contribute to the development of the local economy. While vital to the region containing the university, this contribution would not be captured in rankings, making it highly unlikely that a WCU, or aspiring WCU, would prioritize or even capture this activity. In many regions of the world, the production of well-educated people can promote human capital flight to wealthier parts of the world, suggesting that WCUs may actually have the potential to accelerate the loss of educational capital in a developing economy. Overall, it is far from clear that a well-ranked WCU would be best placed to contribute to a developing economy. An argument could be made that universities such as Ibadan are placed into a deficit position in global rankings for not being *less* relevant to the needs of developing nations. This is hardly the intent of any of the ranking systems.

Conclusion

Overall, the conclusion must be that world university rankings are of dubious value to UGS, either in recognizing their work or providing guidance to them in terms of development. Rankings are an expensive, high-stakes pursuit that may not have clear benefits to the state or locality that supports these institutions. While it may be going a little far to describe rankings as a vanity project for wealthy universities and the states that support them, one can see where such a comment might come from. Rankings may perpetuate a rather pitiful view of the human condition predicated on the assumption that we pay attention to our activities only in a state of competition, a view that is hugely pessimistic due to the implication that some people and institutions must always be considered as "losers."

It seems that UGS are left with two options. One is to withdraw from rankings altogether – there is some cost involved just in participating, for data collection and preparation, etc. – and it is possible those resources could be better allocated. This would lead to a perpetuation of the stratification of global higher education, with the universities who choose not to participate being relegated to a perpetual "unranked" or "also-ran" status. This would leave the world-class universities and the others, which could very well lead to inward-looking cultures within both strata, to the detriment of all. Development could become yet more challenging for the universities working to build human capital in developing economies.

The other option is that UGS develop their own way to demonstrate the value of their work, based on the primary concerns that they hold rather than the WCU ideal. Rather than global reputation, for example, local reputation beyond the university community might be taken into account. The community impact of research might be what matters most. The assessment of teaching could involve the actual student experience rather than a distant evaluation by other academics. There is a lot to be learned from the current rankings systems about how alternative approaches can reflect and reinforce alternative systems of performance and aspiration. The different missions of UGS must be recognized through different performance measures if the rankings are to have utility and value.

One aspect of ideological hegemony is the claim that there is no option but to view the world in a specific way. In my experience as a university administrator in three Western universities, the concept that universities should be ranked, and that the rankings matter, seems to have attained common-sense status. I have had many conversations with people who acknowledge rankings are flawed to the extent they have little real value, but who argue that if other institutions are using them, and assumedly gaining some notional advantage, then they should too. Yet thinkers are challenging the common-sense notion of higher education as a competitive event and asking how else we might think about the role, and the future, of the institution. De Sousa Santos (2014, p. 8) wrote that "counter-hegemonic globalization of the university-as-public-good means that the national reforms of the public university must reflect a country project centred on policy choices that consider the country's insertion in the increasingly transnational contexts of knowledge production and distribution." In other words, there can be an alternative model of global correspondence between institutions, rooted in the needs and priorities of sponsoring states rather than the chimera of international competition.

In closing, I hope that the UGS have an opportunity to express the high standard of their programs and the individuals within them. It seems unlikely to come through the existing ranking systems because they are simply too self-referential and too closed a loop and appear unable to open sufficiently to recognize alternative epistemologies rooted in non-Western (indeed, non-Anglophone) cultures. The degree to which the focus on rankings at NTU actually conceals the other strengths of the university is striking; the point of the rankings is not to show how well institutions score on rankings but to represent those aspects of an institution that form a great environment for teaching, learning, and research. Perhaps one of the surprising lessons of this analysis is not how rankings marginalize institutions outside the wealthy countries, but how many of the key values and activities of high-ranking universities end up being obscured. When there is a real concern that universities in the Global South cannot realistically improve their positions in the rankings due to the relevance of their missions to the needs of national and local communities, there is a real danger that rankings simply reinforce the marginalization of the marginalized.

REFERENCES

Alexander, K., & Alexander, K.W. (2010). *Higher education law: Policy and perspectives*. Routledge.

Altbach, P. (2003). The costs and benefits of world-class universities. *International Higher Education, 33*, 5–8. https://doi.org/10.6017/ihe.2003.33.7381

Altbach, P. (2005). Academic challenges: The American professoriate in comparative perspective. In A. Welch (Ed.), *The professoriate: Profile of a profession* (pp. 147–65). Springer.

Baty, P. (2018). *World university rankings 2018: Now starring a cast of thousands*. Times Higher Education Supplement. https://www.timeshighereducation.com/world-university-rankings-2018-now-starring-cast-thousands

Clark, W. (2006). *Academic charisma and the origins of the research university.* University of Chicago.

De Sousa Santos, B. (2014). *Epistemologies of the South: Justice against epistemicide.* Paradigm.

Drucker, J., & Goldstein, H. (2007). Assessing the regional economic development impacts of universities: A review of current approaches. *International Regional Science Review, 30*(1), 20–46. https://doi.org/10.1177/0160017606296731

Goodhart, C.A.E. (1981). Problems of monetary management: The UK experience. In A.S. Courakis (Ed.), *Inflation, depression and economic policy in the West* (pp. 91–121). Rowman & Littlefield.

Hazelkorn, E. (2011). *Rankings and the reshaping of higher education: The battle for world-class excellence.* Palgrave Macmillan.

Hazelkorn, E. (2014a). Reflections on a decade of global rankings: What we've learned and outstanding issues. *European Journal of Education, 49*(1), 12–28. https://doi.org/10.1111/ejed.12059

Hazelkorn, E. (2014b). Rankings and the global reputation race. In S.S. Bagley & L.M. Portnoi (Eds.), *New directions in higher education 168: Critical perspectives on global competition in higher education* (pp. 13–26). Jossey-Bass.

Ishikawa, M. (2009). University rankings, global models, and emerging hegemony critical analysis from Japan. *Journal of Studies in International Education, 13*(2), 159–73. https://doi.org/10.1177/1028315308330853

Marginson, S. (2016). The global construction of higher education reform. In K. Mundy, A. Green, B. Lingard, & A. Verger (Eds.), *Handbook of global education policy* (pp. 291–311). Wiley-Blackwell.

Nanyang Technological University. (2018a). *Facts and figures.* http://www.ntu.edu.sg /AboutNTU/CorporateInfo/FactsFigures/Pages/FactsandFigures.aspx

Nanyang Technological University. (2018b). *Finding and improving your research impact.* https://www.ntu.edu.sg/library/About_NTULibrary/Pages/Citation-and -Research-Impact.aspx

Nanyang Technological University. (2018c). *Corporate information.* http://www.ntu .edu.sg/AboutNTU/CorporateInfo/Pages/Intro.aspx

Olawoyin, O. (2016, 29 December). Despite lacking infrastructure, recurrent expenditures dominate Nigerian universities' 2017 budgets. *Premium Times.*

Pérez-Peña, R., & Slotnik, D.E. (2012, 31 January). Gaming the college rankings. *New York Times.* https://www.nytimes.com/2012/02/01/education/gaming-the-college -rankings.html

Pizarro Milian, R., & Rizk, J. (2018). Do university rankings matter? A qualitative exploration of institutional selection at three southern Ontario universities. *Journal of Further and Higher Education, 42*(8), 1143–55. https://doi.org/10.1080/0309877x .2017.1349889

QS. (2017). Papers and citations. http://www.iu.qs.com/university-rankings/indicator -papers-citations

Rauhvargers, A. (2013). *Global university rankings and their impacts: Report II.* European University Association.

Swail, W.S. (2011). Building a better mousetrap: A look at higher education ranking systems. *College and University, 86*(4), 28–36.

Times Higher Education. (2014). *The formula for a world-class university revealed.* https://www.timeshighereducation.com/world-university-rankings/news/the-formula-for-a-world-class-university-revealed

Times Higher Education. (2017). *Why do students go to university and how do they choose which one?* https://www.timeshighereducation.com/student/news/why-do-students-go-university-and-how-do-they-choose-which-one#survey-answer

Times Higher Education. (2018). *World university rankings 2019: Methodology.* https://www.timeshighereducation.com/world-university-rankings/methodology-world-university-rankings-2019

Udege, B., & Ekhaguere, G.O.S. (2017). University of Ibadan: A beacon of higher education in Africa. In D. Teferra (Ed.), *Flagship universities in Africa* (pp. 281–332). Palgrave Macmillan.

Vera-Baceta, M., Thelwall, M., & Kousha, K. (2019). Web of Science and Scopus language coverage. *Scientometrics, 121,* 1803–13.

Williams, R., & Leahy, A. (2018). *Universitas21 ranking of national higher education systems.* Universitas21.

World Atlas. (2018). *Nobel Prize winners by country.* https://www.worldatlas.com/articles/top-30-countries-with-nobel-prize-winners.html

THEME 3

Influence of Rankings on Institutional and Individual Well-Being

The contributors to this section remind us that rankings have real impacts on the day-to-day lives of students, faculty, and staff within and beyond the university. Mayumi Ishikawa provides a compelling argument for how rankings have affected the domestic labour market within and outside universities. Within universities, there is more pressure for those who hope to become professors to study abroad. Within industry, positions that were previously for Japanese graduates are now open to people outside of Japan. Gary Barron reminds us that rankings are not done to us by some abstract force but tap into capital that has been central to academia – prestige and reputation. To find an alternative or resist the current framework requires acknowledging why rankings have come to be normalized and largely accepted. And finally, Nathan Hall looks at an area that receives very little attention – mental health and ranking. He looks at how people experience being at differently ranked institutions and what impact this may have on their mental health.

7 Between Local Distinction and Global Reputation: University Rankings and Changing Employment in Japan

MAYUMI ISHIKAWA

This chapter examines the conundrum posed by the popularity of global university rankings and the proliferation of the excellence norms that they promote by examining their incompatibility with the traditional domestic university hierarchy of Japan. Previous studies have identified the delayed internationalization and slow Anglophonization of research and education as factors responsible for the deteriorating performance of Japanese universities in recent years. A culture of "conservatism" and "lack of ambition" among research universities is blamed for the declining rankings. This study sets itself apart from such a culturally essentialist approach and addresses the broader socio-economic factors surrounding university reputation and employment in Japan today. By doing so, it offers another look at the challenges that globalization poses to Japanese higher education and the society at large, specifically, that of constructing a global reputation versus the deconstructing (or eroding) domestic reputation.

Japan's domestic university hierarchy, maintained throughout much of the postwar period, is based largely on exam selectivity of students and the prioritization of producing desirable graduates for the domestic labour market. Although this local system is badly in need of adjustment amid the changing economic climate and labour market practices under globalization, embracing global university rankings at the expense of the domestic system of assigning status can be destructive to employment and career systems that have defined the lives of Japan's middle-class, white-collar workers for decades. The study thus addresses the significant impact and threat that global university rankings may present to the career and life trajectories of individuals in a "periphery" nation on the global higher education map.

Previous studies on global university rankings have been conducted from "institutional" and "national" perspectives, such as those seeking policy solutions to enhance the competitiveness of flagship institutions, or those on talent wars and the implications for the knowledge economy. This study, however, ultimately questions the impact that the prevalence of global excellence norms showcased in world university rankings may have within the context of corporations expanding borderless operations and the global restructuring of national labour markets.

The "Decline" of Ranking Positions and Japanese Universities under Attack

Despite the intense interest and attention to global rankings expressed from national stakeholders (Yonezawa, 2010, p. 122), the overall performance of Japanese universities has declined in recent years. The downward trend is especially notable when compared with the bourgeoning rankings of universities among Asian neighbours such as China. For example, Japan consistently led Asia in the Academic Rankings of World Universities (ARWU) by Shanghai Jiao Tong University until 2015, with seven to nine institutions listed in the top 200. Today, twelve Chinese universities are listed in the top 200 while only seven Japanese universities remain in the same ranking at all, with a majority positioned near the bottom (ARWU, 2015a, 2015b, 2018a, 2018b). Japan's government, which had been ambivalent towards global university rankings due to its inability to sustain financial commitments to uplift positions of domestic universities in the climate of fiscal austerity (Yonezawa, 2010, p. 125), was alarmed by the trend and has since embraced global rankings as national key performance indicators to evaluate domestic universities (Ishikawa, 2014). Subsequently, highly selective, large-scale funding schemes such as the "Top Global University" project has been introduced to boost international competitiveness or, more explicitly, the ranking positions of Japanese universities (Ishikawa & Sun, 2016, pp. 465–6).

Previous studies and criticisms from stakeholders have identified two major factors considered responsible for, or at least related to, the downward trend in the global rankings of Japanese universities. These are (1) a delay in "internationalization" and (2) a lack of "citation" of Japanese academics in international publications (Ministry of Education, Culture, Sports, Science and Technology, Japan [MEXT], 2013).[1] Various stakeholders – including policymakers, business leaders, and those within domestic higher education – point, first and foremost, to delayed and ineffective internationalization of Japanese universities (see, for example, Ishikawa, 2014, p. 6; Yonezawa, 2010; also see Mock et al., 2016). "Internationalization" is typically measured in global university rankings by indicators such as the percentage of international students and faculty, areas in which Japanese universities are reported particularly "weak" (Yonezawa, 2010, p. 127). Japanese universities are said to be dragging behind in rankings due to their failure to internationalize with measures such as promoting the widespread usage of English to diversify student and staff bodies and create international campus environments.

A lack of "citation" is related to the production of academic knowledge and connected to the delay in internationalization. Japanese universities have delayed shifting their faculties' publication language to English, which would enhance global engagements in research and, by extension, boost research publication and citation scores in university rankings. Significant proportions of research outcomes in the humanities and social sciences and important segments of "hard science" research in Japan are published in the Japanese language. Therefore, the "narrowly Anglo-American" (Paasi, 2005) English-language publication data used in global rankings omits a significant amount of Japan's academic research and is thus unfit to accurately assess the performance of scholars in Japan (Ishikawa, 2014; Ishikawa & Sun, 2016). To boost the ranking positions of Japanese universities as the government instructs, however, it is imperative for Japanese research universities to publish more in English in indexed international journals, particularly in areas conventionally undertaken in the national language.

The pursuit of higher positions in rankings by "producing" and "gaming" (Espeland & Sauder, 2007; Shore & Wright, 2015, p. 26) may not only compromise responsibilities to local readership but also be detrimental in fostering innovation and creativity in scientific research (see, for example, Ishikawa, 2014, n. 9). In the areas of both internationalization and citation, Japanese universities are criticized for being plagued with conservatism (Goodman, 2016, p. viii) and a "lack of ambition" (JSPS, 2011, p. 2) in the age of global ratings and position-taking.

This Study: University Hierarchy and Employment

This study addresses a third factor contributing to Japan's declining ratings: the incompatibility of global ranking systems with Japan's domestic university hierarchy, which is based mainly on exam selectivity of students and prioritizing producing desirable graduates for the labour market. As the prestige of a particular university has been inextricably linked to graduates' employment prospects and the associated lifetime security and rewards, replacing the domestic with global reputational hierarchy could upset the existing social stratification mechanism that has defined the lives of white-collar university graduates in much of postwar Japan. This chapter focuses on the "potential threat to the conventional university entrance and exit points of *juken* [taking entrance exams] and *shushoku* [job search and placement]" (Breaden, 2013, p. 183).

The analysis hereafter thus goes beyond the realm of higher education and addresses the broader socio-economic factors surrounding university reputation and employment in Japan. By doing so, this study offers another look at globalization challenges to Japanese higher education and the society at large and, specifically, the dilemma of eroding domestic reputation in order to construct a global reputation. The study contends that Japanese universities' delay or wariness in adhering to the norms of global rankings is not necessarily due to cultural conservatism or lack of ambition, but rather, because of the embeddedness of the domestic university hierarchy in the nation's labour market and the risks of replacing the national system of prestige with global rankings. Embracing global rankings, as policymakers now encourage, may have significant impacts on the well-being of individuals beyond institutional and national policy aspirations and competitions.

Scholarly work on global university rankings rarely pays attention to the relationship between university rankings and career and employment, even though university reputation does matter for the employment and career prospects of graduates in many national contexts. A recent study from the United States, for instance, presents compelling evidence that graduates of elite universities monopolize high-paying jobs (Rivera, 2015). Also, university hierarchy and reputation, of which university rankings are a powerful indicator, influence class formation and the transmission of privilege from one generation to the next (cf. Karabel, 2005; Soares, 2007).

With the exception of a small number of studies (see, for example, Hazelkorn, 2015, pp. 159–62), social analyses of global university rankings tend to be university-centred (see Altbach & Balán, 2007; Yudkevich et al., 2016), and often written from the perspective of an institution's or state's competitiveness rather than that of individual stakeholders. This study from Japan is intended to close this research gap, attempting to show the impacts that global university rankings may have on white-collar jobs as corporations enhance borderless operations and national labour markets are subjected to global restructuring (cf. Brown et al., 2008).

The following case study[2] begins with a description of how the postwar norm of university hierarchy and a system of meritocracy are constructed in Japan. This is followed by an analysis of the increased importance of enrolment at elite domestic universities due to demographic changes and the universalization of higher education. It then discusses the advantages that prestigious universities offer graduates at critical moments of recruitment and promotion at leading corporations. The analysis reveals the high stakes of entrance into four-year undergraduate programs at prestigious universities, as it brings long-term security and better lifetime earnings to Japan's white-collar workers. Furthermore, signs of fundamental change afoot in the labour market, due mostly to globalization, and the implications of such changes for local and global university hierarchies are discussed. Although the conditions are emergent and fluid, the final section discusses the rising prominence of global rankings vis-à-vis domestic university hierarchy and their potential impacts to individual employment, remunerations, promotion prospects, and upward social mobility in Japan – a periphery nation on the global higher education map.

Japan's Postwar University Hierarchy and Intensification of "Which Institution" Competition

Japan has had a hierarchy of universities since the establishment of Western-modelled modern universities in the late nineteenth century. While the status of a university carries significance in both social and economic senses, a university's prestige is not determined by factors such as its long history and traditions, location, the social class of the students, or the faculty's research capacity (Amano, 1997, p. 56). Rather, universities in Japan are ranked according to the entrance exam scores of incoming students. When an increased number of students from broader social strata started to pursue higher education during the postwar period, competition among high school students to pass university entrance examinations heated up. Ronald Dore (1976/1997) once referred to Japan's pyramid-shaped hierarchy, with Tokyo University at the top, as a system based on "enormously elaborated, very expensive intelligence testing" (pp. 48–9). Amano (1997) further noted that what mattered most in Japanese society was "which institution" rather than "what level" (of education) (pp. 56–7). Fierce university exam competition to enter prestigious universities, or "diploma disease," has been the subject of much criticism since the 1970s for being counterproductive to fostering individual creativity (Dore, 1976/1997).

Nevertheless, not only has the basic principle of using exam performance as a means of acquiring social status and prestige remained, but access to prestigious universities has become more important socially and economically during the past decades due to expanded enrolment or universalization of higher education.

University and junior college enrolment expanded rapidly between 1960 and 1975, jumping from 10 to 40 per cent of high school graduates. By about 2005, rates stood at approximately 50 per cent of all students (MEXT, 2017). With the growth in demand, the number of universities and junior colleges increased more than threefold during the past fifty years, from 245 in 1955 to 778 in 2010 (MEXT, 2016). The increasing number of seats coupled with declining birth rates and a shrinking youth population have caused the total entrance capacity of Japan's universities to exceed the total number of applicants or prospective students. By 2010, Japanese higher education had thus reached the *zen'nyu* (or "all in") stage. In other words, as long as they do not choose the "best" schools or stick to a particular area of study, any students can now enter university.

With the arrival of the "all in" era, the relative worth, or "premium," of a university diploma is destined to decline (Tachibanaki, 2010, pp. 33–4). In Japan, the increasing rates of tertiary education attainment (and the decreased competitiveness to get into university) did not translate into pressure to attain more advanced degrees, as it did in many other countries. In Germany, for example, where the "massification of higher education" and degree inflation have proceeded under the Bologna Process and standardization of tertiary qualifications, a bachelor's degree has reportedly become "an all-round qualification that enables its holder to work at a mid-level position on a mid-level income" (Münch, 2010, p. 3). Consequently, the competition to enter master's degree programs has intensified, Münch (2010) argues, as in the case of the United States (p. 3).

In contrast, in Japan, rather than the vertical competition to seek advanced degrees, the horizontal competition to attend a more "superior" university for an undergraduate degree has intensified (Yashiro, 2009, pp. 148–9). In other words, what Amano (1997, p. 57) previously called a "which institution" credential competition has paradoxically intensified. Meanwhile, the pursuit of postgraduate degrees has remained unpopular in Japan except in science and engineering disciplines, where a master's degree is considered a basic attainment and a prerequisite to be hired as a professional.

A recent MEXT study of degree attainment in seven countries (China, France, Germany, Japan, South Korea, the UK, and the US) shows that only in Japan has the number of graduate degree recipients stagnated or even declined over the past decade; all other countries show a clear sign of increase (National Institute of Science and Technology Policy [NISTEP], 2018, 125). The widely accepted notion that graduate degrees do not provide a return on investment persists in Japan, despite recent studies that indicate otherwise (see, for example, Kakizawa et al., 2014; Morikawa, 2013).

The MEXT report even hints at the possibility that young generations in Japan remain underqualified compared to their peers with advanced degrees in other economies. Japan's rather idiosyncratic intensification of horizontal competition for enrolment in the nation's best universities, against the global trend of vertical competition for advanced degrees, needs to be understood in the context of the nation's labour market and the significance of university reputation to social stratification.

Elite Universities and Corporate Jobs

Although Japan's earnings premium indicator for tertiary education (152) as opposed to upper and post-secondary education is relatively modest – and lower than the OECD average of 156 (OECD, 2017, p. 104) – graduates of elite universities enjoy a much bigger premium. Leading universities offer brighter prospects for employment at major companies that are considered to offer higher salaries, employment security, and benefits (Lechevalier & Nanta, 2014, p. 108; Tachibanaki, 2010, pp. 18–20).

Japanese firms recruit employees for managerial positions directly from universities; they therefore "comprise an entering cohort that is homogeneous in age and in education" (Spilerman & Ishida, 1995, p. 7). Major corporations used to recruit only from select institutions, a practice criticized as discriminatory from the 1970s and largely discontinued by the 1990s (Amano, 1997, p. 57; Tachibanaki, 2010, p. 19). Even after companies switched to an "open-door" recruitment process, it is widely believed that privileges, if not outright favours, are still distributed. The advantage of attending an elite university does not just apply to acquiring a job, however. According to economist Toshiaki Tachibanaki, graduates of prestigious universities have greater chances of promotion in listed companies in Japan as well, and thus of higher lifetime earnings (Tachibanaki, 2010, pp. 12–21).

Using alma mater information of the presidents and executives of leading Japanese corporations published in a local business magazine in 2009 as an example, Tachibanaki traces the graduates of "brand universities."[3] Graduates from the seven former imperial (currently national) universities (the Universities of Hokkaido, Kyoto, Kyushu, Nagoya, Tohoku, Tokyo, and Osaka), Hitotsubashi University, and the leading private universities (Waseda and Keio) are more likely to be promoted to the ranks of senior management or leadership in Japan. Among these, graduates of the universities of Hitotsubashi, Kyoto, Tokyo, and Keio are far more likely to become company presidents and executives than graduates of other universities (Tachibanaki, 2010, pp. 12–19). Such positions are a compelling indicator of success; both men and women in managerial and senior management positions receive an additional ¥3 million to ¥5 million in annual income compared to those in non-managerial positions (Tachibanaki, 2010, p. 10; see also Ministry of Health, Labor, and Welfare, 2017). Earnings beyond retirement age may also be affected, as better positions tend to lead to post-retirement positions in affiliated companies (Yashiro, 2011, pp. 139–40). Note that no names of foreign universities are listed, either as an individual institution or as a compilation of all institutions overseas.

Competition is fierce for better positions with higher wages within corporations and in government. Employers positively rate graduates of elite universities; their success on the university entrance exam is considered an indication of the drive, intellectual capacity, and potential for "absorbing the firms' on-the-job training" (Yashiro, 2011, p. 148). Also, graduates of elite universities often benefit from university alumni connections within corporations; bosses tend to treat their juniors who graduated from the same university well and may even give them preferential "sunny side" positions with better prospects for promotion (Tachibanaki, 2010, pp. 18–19). Employers also benefit from such connections: those who graduate from elite universities are considered useful in cultivating ties with high-ranking government officials through common membership in alumni associations (see, for example, Mori, 2004).

The relationship between which university one attends and one's job, promotion, and wages is not so black and white as the above suggests, however (see Takeuchi's [1995/2016] detailed study about Japan's meritocracy, promotion, and layers of intra-company competition). While graduates of elite universities may have higher chances of promotion, by no means do they monopolize executive jobs.[4] It is important to note the influence that business magazine articles about executives and their universities have on mostly white-collar readers and their families. Each time national newspapers publish the latest appointment information of new CEOs and presidents of major corporations, their short CVs typically include the name of the university from which they graduated. The public is thus habitually reminded of elite schools that produce influential business leaders of the past, the present, and perhaps the future.

There is no denying, however, that Japan's labour market constitutes a "matrix of inequalities" (Lechevalier, 2014, p. 96). Since the 1990s, Japan has departed from its earlier model of an egalitarian society. The growing social inequality in Japan from the 1990s to the twenty-first century – widely noted and studied by social scientists (see, for example, Kariya, 2010; Kikkawa, 2006; Lechevalier & Nanta, 2014; Moriguchi, 2017; Moriguchi & Saez, 2008; and Shirahase, 2014) – was induced not by technological advancement, changing labour institutions, and globalization, like in other economies, but rather by wage differentials, employment opportunities, and job security (Lechevalier, 2014, pp. 95–8; see also Moriguchi, 2017; Moriguchi & Saez, 2008). This inequality matrix is, as seen above, heavily influenced by one's alma mater.

Globalization, Changing Labour Recruitment Practices, and Universities

By the year 2010, when the poor performance of Japanese universities in the Times Higher Education World University Rankings made national headlines, Japan's labour market was already exhibiting some signs of fundamental changes. These were due mostly to globalizing business operations. This section will outline the ongoing changes in the domestic labour market and how such changes may affect the conventional university hierarchy. The three changes outlined below all relate to the recruitment of new college graduates by employers.

First, the practice of searching for and hiring non-Japanese employees, or so-called "global human resources," from both within and outside of Japan has been spreading. In 2010 – the same year Japan's universities fell in global ranking positions – Japanese corporations announced new initiatives to hire more non-Japanese beginning in the spring of 2011. This marked the beginning of outsourcing domestic jobs previously reserved for candidates within the country.

Several articles appeared in leading national dailies quoting major corporations announcing that they would be hiring new workers from overseas and in some cases would establish offshore recruiting offices. Panasonic Corporation, one of Japan's largest recruiters of new college graduates, announced its plan to allocate 80 per cent (1,100 of 1,390) of its spring 2011 job openings to overseas candidates (*Asahi Shimbun*, 2010), while reducing domestic recruits by 40 per cent (*Nihon Keizai Shimbun*, 2010). Other significant recruiters, such as Mitsubishi Heavy Industries Group and Toyo Engineering Corporation, followed suit (*Nihon Keizai Shimbun*, 2010). Unlike previous foreign recruits, most of whom were posted in manufacturing and worked in overseas branch offices, new overseas recruits were said to become key technical and design personnel and were expected to become part of the management in the near future.

These outsourcing moves occurred years earlier in some neighbouring Asian countries but were new to Japan. Today, recruiting staff from overseas has become commonplace and ceases to make headlines. By 2015, just over 37 per cent of 2,138 Japanese corporations surveyed had already recruited international staff, including graduates from institutions overseas and foreign students in Japan (*Nihon Keizai Shimbun*, 2015).[5]

Second, concurrent to the change in *who* was recruited for available jobs, corporations are increasingly recognizing the impracticality of *when* new hires are recruited. Traditionally, new employees began working on 1 April in Japan, immediately upon graduation from college. As part of the drive to attract "global talent," however, recruiters now offer interview opportunities between June and August to hire Japanese students who study abroad and therefore miss the early spring job-hunting season. These recruits are hired along with mostly non-Japanese candidates and begin working between July and October, rather than waiting until April of the following year, which was the previous practice (*Nihon Keizai Shimbun*, 2015). The adjustment reflects the increasing competition in the global as well as the local markets for high-skilled jobs.

Finally, recent challenges to the norm of equal pay for all new entrants in the Japanese labour market indicate another significant change on the horizon. In the fall of 2017, Huawei Technologies, a Chinese ICT firm, offered a monthly salary of ¥400,000 for prospective bachelor's degree holders in science and engineering; this was double the standard starting salary offered by Japanese companies (*Nikkei Asian Review*, 2017). Huawei was reportedly seeking Japanese technology graduates to work in its new research lab near Tokyo, who would be compensated according to the "global standard" (*Nikkei Asian Review*, 2017).[6] Not only did this episode receive attention among prospective graduates and recruiters. It was seen as a challenge to the long-term practices of seniority-based wages and employment security, the two pillars of Japanese postwar employment.

Under the conventional two pillars, a regular, full-time employee of a private Japanese corporation or the public sector enjoys job security until retirement age. The trade-off of this security is a "work now, get paid later" salary system in which young workers are paid less than their contribution to the firm and are compensated through higher wages in their middle age and a large lump-sum retirement benefit (Yashiro, 2011, pp. 136–8). While seniority-based wages are not unique to Japan, the wage gap between senior and junior workers in Japan is significantly higher than in countries such as Germany, France, and the UK (Yashiro, 2011, pp. 136–7). Thus, chances are that young workers employed by Japanese corporations initially earn less than their counterparts in other advanced economies or, in this case, China.

Old labour practices, specific to most Japanese corporations, might have worked well during periods of steady economic growth. For young workers today, however, the "paid later" model is increasingly unattractive and implausible when information technology and technological innovation such as artificial intelligence (AI) are continually changing labour requirements and are expected to reduce jobs. In addition, international mergers and acquisitions deals and global management teams are already changing the Japanese corporate landscape. Good old Japanese employment practices can wither sooner than one expects.

Impacts of Globalization on the Labour Market

Despite ongoing changes in the labour market, Japan's white-collar employees continue to be recruited directly from universities and still compose an entering cohort that is homogeneous in age and education qualifications. A degree from a prestigious domestic university is still believed to bestow on its graduates a ticket to success at the critical point of entering the labour market and in subsequent promotion opportunities. The worrisome trend of outsourcing jobs, that is, allocating more positions to international rather than domestic graduates, has not yet invited voices of protest or translated into antagonism from domestic stakeholders, mainly students and families.

The impacts of the recent changes in the labour market noted above have been downplayed, primarily due to improving labour prospects for new graduates after a prolonged period of contraction in the aftermath of the 2008 financial crisis and the Great Eastern Earthquake and Tsunami that hit the northern region of Japan in 2011.[7] Employment conditions improved considerably after 2010, judging from various public and private statistics (see, for example, Japanese Institute for Labour Policy and Training [JILPT], 2020; Recruit Works, 2019). Since 2012, the job offers-to-seekers ratio for new college graduates has continued to rise and reached 1.88 for the spring of 2019 (Recruit Works, 2019).

Although Japanese corporations are developing new hiring practices, the conventional path for new graduates to search for a job remains. Despite the expansion of international human resource recruitment for Japanese corporations' white-collar jobs, domestic job seekers have yet to be seriously impacted by global competition. Hence, the local labour market has not been globalized; instead, there is now a "new track" to attract more international talent into the market. While the traffic is increasing on this side track, as long as the general labour market conditions remain good, it continues to receive little attention, if any.

Hence, two tracks of employee recruitment exist in parallel, with no sign of convergence.[8] However, new practices in the labour market will inevitably bring entrants from both tracks together in the same workplaces. International graduates are likely to demand wages commensurate with their specialized training and advanced degrees, resist the "paid later" salary structure, and compete for better positions and promotion opportunities with Japanese employees. Some will also bring the benefits of the global networks of elite, world-class universities to domestic corporations and expect compensation for doing so.

Although the two recruitment tracks remain separate, practices in the "side track" may already be affecting domestic recruitment practices in the main track. Recently, Hiroaki Nakanishi, chairman of the Japan Business Federation (Keidanren), publicly voiced doubts that Japan's rigid recruitment and employment practices were in the best interest of the country's new college graduates (Japan Business Federation, 2018). His comments surprised the public, as regulations concerning recruitment and employment had thus far been set forth by business associations such as Keidanren, which also monitors their implementation among major member corporations. Nakanishi was quite blunt, saying, "Conventional Japanese methods such as lifetime employment and simultaneous hiring of new graduates are gradually ceasing to function effectively." Instead, each company should practise its own recruitment policy at its discretion (Japan Business Federation, 2018). He then ordered the federation to fundamentally review its recruitment and employment policy rather than simply adjusting timetables and schedules as previous reviews had done.

Discussion and Conclusion

This final section revisits significant points of argument concerning Japan's system of university hierarchy and emerging changes surrounding the very labour market that has rationalized such a hierarchy. It aims to capture the salient features in the undercurrents of change as well as the contradictions that emerge when constructing university reputation amid both globalizing and conventional labour market practices.

First, Japan's university hierarchy and prestige system are badly in need of adjustment. This need comes not so much from the social and political pressure concerning global university rankings, but more is due to the structural incapacity to train graduates to meet the demands and realities of a globalizing world. The conventional practice that disproportionately emphasizes the entry point into university and into the labour market as determinants of success is outdated. Such practices discourage the continuation of studies and advancement to higher levels of inquiry, thus disadvantaging Japan in the post-industrial, knowledge-based economy, where science and technology are considered to hold the key to innovation and economic development. Emphasis on "points of entry" accords a skewed amount of benefit to those who succeed at the critical points of entering university and the job market: winners enjoy privileges that may last for their entire career or life, while losers may be disadvantaged for life without a second chance. Such inflexibility not only fosters conservatism, but it also inhibits inclusive study and work environments that accommodate diverse talent regardless of age, gender, and nationality.

In short, the need is inherent, and challenges are far greater and more urgent than a superficial pursuit of world-class fame through elevating Japan's world university rankings positions. However, no matter how outdated the current national system of university prestige seems, replacing it with the norms and standards of global rankings would be not only unfit for improving the quality of Japan's higher education and scholarship but also unconducive to solving the fundamental social challenges in the era of global engagements. Global university rankings simply are not tools to promote justice and equity, as they cannot reexamine existing privileges and increase merit-based opportunities regardless of one's alma mater. Instead, they may even promote "social exclusion" (Amsler & Bolsmann, 2012).

Second, Japan's domestic university hierarchy has so far remained valid in the national community. It has yet to be "deconstructed" vis-à-vis the globally constructed rankings reputation regime because the domestic university hierarchy is inextricably linked to employment and career systems that have defined the lives of Japan's middle-class, white-collar workers. The stakes are too high for its demise. National hierarchy and the power of domestic elite schools have thus remained resilient to the pressures of globalization. As Japan shifts from an egalitarian middle-class society to one more stratified along class lines, any "potential threat" to the remaining security passage between conventional university entrance and exit points is a grave concern for white-collar employees and their families. Such concern perhaps is at the core of the "conservatism" discussed at the beginning of this chapter.

Domestic universities, rather than their counterparts overseas, continue to provide a steady linkage from school to corporations. Domestic universities are reputed to produce students with the trainability, basic intellectual capacity, and traits that continue to be appreciated and sought out by Japanese corporate recruiters. In this sense, the local hierarchy system is also more relevant to corporate needs than the rules of global university rankings, which primarily measure faculty research performance and international profiles of institutions.

Increasingly, however, the public is sensitive to signs that the prestige and ability of elite universities to bestow advantages to graduates may be eroding. Hence, the poorer performance of Japanese leading universities in global university rankings creates "much ado" (Yonezawa, 2010). The stakeholders' response reflects the public awareness that home-based university credentials are unlikely to continue to offer the kind of lifetime rewards taken for granted by the previous generations of Japanese corporate elites.

Such awareness is perhaps related to the third and final point. Major forces to alter the conventional university hierarchy in Japan are likely to originate from the labour market, rather than university campuses. The domestic labour market is increasingly incorporated into international, global labour markets, which are restructured and divided along global and national lines and principles. Japan's leading listed corporations have been discreetly offshoring jobs and recruiting more employees from overseas labour markets since 2010, cutting shares of domestic recruits. The upper echelon of the domestic labour market is fast globalizing, while practices of the local employment track remain unchanged, though surely shrinking in the long run.

As conditions are fluid and changes are emergent, this chapter intends to capture some of the contingencies rather than presenting empirically grounded evidence. There seems to be an imminent danger that one inflexible, outdated local system of prestige is replaced by another, namely the hegemonic "world-class" model prescribed by rankings organizations (Ishikawa, 2009). If this happens, domestic qualifications may also risk becoming subordinated to global excellence norms represented most typically by world-class rankings. This is likely to have a significant impact on the employment, remunerations, career-building and promotion prospects, and upward social mobility of individuals, as the domestic example from Japan showcases. Japan's case perhaps has relevance to other national contexts in the world.

Just as universities are expected to use their own agency to maximize their standing in the rankings, according to Susan Wright (2012), individuals are "responsible for creating their own CV, gaining the best credentials and outputs (or appearance of outputs) that count, which importantly includes the 'brand' of their university, marketing them and networking to gain access to an elite, globalised labour market" (p. 99). Global university rankings are basically "Harvard-ometers" (Ordorika & Lloyd, 2015, p. 392) and measure how closely an institution resembles Ivy League universities such as Harvard. Their graduates possess the "world-leading" credentials already reported to monopolize high-paying jobs in the US labour market (Rivera, 2015) and very likely far beyond the national borders.

Japan has built and maintained a highly autonomous higher education sector during the past century. Until now, domestic universities have been able to uphold an independent system of training faculty without requiring them to attend Western institutions to attain higher degrees or garner prestige (cf. Amano, 2009; Ishikawa & Sun, 2016, pp. 463–4). It also is a country that once boasted that it was an egalitarian society, in which 80 per cent of the population believed it was part of the middle class. That predominantly middle-class society was achieved thanks not only to the economic development, narrow wage differences, and standardized salary levels but also to universal education and democratization over the last century (cf. Amano, 1997, p. 53). Improved access to university education and globalization in the twenty-first century may as well bring about positive social changes. To this end, the existing hierarchy that monopolizes prestige and opportunities is better replaced with a system that ensures equity and openness towards global society, rather than a new global hierarchy based on rankings.

NOTES

1 There is no doubt that low and ever-decreasing public spending on higher education as per OECD average, the financial crisis, and the reduction in the workforce are major causes of deteriorating ranking positions of Japanese universities. Such policy issues, however, demand a separate analysis and thus are not covered in this article.

2 The study is based on more than ten years of anthropological research (including participant observation and analysis of media and policy documents) in one of Japan's leading research universities and other similar research-oriented institutions. It also draws upon research in the fields of education, sociology, anthropology, and labour economics published in Japanese.

3 Tachibanaki (2010, p. 13) uses the term *burando daigaku* (brand universities) to denote Japan's most prestigious universities such as those listed here. "Brand" here does not necessarily mean an "image management tool for marketing" increasingly used proactively by higher education institutions globally but rather an "identity definition" (Wæraas & Solbakk, 2008) of superiority and prestige shared by the public in Japan.

4 According to Tachibanaki (2010, pp. 20–1), less than 50 per cent of executive officers of listed companies are graduates of the twelve leading universities. He interprets this figure as a testimony that after all merit matters to go up the corporate ladder.

5 The trend since 2010 is a significant departure from the unfriendly recruitment and employment conditions for foreign recruits less than a decade ago. Breaden (2013,

p. 120) cites a 2008 Japanese government report in which almost half of the Japanese employers stated "they did nothing special to help new non-Japanese employees to adjust to the workplace" and describes efforts on the part of a Japanese private institution in offering special job placement services and lessons for international students.

6 Kenichi Ohmae, a well-known business consultant and social critic, deplores the state of Japanese corporate rivals that could not match Huawei's offer (Ohmae, 2018). He also criticizes the naïve Japanese engineering graduates who jumped at the Huawei salary rates without knowing that their counterparts based at the company's headquarters in Shenzhen, China, are paid twice as much. The Japanese hires seem to receive only half the "global standard" the company boasted it would provide.

7 Even prior to these, the tightened labour market disproportionately affected young people during a prolonged recession of the mid-1990s through the early 2000s, and the proportion of young workers not engaged in regular full-time employment has sharply increased since the 1990s (cf. Genda et al., 2010, p. 159; Ohtake & Inoki, 1997).

8 Although the two tracks are distinctively different, two groups of graduates that qualify for both tracks are (1) Japanese students who receive degrees from universities abroad and (2) international students in Japan. They can choose either the international or domestic recruitment pathway with their local language skills and knowledge of conventional hiring practices of Japanese corporations.

REFERENCES

Academic Ranking of World Universities (ARWU). (2015a). Country ranks, China. http://www.shanghairanking.com/World-University-Rankings-2015/China.html

ARWU. (2015b). Country ranks, Japan. http://www.shanghairanking.com/World-University-Rankings-2015/Japan.html

ARWU. (2018a). Country ranks, China. http://www.shanghairanking.com/World-University-Rankings-2018/China.html

ARWU. (2018b). Country ranks, Japan. http://www.shanghairanking.com/World-University-Rankings-2018/Japan.html

Altbach, P.G., & Balán, J. (2007). *World class worldwide: Transforming research universities in Asia and Latin America.* Johns Hopkins University Press.

Amano, I. (1997). Education in a more affluent Japan. *Assessment in Education: Principles, Policy & Practice, 4*(1), 51–66. https://doi.org/10.1080/0969594970040104

Amano, I. (2009). *Daigaku no tanjō (jō): Teikokudaigaku no jidai* [The birth of universities vol. 1: The age of imperial universities]. Chūōkōron shinsha.

Amsler, S.S., & Bolsmann, C. (2012). University ranking as social exclusion. *British Journal of Sociology of Education, 33*(2), 283–301. https://doi.org/10.1080/01425692.2011.649835

Asahi Shimbun. (2010, 25 March). Panasonic kokunai saiyō yon-wari gen [Panasonic reducing domestic recruits by 40 per cent]. http://www.asahi.com/special/08017 /OSK201003240131.html

Breaden, J. (2013). *The organisational dynamics of university reform in Japan: International inside out*. Routledge.

Brown, P., Lauder, H., & Ashton, D. (2008). Education, globalisation and the future of knowledge economy. *European Educational Research Journal, 7*(2), 131–47. https:// doi.org/10.2304/eerj.2008.7.2.131

Dore, R. (1997). *The diploma disease: Education, qualification and development* (2nd ed.). Institute of Education, University of London. (Original work published 1976)

Espeland, W.N., & Sauder, M. (2007). Rankings and reactivity: How public measures recreate social worlds. *American Journal of Sociology, 113*(1), 1–40. https://doi .org/10.1086/517897

Genda, Y., Kondo, A., & Ohta, S. (2010). Long-term effects of a recession at labor market entry in Japan and the United States. *Journal of Human Resources, 45*(1), 157–96. https://doi.org/10.3368/jhr.45.1.157

Goodman, R. (2016). Foreword. In J. Mock, H. Kawamura, & N. Naganuma (Eds.), *The impact of internationalization on Japanese higher education: Is Japanese education really changing? Global perspectives on higher education* (pp. vii–ix). Sense Publishers.

Hazelkorn, E. (2015). *Rankings and the reshaping of higher education: Battle for world-class excellence* (2nd ed). Palgrave Macmillan.

Ishikawa, M. (2009). University rankings, global models, and emerging hegemony critical analysis from Japan. *Journal of Studies in International Education, 13*(2), 159–73. https://doi.org/10.1177/1028315308330853

Ishikawa, M. (2014). Ranking regime and the future of vernacular scholarship. *Education Policy Analysis Archives, 22*(30), 1–27. https://doi.org/10.14507/epaa .v22n30.2014

Ishikawa, M., & Sun, C. (2016). The paradox of autonomy: Japan's vernacular scholarship and the policy pursuit of "super global." *Higher Education Policy, 29*(4), 451–72. https://doi.org/10.1057/s41307-016-0014-8

Japan Business Federation. (2018, 3 September). Chairman Nakanishi's statements and comments at his press conference. http://www.keidanren.or.jp/en/speech /kaiken/2018/0903.html

Japan Institute for Labour Policy and Training (JILPT). (2020). Figure 1: Kanzen shitsugyō ritsu, yūkō kyūjin bairitsu [Unemployment rates and active job openings to applicants ratio]. http://www.jil.go.jp/kokunai/statistics/timeseries/html/g0301 .html

Japan Society for the Promotion of Science (JSPS). (2011). Jinbungaku shakaikagaku no kokusaika ni tsuite (in Japanese) [Internationalization of humanities and social sciences]. https://www.jsps.go.jp/j-kenkyukai/data/02houkokusho/houkokusho.pdf

Kakizawa, H., Hirao, T., Matsushige, H., Yamasaki, I., & Inui, T. (2014). Daigakuin sotsu no chingin puremiamu: Micro data ni yoru nenrei chingin purofairu no bunseki [The postgraduate wage premium: Estimating the age-wage profiles using 2007 employment status survey]. Economic and Social Research Institute, Cabinet Office Tokyo. http://www.esri.go.jp/jp/archive/e_dis/e_dis310/e_dis310.pdf

Karabel, J. (2005). *The chosen: The hidden history of admission and exclusion at Harvard, Yale, and Princeton*. Houghton Mifflin.

Kariya, T. (2010). From credential society to "learning capital" society: A rearticulation of class formation in Japanese education and society. In H. Ishida & D.H. Slateds (Eds.), *Social class in contemporary Japan* (pp. 87–113). Routledge.

Kikkawa, T. (2006). *Gakureki to kakusa-fubyōdō: Seijukusuru nihongata gakureki shakai* [Education and social inequality: Contemporary educational credentialism in Japan]. University of Tokyo Press.

Lechevalier, S. (2014). What is the nature of the Japanese social compromise today? In S. Lechevalier (Ed.), *The great transformation of Japanese capitalism* (pp. 86–105). Routledge.

Lechevalier, S., & Nanta, A. (2014). Which education system in a neo-liberal world? In S. Lechevalier (Ed.), *The great transformation of Japanese capitalism* (pp. 106–18). Routledge.

Ministry of Education, Culture, Sports, Science and Technology, Japan (MEXT). (2013, 23 April). Jinzai ryoku kyōka no tameno kyōiku kaikaku puran [Plans for educational reform to enhance the power of human resources]. A document submitted by Minister H. Shimomura to the 7th meeting of the Industrial Competitiveness Council. http://www.kantei.go.jp/jp/singi/keizaisaisei/skkkaigi /dai7/siryou07.pdf

MEXT. (2016). *Statistical abstract 2016 edition*. http://www.mext.go.jp/en/publication /statistics/title02/detail02/1379369.htm

MEXT. (2017). *2017 Gakkō kihon chōsa* [2017 basic statistics of schools]. http://www .mext.go.jp/component/b_menu/other/__icsFiles/afieldfile/2018/02/05/1388639_1.pdf

Ministry of Health, Labor, and Welfare. (2017). Yakushoku betsu ni mita chingin [Wage differences by job titles]. In *Chingin kōzō kihon tōkei chōsa [Basic statistics in labour and wages]*. https://www.mhlw.go.jp/toukei/list/chinginkouzou.html

Mock, J., Kawamura, H., & Naganuma, N. (Eds.). (2016). *The impact of internationalization on Japanese higher education: Is Japanese education really changing? Global perspectives on higher education*. Sense Publishers.

Mori, S. (2004). What happens when they come back: How Japanese young people with foreign university degrees experience the Japanese workplace. In G. Mathews & B. White (Eds.), *Japan's changing generations: Are young people creating a new society?* (pp. 155–70). Routledge Curzon.

Moriguchi, C. (2017). Nihon wa kakusa shakai ni nattano ka: Hikaku keizaishi ni miru nihon no shotoku kakusa [Did Japan become an unequal society? Japan's income disparity in comparative historical perspective]. Discussion Paper Series A, No. 666, Institute of Economic Research, Hitotsubashi University.

Moriguchi, C., & Saez, E. (2008). The evolution of income concentration in Japan, 1886–2005: Evidence from income tax statistics. *Review of Economics and Statistics, 90*(4), 713–34. https://doi.org/10.1162/rest.90.4.713

Morikawa, M. (2013). Postgraduate education, labor participation, and wages: An empirical analysis using micro data from Japan RIETI. Discussion Paper Series 13-E-065, Research Institute of Economy, Trade and Industry (RIETI). https://www .rieti.go.jp/jp/publications/dp/13e065.pdf

Münch, R. (2010). Bologna, or the capitalization of education. *Eurozine.* https://www .eurozine.com/bologna-or-the-capitalization-of-education

National Institute of Science and Technology Policy (NISTEP), Japan. (2018). Japanese science and technology indicators 2018 (NISTEP research material No. 274). http:// doi.org/10.15108/rm274

Nihon Keizai Shimbun. (2010, 15 June). Kaigai de kambu kōho tairyō saiyō [Massive recruitment of overseas candidates]. https://www.nikkei.com/news/print-article/?R _FLG=0&bf=0&ng=DGXNASDD1406A_U0A610C1MM8000

Nihon Keizai Shimbun. (2015, 29 March). Gurōbaru saiyō ga honkaku ka: 37% no kigyō waku mōkeru [Global recruitment gaining momentum: 37% of companies surveyed hire international staff]. https://www.nikkei.com/article /DGXLASDZ23IMQ_U5A320C1M12900

Nikkei Asian Review. (2017, 21 September). Huawei's hefty paychecks make a splash in Japan: Chinese IT company doubles the typical starting salary for tech grads. https:// asia.nikkei.com/Business/Huawei-s-hefty-paychecks-make-a-splash-in-Japan

OECD. (2017). Education at a glance 2017 OECD Indicators. https://www.oecd -ilibrary.org/docserver/eag-2017-en.pdf

Ohmae, K. (2018, 5 March). Nihonjin engineer no kyūryō ga agaranai riyū [The reason why the salary of Japanese engineers does not increase]. *President Online.* https:// president.jp/articles/-/24409

Ohtake, F., & Inoki, T. (1997). Rōdōshijō ni okeru sedai kōka [Cohort effects in the labour market]. In K. Asako, N. Yoshino, & S. Fukuda (Eds.), *Gendai macro keizai bunseki: Tenkanki no nihon keizai (Analysis of contemporary macroeconomics: Japanese economy in transition).* University of Tokyo Press.

Ordorika, I., & Lloyd, M. (2015). International rankings and the contest for university hegemony. *Journal of Education Policy, 30*(3), 385–405. https://doi.org/10.1080/0268 0939.2014.979247

Paasi, A. (2005). Globalisation, academic capitalism, and the uneven geographies of international journal publishing spaces. *Environment and Planning A, 37*(5), 769–89. https://doi.org/10.1068/a3769

Recruit Works. (2019). Dai 36 kai daisotsu kyūjin bairitsu chōsa [The 36th annual report on the job offers-to-seekers ratios]. https://www.works-i.com/research /works-report/item/190424_kyujin.pdf

Rivera, L.A. (2015). *Pedigree: How elite students get elite jobs.* Princeton University Press.

Shin, J.C., & Kehm, B.M. (Eds.). (2013). *Institutionalization of world-class university in global competition.* Springer.

Shirahase, S. (2014). *Social inequality in Japan.* Routledge.

Shore, C., & Wright, S. (2015). Governing by numbers: Audit culture, rankings and the new world order. *Social Anthropology, 23*(1), 22–8.

Soares, J.A. (2007). *The power of privilege: Yale and America's elite colleges.* Stanford University Press.

Spilerman, S., & Ishida, H. (1995). Stratification and attainment in a large Japanese firm. Working Paper No. 91, Center on Japanese Economy and Business, Graduate School of Business, Columbia University.

Tachibanaki, T. (2010). *Nihon no kyōiku kakusa* [Educational inequality in Japan]. Iwanami Shoten.

Takeuchi, Y. (2016). *Nihon no meritocracy: kōzō to shinsei* [Japan's meritocracy: Structure and mentality]. University of Tokyo Press. (Originally published 1995)

Wæraas, A., & Solbakk, M.N. (2008). Defining the essence of a university: Lessons from higher education branding. *Higher Education, 57*(4), 449. https://doi.org /10.1007/s10734-008-9155-z

Wright, S. (2012). Ranking universities within a globalised world of competition states: To what purpose, and with what implications for students? In H.L.A.J.C. Jacobsen (Ed.), *Uddannelseskvalitet i det 21. Århundrede* (pp. 79–100). Samfundslitteratur.

Yashiro, N. (2009). *Rōdōshijō kaikaku no keizaigaku* [Reforming the Japanese labour markets]. Tōyō Keizai Shimpōsha.

Yashiro, N. (2011). Myths about Japanese employment practices: An increasing insider–outsider conflict of interests. *Contemporary Japan, 23*(2), 133–55. https:// doi.org/10.1515/cj.2011.008

Yonezawa, A. (2010). Much ado about ranking: Why can't Japanese universities internationalize? *Japan Forum, 22*(1–2), 121–37. https://doi.org/10.1080/09555803 .2010.488948

Yudkevich, M., Altbach, P.G., & Rumbley, L.E. (Eds.). (2016). *The global academic rankings game.* Routledge.

8 Rankings as Surveillance Assemblage

GARY R.S. BARRON

"No one, no thing, no class, no gender, can 'have power' unless a set of relations is constituted and held in place: a set of relations that distinguishes between this and that (distribution), and then goes on to regulate the relations between this and that ... The argument, then, is that power, whatever form it may take, is recursively woven into the intricate dance that unites the social and the technical."

John Law, *A Sociology of Monsters*, p. 16

"Lacking a vision to replace those that foundered on the shoals of repression and corruption in the twentieth century, we are reduced to reform and resistance – the latter being a favored term today in part because it permits action as reaction, rather than as crafting an alternative."

Wendy Brown, *Undoing the Demos*, p. 220

The epigraphs to this chapter articulate a problem for those of us who regard university rankings, metrics, and their politics to be undesirable, or perhaps even destructive to our freedoms to choose what research we conduct, where we publish, and how our universities are governed and to have valid information to make personal and governmental policy decisions. Yet rankings are as much a part of academic history and culture as they are governmental or business tools for oversight and profit generation. The problem is this: the material and cultural relations in which rankings are entwined make them all at once seductive, coercive, and profane to academics, who are not only subject to them but whose very work feeds their production. That is, they are not only embedded within long-standing academic practices and interests, they are increasingly integrated into routine ways of knowing, thinking about, and recognizing legitimate universities and academic work. The university's entanglement with rankings makes a world without them seem unimaginable. In this chapter I discuss rankings within actor-network theory and explain the implications of this perspective for articulating junctures between rankings, metrics, and university life that require personal and collective reflection, per Wendy Brown's point – to instigate thought as to what alternative values, ethics, and means of recognition might be possible. Rather than presume to know what alternative values and interests are best, I simply outline the current state of affairs and, in so doing, intimate points of departure.

In what follows I provide a brief overview of rankings in popular culture and academia and situate them as a form of global surveillance assemblage. I then engage with data that includes documents, news media, and interviews to illustrate three of numerous points within the global rankings assemblage that have consequences for how universities are currently known and enacted, but also for how any alternative may or may not align with such an assemblage. The three instances I examine are academic standards of merit, university data collection and reporting, and public claims-making. I also draw on data that illustrate concerns with ranking methods in an attempt to discredit them so as to show how action against them merely alters the relations through which academics are tied to rankings while intensifying the assemblage.

Theoretical Perspective

My analysis of global university rankings and related metrics is informed by actor-network theory (Callon, 1986; Callon & Latour, 1981; Latour, 1987; Latour, 2007; Law, 1994; Law, 2012). From this perspective rankings can be conceptualized as an assemblage that includes human and non-human actors that make use of symbolic and material resources to hold relations between them together or break them apart. The effects of such networks are the realities that we observe and experience in day-to-day life. Actor-networks are somewhat stabilized but always shifting as a result of the ongoing negotiations between their components. Within actor-network theory, action is always mediated through the relations in which actors are embedded. For example, rankings lists that appear each year in the *Times Higher Education* are a product of globally mediated action. Rankings are an effect of professors doing research that is published in journals and books, of metadata scraped from these to form databases such as Elsevier's SciVal and Scopus. Rankings are also derived from surveys that ask professors and administrators to submit their opinions on which universities are best. Further, they incorporate institutional data produced at each university around the globe which are submitted to the *Times Higher Education* via standard templates each year. All of the universities, professors, databases, survey respondents, staff that produce institutional data, and rankings organization employees are tied together in a set of relations that produce the annual rankings. Each actor in this web mediates relationships with others, and each of their actions along the information flows potentially affects the others. The effects are rarely observable other than when one university decreases in the rankings as another increases. No single actor in the web can know for certain why any movement in the rankings occurred. It could be the *Times Higher Education* changed its method. It could be that a group of professors gamed their publication metrics, or it could be that a concerted effort was made by a university to have many friendly people rank their university highly in the annual survey.

Haggerty and Ericson (2000) have described a "surveillance assemblage" composed of individual personal data that flows through various centres of calculation, databases, and information infrastructure to affect people's lives in ways they cannot know. Haggerty and Ericson's notion of surveillance here is intended to refer to broad relations of visibility and scrutiny, or "systems of observation" (p. 606). As David Lyon (2002) has noted, "Surveillance studies covers a huge range of activities and processes" to do with "personal details, that are monitored, recorded, checked, stored, retrieved and compared ... processed in many different ways" (p. 2). The surveillance assemblage is positioned in relation to familiar hierarchical forms of monitoring, where managers observed employees on the factory floor or guards watched prisoners in their cells. While these forms of monitoring continue to exist, the surveillance assemblage points to the obscurity of data-based surveillance, to the ways in which individuals under observation may not be aware they are being watched, and, citing Bauman (1992), to how "the population is increasingly constituted as consumers and seduced into the market economy" (in Haggerty & Ericson, 2000, p. 615). Haggerty and Ericson (2000) then elaborate that this is a situation "where individuals monitor their behaviour in light of the thresholds established by such surveillance systems ... often involved in efforts to maintain or augment various social perks" (p. 615). People submit themselves to surveillance systems as a matter of routine, going about their jobs, leisure activities, and personal relationships. Importantly, attempts to evade the assemblage involve trade-offs regarding access to resources and benefits.

The global rankings assemblage is a particular sort of surveillance assemblage that pertains to global higher education. Professors and students unknowingly become connected to the assemblage by registering at a university, being hired to teach a course, or publishing a paper. Even when students graduate or professors quit a university for new employment, their traces – data pertaining to their existence, past work, interests – continue to flow through the assemblage in ways they cannot know. I contend that it is this complex web of mediated relations – the global rankings surveillance assemblage – embedded within local and global academic histories and cultures that must be considered for any alternative global system of higher education. Individuals, universities, or nation-states might consider altering their role within the assemblage or rejecting it completely to disentangle themselves from it.

For many analysts, actor-network theory raises concerns with agency and structure (Corman & Barron, 2017; Sayes, 2013). From an actor-network perspective agency does not require intentionality, is not located within an individual actor, and is not understood as something distinctive of humans. Rather, it proffers a broader notion of agency that can involve resistances and effects that are embedded within, and are a product of, networked relations (Sayes, 2013). Similarly, in instances where non-human actors cannot speak for themselves, humans often make claims on their behalf. In regard to the global rankings assemblage, for example, people may refer to data as "objective," meaning they should speak for themselves as undeniable facts. However, from this perspective there is also no necessarily objective truth to rankings or any data. Rather, they are a product of assumptions and decisions made by specific individuals and organizations. Rankings are dependent on actors across the globe – the professors, staff, databases, and others – that assemble and submit information for their calculation. Importantly, artifacts such as data, information infrastructure (e.g., templates, tables, databases, spreadsheets, network servers) carry interests and act upon their users to limit or facilitate particular capacities. For example, the *Times Higher Education* annually sends a data request to universities with a template that has definitions of student-faculty ratio, research funding, and so on. These define what is important and ought to be legible within the rankings system. Institutional analysts must then take their local categories and definitions and translate them into those that the *Times Higher Education* requires. The templates, definitions, data, and databases that the institutional analyst uses are all a part of the actor-network; they tie together universities around the world and – in part – create the effects of the global rankings surveillance assemblage. Such artifacts work with professors and administrators to make rankings and the network. The actor-network is further strengthened as students and parents consume rankings and administrators engage in public identity management.

Thinking about rankings through actor-network theory has implications for conceptualizing alternative relations. Will we merely alter the relations we observe ourselves embedded within, or might we imagine ways to disengage and create an alternative? It is not rankings alone that must be considered, but the complex of relations in which they are embedded. These include the traditional values and interests of academia, day-to-day work of professors and support staff at universities, students' and parents' concerns to choose a university, the business interests of publishers and rankings organizations, and the political interests of governments. All these organizations and people work with data and information infrastructure to learn about rankings, submit data for their production, and package them into a variety of consumable products. For example, in addition to the direct data request that rankers make to universities, professors around the world regularly submit their papers to academic journals so that they can be published, often in hopes of being cited in order to increase their own reputation and grow their careers. Metadata is scraped from these publications to create metrics such as citations, and these metrics are then combined with the data submitted by universities to create rankings. The data are also used to develop additional products – such as Elsevier's SciVal and Thomson Reuters' InCites – that are sold to universities for further monitoring professorial and organizational performance. These academic and business interests, data flows, and work must all be considered in any project against the global rankings assemblage. Similarly, strategically crafting an alternative might require evading interfaces with the global rankings assemblage, as the alternative might not truly be one at all.

For the project at hand I examine three of many practices that piece together the actor-network in which the global rankings assemblage exists. Callon (1986) has demonstrated several processes that are important for network formation, including a definition of a problem or situation, the fixation of actors into proposed roles, clarification of knowledge and relations for all involved in these roles, and the actions of the stabilized set of actors as one. Here I examine how problems and roles related to rankings are defined and situated in public claims-making activities. The examples I provide illustrate how actors can alter their networked relations with the global rankings assemblage against a background of how the assemblage itself simultaneously shapes those relations.

An analysis of claims-making can be effective at helping to situate actors within a set of symbolic and material relations because results implicate how actors and resources are enmeshed with one another while also illustrating their values. Strategies for conceiving alternatives might then be a matter of considering what values are problematic, the resources at hand, and any possible costs to altering relations or constructing new ones. My analysis of claims-making shows that the definitions of situations related to academia and rankings are often aimed only at specific parts of the complex global rankings assemblage and that, in the instances I share, the assemblage intensifies.

Situating Rankings

Rankings have a long history in Western societies. Rankings are cultural artifacts derived from human work at categorizing and quantifying a set of ostensibly similar objects, then ordering them according to a qualitative distinction – best to worst, for example. Readers are likely to be familiar with rankings as they are now a common social form that seems to be applied to every object, organization, and institution. We have rankings for sports, economic freedom, beauty, professors, cars, cities, and animals. Rankings are not value-neutral tools for assessing the true quality of phenomena; rather, they are imbued with the values and biases of the people and data that make them up. Thus, rankings are always political, creating new hierarchies while maintaining old ones (Barron, 2017). Rankings are productive in that they create new orders of people and things, direct attention, and reinforce their reality through reactivity – organizational and individual responses that shift expectations and practices in attempts to manage identities and situations that rankings create (Espeland & Sauder, 2007, 2016). Yet rankings are also destructive in that they ignore, suppress, or truncate information regarded as unimportant to their production and consumption. Rankings can erode professional authority and solidarity, exclude individuals and universities from their lists, and delegitimize local or traditional knowledge. This is because rankings are simple tools for visibility that articulate comparisons in terms of relative quality – they work upon personal and collective identities and representations. In doing so, they become a point of reference that shapes future interpretations of the very same identities and representations.

Rankings draw on academic traditions and discourses of peer review, excellence, and self-promotion, but in ways that are not situated within other academic cultural practices. In its formal standards, academic peer review attempts to recognize diverse forms of excellence and incorporate context into assessments of quality, for example, in assignment of prestigious fellowships and awards (Lamont, 2010) and for tenure and promotion (Sayer, 2016). Academic culture is fundamentally concerned with recognizing excellence and promotion through status hierarchies to which symbolic and material rewards are attached – as are rankings. However, rankings conflict with academic traditions that recognize excellence as taking diverse forms. Universities have been recognized as having the unique organizational property of incorporating diversity, rather than maintaining a singular focus or mission (Smelser, 2013). Rankings discourse and method are not foreign to universities; they are embedded in academic concerns for prestige and distinction but are dissonant with other academic traditions that recognize and support diversity. Rankings impose universal standards and a single mission: a competition for visibility in terms of world-class status. As universities become represented and identified by the global rankings surveillance assemblage, the opportunities to represent themselves become limited to techniques of manipulating data submitted to categories defined by rankings organizations. As such, rankings can also interfere with academic freedom – the liberty to self-govern academic institutions and to pursue uninterested inquiry. By defining situations, rankings simultaneously articulate winners and losers, objectifying subjective interpretations of quality, and in doing so may affect the distribution of material rewards such as student applications and government funding. Rather than traditional interaction rituals whereby humans can directly engage with one another to represent themselves strategically (Goffman, 1959, 1969, 1986), rankings mediate such interactions and thereby define the terms by which interactions are structured and place limits on possibilities for how they can unfold. As a global system of surveillance, rankings apply their values and definitions to everyone around the world – regardless of whether those values and definitions are shared.

Method

The current analysis is based on a broader research project that examined university rankings as a globally coordinated phenomenon. In that broader project I focused on data work, information infrastructure, and academic culture. My research involved semi-structured interviews with sixty-one deans, department heads, recruiters, institutional analysts at several universities, and rankings organization employees to understand the coordination of global academic activity. The study also included observations at several rankings-focused conferences and promotional events, such as the International Ranking Expert Group (IREG) annual conference, a *Times Higher Education* university summit, and a QS conference on re-imagining education. At the events I also met professors and university administrators from around the world and spoke to them about why they attended the event, why they were interested in rankings, what their local university was like, and how rankings affected them. The interviews and observations helped me understand how academic and non-academic actors in different organizations and roles around the world conceptualize, speak about, make claims in regard to, or publicly share their concerns with rankings and related metrics such as citations and impact factor.

Because of my own standpoint as a graduate student, it made sense to begin my investigation with the University of Alberta, where I was enrolled in a PhD program. I chose Mount Royal University – a small university in Calgary, Alberta – as an additional location for interviews. I believed that its recent transition from a teaching-focused college to a research university, and the fact that it was not included in any rankings, might provide an interesting comparison to ranked universities. Other organizations and sites were chosen primarily for convenience. I invited representatives of several rankings organizations to take part in interviews, but only Phil Baty of the *Times Higher Education* made himself available. Convenience samples of this sort are a pragmatic matter, not purely methodological, in that they provide points of entry into examining and analysing the networks in which each informant is embedded.

My primary approach to interviews was to tell my participants about the topics I was interested in and then let them talk (see Devault & McCoy, 2006). I would describe my interest in the university, rankings, performance metrics, and the day-to-day work that the participant does, then ask them to tell me about their job. As participants described their job titles, I would ask who they work with, who they report to, who reports to them, how they communicate and get information to complete their work. I listened for references to other processes and texts, asked how such items work, what purpose they serve, whether I could have a copy of an item of interest, whether I could observe the informant using the item or if they could describe how it was typically used. I also asked who I should speak with to learn more about the process or item in question. In this way, I was able to trace the infrastructure that my participants create and use as they go about their daily work. I would then follow these relationships to the next person in the chain who could fill information gaps. This process continued until I had established a sense that any further interviews would yield few new details.

I conducted a search for popular media and news articles in January 2014, using Factiva, an online database that contains global media including newspapers, broadcast news, blogs, images, and videos. I intended a broad search, so the only search term I used was "university rankings." I limited media to those created between 1990 and 2014, as many regional or local university rankings emerged in the late 1980s and 1990s, while global rankings became popularized between 2005 and 2010. I also excluded financial news, blogs, videos, audio, obituaries, and other types of media in the database that were not apparently relevant to text-based analysis of media regarding university rankings controversies. The original search included media from Asia, South America, and Africa, but I excluded these from this study as I am only literate in English and many items were not available in English. The search resulted in 1,592 items, but after using my stated exclusion criteria and eliminating duplicates, I had 600 text-based articles: 201 from the United States, 99 from the United Kingdom, 201 from Canada, and 99 from Australia. Many of the articles I retrieved were from newswires such as Canada Newswire and Associated Press Newswire; well-known national papers such as the *Globe and Mail*, the *Guardian*, and the *Australian*; local papers like the *Ottawa Citizen*, the *Bedford Times and Citizen*, and the *Santa Fe New Mexican*. I used the qualitative analysis software R package for Qualitative Data Analysis, commonly known as RQDA (Huang, 2016), to keep track of issues, problems, criticisms, and other aspects of what I refer to broadly as "the rankings controversy" that appeared in the media. Box 8.1 illustrates broad categories of arguments against rankings and their frequency of occurrence in the articles that I collected.

My interest in the media analysis was not a deep examination of themes and sub-themes and their relationships. Rather, it was to clarify how public

Box 8.1. Public Problems and Issues in University Ranking News Media, Ordered by Frequency

Methods Issues – 140	Language – 7
Decision-Making – 36	More Research – 7
Alternative Ranking System – 34	Rank Focus – 7
Accountability – 24	UK/US Bias – 7
Top 10/100/200 – 19	Specialization – 6
Teaching vs. Research – 18	Economic Growth – 6
Funding Increases – 18	Fee Increases – 6
Diversity in University Mission – 17	Costs – 4
Gaming – 16	No Controversy – 4
Cuts – 15	Inevitable, Here to Stay – 4
Performance-Based Funding – 14	Knowledge Society/Economy – 3
Simplicity/Complexity – 14	University Autonomy – 2
Resistance – 14	Alternative Revenues – 2
Access – 12	Deregulation – 2
Collaboration/Competition – 11	Efficiency – 1
Drop in Rank – 11	Hiring Freeze – 1
Standards – 11	Increase Student Enrolment – 1
Internationalization – 10	Public Good – 1
Leadership – 10	Restructuring – 1
International Excellence – 8	

claims were stated in the media and, as such, the ways in which problems with rankings were defined. My interest was in public engagement with rankings and in controversies, not the process of constructing the controversy or problem itself – which is more typical of studies in social problems (see Altheide, 2002). I was interested in concerns with rankings, broadly conceived. The themes I report here represent broad categories, operating as inclusively as possible of any statements that fit within the topic to which they refer. For example, "methods issues" includes all statements regarding limitations, weaknesses, strengths, objectivity, bias, or adaptations to methods; "decision-making" includes any statements pertaining to students, faculty, administrators, or governments making decisions in regard to rankings; "gaming" includes any statements I found related to the notion that people were cynically manipulating rankings surveys or data they submit for rankings calculations. I use these categories merely as a point of departure for a more particular concern to reflect strategically on specific parts of the global rankings assemblage.

Discussion

Academic Standards

Universities have engaged in some form of ranking since at least the eighteenth century, when engineering school administrators quantified and ranked student performance (Alder, 1997). More recently, Hazelkorn (2015) has documented three eras of university rankings, beginning in 1910 with an "American Men of Science" ranking that examined schools based on the ratio of "star faculty" to all faculty, followed by regional reputation rankings and global rankings. Concern with reputation likely has its roots at least as far back as the first days of scientific experimentation, when only men of recognized noble status were considered worthy of witnessing and testifying to the veracity of an experiment's results (Shapin, 1994). These examples are illustrative of professors' long-standing concern with reputation, which is a primary form of symbolic capital (Bourdieu, 1980, 1984) within academia through which individuals are hired, granted tenure, and promoted. This concern with reputation is one of the conditions that make the global rankings assemblage possible but also salient within global higher education. It is not a coincidence that appealing to concerns with reputation is a standard marketing technique used by publishing and rankings organizations.

Faculty are evaluated on criteria that emphasize quality and quantity of their work, which, if assessed positively, leads to increasing reputation and prestige. Concerns with reputation and prestige are further reinforced within universities through strategic plans and benchmarking practices. Professors are assessed for tenure and promotion based on increasing reputation and reach of their work. At the University of Alberta, the first stage of promotion is when tenure is granted and the rank of associate professor is awarded (from assistant professor), while the second stage involves promotion to full professor. Tenure is typically awarded on the promise of things to come, as evidenced by the total work over a professor's career to the date of application for tenure and as determined by peer review. In the Faculty of Arts at the University of Alberta, "Tenure is justifiably awarded only where it can be demonstrated that a staff member has research programs of clearly recognized promise and concrete scholarly achievements, in the form of published research or publicly performed or exhibited creative work, of a magnitude and quality that makes it highly probable that there will be continuing significant contributions to the staff member's discipline through a whole career" (University of Alberta, Faculty of Arts, 2014, p. 12). This is more or less consistent across the faculties including science, where the standards for tenure are, "The individual is expected to take an active part in research and scholarly activities, as evidenced by research publications in refereed venues of international repute" (University of Alberta, Faculty of Science, 2012, p. 5). In this case journals must have international reputation. The international repute of journals is conveyed to the professor who publishes in them and who is then recognized as achieving tenure-worthy status.

For promotion to full professor, the importance of reputation and prestige is more clearly articulated, again from the Faculty of Arts: "Promotion on the primary criterion of research or creative work requires prominence in the applicant's scholarly or creative community as that community might extend ... of sufficient scope and intensity to maintain the prominence already achieved" (University of Alberta, Faculty of Arts, 2014, p. 13). For promotion to full professor in the Faculty of Science, "The individual must demonstrate high quality and mature scholarship as evidenced by international recognition of research contributions" (University of Alberta, Faculty of Science, 2012, p. 6). Promotion at the University of Toronto is captured as follows: "The successful candidate for promotion will be expected to have established a wide reputation in his or her field of interest, to be deeply engaged in scholarly work, and to have shown himself or herself to be an effective teacher" (University of Toronto, 2016). These criteria are also used at many North American universities (Sayer, 2016) and elsewhere as standards that colleagues refer to in order to assess one another's worthiness for promotion and tenure. Scholarly excellence operates as an international symbolic economy through which reputation can circulate in exchange for rewards. Rankings align with these interests, using many similar indicators, such as quantity of publications which are measured by citations. The evaluative criteria for professorial work are explicitly and tightly coupled with those of university rankings in regard to their concern for prestige and visibility. By hiring and promoting faculty based on these criteria, universities have interests and values that are well aligned with the global rankings assemblage.

Academic performance standards position reputation as something professors must work towards. Publishing in well-reputed journals is an indicator of quality work; having one's work recognized as such improves the professor's reputation and is considered an indicator of future potential. Reputation coordinates academic work but also circulates through it as a means to acquire rewards such as promotion. Global university rankings are embedded within academic interest in reputation. They incorporate reputation by having academics report on it through surveys and then advertise this reputation in their annual releases. As professors continue to be rewarded based on indicators of reputation and incorporate such concerns into their identities, they become discursively aligned with rankings and their purposes. Reputation is one mechanism by which the global rankings surveillance assemblage coordinates academic work and aligns it with its purposes. Universities also take part in rankings and related metric practices, in part due to the reputation risk posed by not participating (Power et al., 2009). Reputation – and the use of rankings to convey status – has been a part of university culture for a long time. Any alternative to the global rankings surveillance assemblage must contend with these practices that are strongly embedded in processes used to promote individual professors, as well as personal and collective academic identities.

Actor-network theory sensitizes analysts to the multiplicity of relations in which actors are embedded and how a reality can be enacted and observed (see Mol, 2002). Professors and universities are concerned with not only visibility and reputation but also novel contributions to knowledge. Assessing contributions to knowledge can be done independently of metrics and rankings, which – within the global rankings surveillance assemblage – often dictate what counts as a worthy and reputable body of work. Lamont (2010), for example, in her study of peer review in the allocation of prestigious awards, has demonstrated that academic judgment achieves a pragmatic fairness through inter-subjective negotiation and dialogue to determine quality work. Such practices do not require any reference to metrics or rankings. Crafting alternative ways of valuing scholarship and education must contend with allowing the global rankings assemblage to influence processes of recognition and reward.

University Data Collection and Reporting

Universities create a great deal of data used for many purposes. Institutional analysts and research facilitators work with data and build information infrastructure to assess academic performance, communicate to the public, and support decisions like budget allocations. Institutional analysts are important actors in the global rankings surveillance assemblage in that they produce much of the data that feeds into rankings, but also adapt local data practices and information infrastructure to effectively respond to and work within the rankings assemblage. Where infrastructure is adapted or built to respond to rankings and related indicators, work within universities incorporates their logics, orienting future work. I draw on a university's data warehouse to illustrate this point. Importantly, local data practices and infrastructure can be a site of resistance or outright refusal against rankings organizations and their attempts to align individual universities with their interests. Having data is necessary to perform the university's identity to audiences. Without working information systems, no data can be shared with rankings organizations, accreditation bodies, or potential collaborators. One representative from a large publishing corporation that I spoke with spent much of his time working with universities to do such work. At the University of Alberta, a data warehouse was developed to be the ultimate source of rationalized data across the organization. Once a new data source is created, people begin to ask new questions of it and it often begins to incorporate new functions and be adapted to new purposes. This is why the data warehouse was named Acorn: "It's just the little seed that grows," I was told by an analyst who helped create it. As data systems like Acorn grow and begin to interface with rankings and publisher systems like Scopus, they become aligned with the global rankings assemblage and incorporate its categories of knowledge, shaping future work within the university.

Rankings organizations also request administrative data of the sort that Acorn was designed to standardize and report on. I was fortunate to connect with one institutional analyst who regularly provided these reports to rankings organizations. She shared the template she used for the submission to the *Times Higher Education* rankings, a portion of which I have illustrated in box 8.2. The template required her to copy and paste data from her own sources into the template, then copy them from that template into the THE rankings online form. The template asks for the university's number of academic staff and students of different categories (international, research, undergraduate, graduate), number of degrees awarded (doctoral, undergraduate), overall institutional income, research income, and research income from industry.

Just as Acorn requires specific definitions to ensure consistency and comparability across departments and faculties, the THE template also contains definitions to ensure that analysts across the globe understand how to make their counts for each category, which will be submitted and combined with other data to create the ranking. Asked where the definitions in the template came from, the analyst said, "The ranking agency develops them and then we apply them as best we can." Another analyst explained that creating counts of employees is a complicated process. Definitions of full-time equivalence (FTE) and medical staff are categories that need to be better understood and standardized. A head count of employees would give one total, but the sum of full-time equivalent employees would give another. Imagine that a university had only ten employees; that number would be the same as the total head count. But if five employees were FTE 1.0, two were 0.2, and three were 0.5, the FTE sum would be 6.9 FTE. The FTE is a more precise representation of how many employees spend their time working on campus, but it is not the total number of employees. Medical faculty added another layer of complication because many worked at the university but were paid entirely or in part by Alberta Health Services – the provincial health system. Notice also that the template in box 8.2 has notes for the analyst: "the term varies across countries," "only doing research," and so on. These notes illustrate how analysts apply definitions "as best as we can." The local data sources such as Acorn are traditionally organized by locally meaningful definitions and categories that don't necessarily fit with those required by rankings and which must be translated as closely as possible. The template

Box 8.2. THE Institutional Data Submission Template: Section and THE Definitions

---

Academic Staff

This is the FTE [full-time equivalence] number of staff that are employed for an academic post. Typically they will have a post such as: lecturer, reader, assistant/ associate professor or professor.

Notes:

- This should include permanent staff and staff that are employed on a long-term contract basis.
- This will NOT include: non-teaching "fellows" (the term varies across countries), researchers (only doing research), post-doctoral researchers, research assistants, clinicians of all types (unless they also have an academic post), technicians and staff that support the general infrastructure of the institution or students (of all levels).
- This will NOT include staff that hold an academic post but are no longer active (e.g., honorary posts or retired staff) or visiting staff.

Number of Academic Staff

operating only

Of which are international/overseas origin

The FTE number of "academic staff" (see above) whose nationality is different from the country in which your institution is based

Research Staff

This is the FTE number of people who are employed only to perform research. *Typically they will not have a permanent post at a university*; often they are contracted specifically for purposes of doing research or similar activity.

Notes:

- This will include researchers, research fellows, and post-doctoral researchers.

---

is also illustrative of what I mean by a global assemblage of mediated relations. In this instance local meanings and action are mediated by the template and rankings definitions, transmitted to another location, and then manipulated in ways the analysts cannot know.

Businesses like Elsevier and Thomson Reuters also offer ready-made data solutions to track faculty and productivity at universities based on their citation metrics, impact factors of journals, and relational data such as co-authorship across institutions. However, categories that organize databases tend to be incongruous with local definitions. Just as counts of staff pose problems, governing and organizational structure may as well. For example, one university may have a department of sociology and psychology, whereas another may have separate departments for each discipline, and there may not be any straightforward way to use the ready-made data source to reconcile these differences. Such complications were why the University of Alberta embarked on creating its own data warehouse. Similarly, common concerns with rankings and related products are that they are based on privately owned data and infrastructure, that access is sold through licensed or ready-made products, and that their effects cannot be undone once released to the public. The aim of the data warehouse was much like the purported utility of rankings and tools like SciVal that produce rapidly consumable and interpretable information. An analyst explained, "That is the purpose of the data warehouse ... and that's what we're also trying to do ... so at one glance, 'oh, that's the trend.'"

The data warehouse produces information that can be understood at a glance as conveniently as ready-made products. However, in instances where data seem wrong or categories do not match with what was expected, there were clear rules to trace back how figures were produced: "the advantage for the deans is everybody's got the same business rules ... Because we've defined the business rules and everything behind it, if they want to question, we can tell them what we did." Business rules were developed to ensure anyone could trace back how data in reports were assembled. There are three interesting points here in considering alternatives to integration with the global rankings assemblage. First, local categories and meanings that are not immediately well aligned with those promoted by rankings organizations and publishers do some work against aligning with rankings. Second, by building their own solution, the University of Alberta avoided supporting the rankings and publication industry by not paying for one of their data products. Third, and perhaps most importantly, is that the local forms of organization, category definitions, and organizational units remained while their translation into reports to audiences was also made possible. An alternative might have been to reorganize the university and its interpretation of itself in order to conform with the categories and definitions that rankings and products like SciVal require.

As Acorn use expands, it has implications for future work at the University of Alberta, how administrators and institutional analysts can think about and represent their individual and collective identities. These may become more aligned with rankings and their business interests, or less so, over time. Information infrastructure, data, and the work done to make these have implications for alternative ways of organizing global higher education in regard to the global rankings surveillance assemblage.

Importantly, global higher education and individual universities like the University of Alberta are often only partially aligned with, incorporated into, and controlled by the global rankings assemblage. Acorn had begun to feed the rankings assemblage with data regarding the University of Alberta, but at the time of my research it had been explicitly designed on the terms of local actors with their own interests and concerns. Despite their alignments, local networks may continue to act without being entirely dominated by distant ones to which they are loosely connected.

When Methods Define the Problem

The final nexus with the global rankings surveillance assemblage I will consider here is public controversies that play out in popular media. These controversies intensify and multiply the reach of the global rankings assemblage and facilitate its incorporation into previously ignored domains. As I have illustrated in box 8.1, the broad themes of news articles that I created demonstrate that the primary approach to claims-making against rankings is to attack their method, illustrated not only in the dominant "methods issues" theme but also in concerns with a focus on alternative rankings systems; research rather than teaching; gaming; standards; and language. Hazelkorn (2015) has also noted that a great deal of concern with rankings can be traced to methodology. For example, in 2004 an article in the *Australian* argued against rankings that use survey data: "Regrettably, those who looked only at the table will not be aware of the survey's limitations" (Walker, 2004). In one of his articles on the subject of method, the *Times Higher Education* ranking editor Phil Baty, conveyed a warning by the South African higher education minister that rankings were "limited in their biased use of a range of indicators" (Baty, 2010). In Canada, the Maclean's rankings have also been disputed based on methodology: "While Maclean's university rankings are popular among high schoolers and anxious parents alike, it has drawn some criticism from the academic community for its methodology" (Yang, 2009). Similarly, deans and institutional analysts I spoke with frequently expressed their opinion of rankings in methodological terms. One senior scholar/administrator stated, "You can dislike them, you can find them methodologically flawed in all kinds of ways ... they seem to be a very rough, imperfect tool." As I have explained, institutional analysts are the ones who are most often tasked with studying rankings and regularly submitting data to them. One senior institutional analyst I interviewed gave the example that rankings organizations "change the normalization of the citation to consider the population in whatever you write in. So of course [some people] skyrocket. I get that it's not that they've changed how well they do, it is change in the underlying metric." My interviews illustrate that beyond public claims-making, individuals working within universities also commonly concern themselves with rankings methods. Espeland and Sauder (2016) found this was the case in their study of law school rankings in the United States. I found in public claims and in conversations that critiques based on method regularly lead to the conclusion that adjusting method will create a more effective ranking system. This approach is also taken by academics who study rankings closely and have argued that it would be better to rank national higher education systems so as to make them more objective and less biased (Hazelkorn, 2015).

The problems I mentioned with translating local meanings and categories into the standardized versions that rankings organizations promote and require for their data systems are also methodological. The process involves turning one's vision of oneself and one's organization into something it is not – local understandings and systems of performance measurement have to be adapted or transformed to effectively submit data to rankings. An analyst at an Ontario university explained that her team does not submit some types of data. The decision was made because the data from their source is not comparable to those from other countries, and if they were to transform it in the ways that rankings agencies require it would not match what they publish in their local annual reports. She explained, "Every year the rankings organizations will issue an invitation to universities to participate. And if you decide to participate then you get a template that says we would like you to submit this data ... And specific definitions are being laid out. And so we would just pull out that data based on the definition ... there's some cases where we would make an additional call saying this indicator is incomparable across countries, so we are not going to submit." Much of the analysts' work to monitor and report to rankings is focused on ensuring that their public image is managed and is as consistent as possible with their local understanding of their university's identity. It is through such work that new relations with actors across networks are formed; as new problems are identified, identities and roles are assigned (Callon, 1986).

I cite these conversations with analysts about their work transforming data for several reasons. First, in addition to methods that rankings organizations publish with their annual tables – the weightings, information about survey data, citations data, and so on – they also convey specific methods to universities in data requests. Second, each university has its own data, its own interpretation practices and means to submit them to the rankings organizations. When critiques are made against rankings organizations for their methods, the methods of all universities taking part in the rankings are rarely considered. Third, the interviews illustrate the fundamental problem that rankings methods pose for universities: they impose standards on a diverse world. Methods have implications for how local identities are conveyed to a global audience. One model may be meaningful or useful to some groups but not others; someone is always left out.

By recognizing what is left out, the rankings surveillance assemblage can grow as new rankings are made.

Further to my point, organizations that produce rankings and metrics regularly respond to criticism by introducing new standards and products. For example, IREG has developed "The Berlin Principles on Ranking Higher Education Institutions," which list principles for good ranking practices and are the basis of their rankings audit (IREG Observatory on Academic Ranking and Excellence, 2014). One of the principles states that rankings need to recognize diversity in mission and goal. The principle is a response to the critique that rankings have a homogenizing effect by promoting a single model of what a university should be (see Marginson, 2007). Recognizing diversity in higher education institutions works well with rankings businesses' marketing and niche standardization to create more types of rankings, or the adaptation of rankings to present them in multiple categories. For instance, global rankings offer a breakdown by academic area such as business management or sciences, university age (under fifty years), region (e.g., Africa, Japan), or emerging economies such as Brazil, India, Russia, China, and South Africa (BRICS) ranking. Slicing up the higher education sector creates new hierarchies while maintaining existing ones. These proliferating niches do not recognize unique characteristics so much as create new groups that facilitate further marketing and surveillance (see Timmermans & Epstein, 2010). The effect is more ranking-related products to sell and further stratification of universities into new status groups. Rather than having one hierarchy where all universities could be recognized, there are now many lists that are hierarchically organized (Barron, 2017) and the global rankings surveillance assemblage touches more of the world than it once did.

One other caveat evident in the examples related to methods: they demonstrate the partial connections within the global rankings assemblage. Only some parts of activity and work are ever included, and occasionally some are left out intentionally. The assemblage is not totalizing in its integration with local activity and realities. This final observation is an important one in that those parts of local networks that are connected to the global rankings assemblage may proliferate it without altering local relations that determine work and identity. Espeland and Sauder (2016) have argued that the proliferation of rankings may actually delegitimize all rankings and reduce the hold that any one ranking may have over universities.

Conclusion

In this chapter, I have argued that university rankings represent a global surveillance assemblage embedded within academic traditions, cultural practices, routine day-to-day work, and the publishing industry. I have briefly described some of the many networked actors and relationships in this global assemblage. I have also drawn on a selection of data from my broader study to illustrate three specific points within the assemblage that offer insight into its appeal and ongoing intensification. I have demonstrated some of the complexities that must be considered if any alternative future for higher education in relation to rankings and related metrics is to be considered. Routine work in universities enrols students, professors, and their activities into the global surveillance assemblage. Beyond any regular reporting or performance review within a particular university, data is shared or even scraped from universities, professorial work such as publications, and student enrolments. These flow into rankings and other global data systems in ways that are incredibly difficult to trace and understand. The acts of resistance I have described demonstrate forms of refusal that only partially prevent entanglement with the global assemblage. For example, while there are instances of universities refusing to submit some data that does not conform well to rankings organization standards, they still submitted data that do. Perhaps more importantly, independent of any active refusal by a single actor – professor, analyst, university, student – distant actors within the global rankings assemblage can enrol other actors without their knowledge. To clarify, if the University of British Columbia were to refuse to partake in rankings, its citation data could still be scraped from Elsevier's SciVal, reputation data would be submitted by professors around the world who take part in the annual surveys, and university enrolment data would almost certainly be scraped from open data on the university's website. Beyond data, the values and interests that the rankings assemblage promotes are tied to long-standing practices and interests of professors and universities to increase reputation and prestige. I argue that the global rankings surveillance assemblage operates independently of any single actor and that this must be considered in imagining alternatives to rankings and their values. As Michel Foucault once noted, "We are neither in the amphitheatre, nor on the stage, but in the panoptic machine … which we bring to ourselves since we are part of its mechanism" (Foucault, 1977, p. 217). We tie ourselves into power relations based on our own interests and motivations and are often unaware of the ways in which we do so. We constitute our own relations of visibility, legibility, and knowledge with the discursive and material resources available as we pursue our interests – publishing papers in highly cited journals, for example.

Reputation – as a form of symbolic capital (Bourdieu, 1980, 1984) – is not only a means by which academics grow their careers; it is also a mechanism by which the rankings surveillance assemblage coordinates actors' interests and work and generates profit for corporations. Information infrastructure and data work at universities also tie academics, university administrators, and staff into the global rankings assemblage as they translate their work and identities into forms that rankings require. Similarly, contesting rankings either in public controversies or in private debates on how to manage data can intensify the assemblage, not only by leading to the creation of more rankings and related products but also by encouraging their modification so as to make them more "objective." As the epigraphs to this chapter indicate, the intensity and appeal of the global rankings assemblage have many complications. In addition to monitoring and punishing, the global rankings assemblage rewards, appeals to our interests, and is tightly woven into day-to-day work in ways that are not always obvious. We who live and build our careers within academia are a part of the assemblage that give rankings their pervasiveness and ability to grow and adapt, as much as we might be agents of change. Any consideration of alternatives to the current state of affairs must contend with how the university and its traditions are tied up with the global rankings assemblage.

The notion of the surveillance assemblage has its limits as it draws on Deleuze's (1992) concept of societies of control and places importance on the notion of "dividuals," disaggregated parts of whole individuals. Of course what happens to our component parts can be consequential, and we may care deeply about how aspects of our identities and activities are treated by others, but to regard humans and organizations as less than the sum of their parts is to ignore a great deal of agency. Indeed, what I have articulated about the global higher education surveillance assemblage illustrates that it is often the case that only traces, proxies, and quanta derived from individual and collective bodies are aligned or integrated into it. It is possible to exist within the global rankings assemblage and live according to an ethic independent of it. For example, professors might be committed to values other than increasing reputation for its own sake and producing work published in highly cited journals.

ACKNOWLEDGMENTS

Many thanks to Michael Granzow for his reference to John Law on "power" and his ongoing reminders that "the stakes are low." I also recognize the research and reporting team that I work with for keeping it real, making me a better social scientist, and helping impact the lives of common folk like me for the better.

REFERENCES

Alder, K. (1997). *Engineering the Revolution: Arms and enlightenment in France, 1763–1815.* Princeton University Press.

Altheide, D.L. (2002). *Creating fear: News and the construction of crisis.* Aldine de Gruyter.

Barron, G.R.S. (2017). The Berlin Principles on ranking higher education institutions: Limitations, legitimacy, and value conflict. *Higher Education, 73*(2), 317–33. https://doi.org/10.1007/s10734-016-0022-z

Baty, P. (2010, 23 September). Global impact: Revamped rankings cause elation and consternation. *Times Higher Education Supplement*, p. 892.

Bauman, Z. (1992). *Intimations of postmodernity.* Psychology Press.

Bourdieu, P. (1980). *The logic of practice.* (R. Nice, Trans.). Stanford University Press.

Bourdieu, P. (1984). *Distinction: A social critique of the judgement of taste.* (R. Nice, Trans.). Harvard University Press.

Brown, W. (2015). *Undoing the demos: Neoliberalism's stealth revolution.* Zone Books.

Callon, M. (1986). Some elements of a sociology of translation: Domestication of the scallops and the fisherman of St Brieuc Bay. In J. Law (Ed.), *Power, action and belief: A new sociology of knowledge?* (pp. 196–223). Routledge.

Callon, M., & Latour, B. (1981). Unscrewing the big leviathan: How actors macro-structure reality and how sociologists help them to do so. In K. Knorr-Cetina & A.V. Cicourel (Eds.), *Advances in social theory and methodology: Towards an integration of micro- and macro-sociologies* (pp. 277–303). Routledge.

Corman, M.K., & Barron, G.R.S. (2017). Institutional ethnography and actor-network theory: In dialogue. In J. Reid & L. Russell (Eds.), *Perspectives on and from institutional ethnography* (pp. 49–70). Emerald Publishing. https://doi.org/10.1108/S1042-319220170000015006

Deleuze, G. (1992). Postscript on the societies of control. *October, 59*(Winter), 3–7. https://doi.org/10.4324/9781315242002-3

DeVault, M.L., & McCoy, L. (2006). Institutional ethnography: Using interviews to investigate ruling relations. In D.E. Smith (Ed.), *Institutional ethnography as practice* (pp. 15–44). Rowman & Littlefield.

Espeland, W.N., & Sauder, M. (2007). Rankings and reactivity: How public measures recreate social worlds. *American Journal of Sociology, 113*(1), 1–40. https://doi.org/10.1086/517897

Espeland, W.N., & Sauder, M. (2016). *Engines of anxiety: Academic rankings, reputation, and accountability.* Russell Sage Foundation. http://www.russellsage.org/engines-anxiety

Foucault, M. (1977). *Discipline & punish: The birth of the prison.* Random House.

Goffman, E. (1959). *The presentation of self in everyday life* (1st ed.). Anchor.

Goffman, E. (1969). *Strategic interaction* (1st ed.). University of Pennsylvania Press.

Goffman, E. (1986). *Stigma: Notes on the management of spoiled identity* (reissue ed.). Touchstone.

Haggerty, K.D., & Ericson, R.V. (2000). The surveillance assemblage. *British Journal of Sociology, 51*(4), 605–22. https://doi.org/10.1080/00071310020015280

Hazelkorn, E. (2015). *Rankings and the reshaping of higher education: The battle for world-class excellence* (2nd ed.). Palgrave Macmillan.

Huang, R. 2016. "RQDA: R-based qualitative data analysis." R package version 0.2-8.
http://rqda.r-forge.r-project.org

IREG Observatory on Academic Ranking and Excellence. (2014). Berlin Principles on
ranking of higher education institutions. http://ireg-observatory.org/en_old/berlin
-principles

Lamont, M. (2010). *How professors think: Inside the curious world of academic judgment.*
Harvard University Press.

Latour, B. (1987). *Science in action: How to follow scientists and engineers through society.*
Harvard University Press.

Latour, B. (2007). *Reassembling the social: An introduction to actor-network-theory.*
Oxford University Press.

Law, J. (1991). *A sociology of monsters: Essays on power, technology, and domination.*
Routledge.

Law, J. (1994). *Organizing modernity.* Blackwell.

Law, J. (2012). Technology and heterogeneous engineering: The case of Portuguese
expansion. In W.E. Bijker, T.P. Hughes, & T. Pinch (Eds.), *The social construction of
technological systems: New directions in the sociology and history of technology* (25th
anniversary ed., pp. 105–28). MIT Press.

Lyon, D. (2002). Surveillance studies: Understanding visibility, mobility and the
phenetic fix. *Surveillance & Society, 1*(1), 1–7. https://doi.org/10.24908/ss.v1i1.3390

Marginson, S. (2007). Global university rankings: Implications in general and for
Australia. *Journal of Higher Education Policy and Management, 29*(2), 131–42.
https://doi.org/10.1080/13600800701351660

Mol, A. (2002). *The body multiple: Ontology in medical practice.* Durham University Press.

Power, M., Scheytt, T., Soin, K., & Sahlin, K. (2009). Reputational risk as a logic of
organizing in late modernity. *Organization Studies, 30*(2–3), 301–24. https://doi
.org/10.1177/0170840608101482

Sayer, D. (2016). *Rank hypocrisies: The insult of the REF.* SAGE. https://us.sagepub
.com/en-us/nam/rank-hypocrisies/book244105

Sayes, E.M. (2013). Actor-network theory and methodology: Just what does it
mean to say that nonhumans have agency? *Social Studies of Science.* https://doi
.org/10.1177/0306312713511867

Shapin, S. (1994). *A social history of truth: Civility and science in seventeenth-century
England.* University of Chicago Press.

Smelser, N.J. (2013). *Dynamics of the contemporary university: Growth, accretion, and
conflict.* University of California Press.

Timmermans, S., & Epstein, S. (2010). A world of standards but not a standard world:
Toward a sociology of standards and standardization*. *Annual Review of Sociology,
36*(1), 69–89. https://doi.org/10.1146/annurev.soc.012809.102629

University of Alberta, Faculty of Arts. (2014). Faculty of Arts faculty evaluation
committee: Standards for the evaluation of academic staff assessed for tenure,
promotion and incrementation.

University of Alberta, Faculty of Science. (2012). Standards of performance and procedures for merit increments, continuing appointment, and promotion for faculty service officers (FSOs) document. https://cloudfront.ualberta.ca/-/media/science/aboutus/documents/faculty-and-staff-resources/human-resources/efec/fso-standards-of-performance-and-procedures.pdf

University of Toronto. (2016). Promotion to full professor. Office of the Vice-Provost, Faculty & Academic Life. http://www.faculty.utoronto.ca/academic-life/full-professor

Walker, S. (2004, 1 December). University ranking criteria should include value judgments, argues Sally Walker. *Australian*, p. 42.

Yang, J. (2009, 5 November). Oshawa cracks Maclean's annual list; school cited for grants, spending on services. *Toronto Star*, p. GTO2.

9 Motivation and Well-Being of Faculty and Graduate Students: Empirical Relations with University Rankings

NATHAN C. HALL

Over the past few decades, researchers have increasingly examined how faculty and graduate students are responding psychologically to the rapidly changing nature of learning, instruction, and scholarship in higher education. Following from the massification of instruction and open scholarship due to remarkable gains in information technology (Lundberg & Cooper, 2010), combined with the widespread adoption of private-sector principles of consumer satisfaction, deliverables, and public accountability (Anderson, 2006; Pollitt & Bouckaert, 2004), post-secondary institutions now compete for students, faculty, and resources on an international scale. However, this shift in focus on post-secondary visibility and comparisons has corresponded with significant changes in the nature of academic work and training, with faculty and graduate students facing heightened demands for teaching excellence and research productivity despite a lack of commensurate resources (Biron et al., 2008; Kinman, 2008; McAlpine & Akerlind, 2010; Rothmann & Barkhuizen, 2008).

Given the critical role of university rankings in bolstering institutional viability by way of undergraduate recruitment, it is not surprising that existing international research on university rankings has focused mainly on their efficacy as undergraduate recruitment tools as moderated by student demographics (e.g., socio-economic status, achievement; Clarke, 2007; Davies et al., 2014; Horst-schräer, 2012), as along with declines in rank, institution size, and proximity (Broecke, 2015; Carroll, 2014; Drewes & Michael, 2006; Mangan et al., 2010). Limited research has additionally examined the psychological correlates of university rankings, with this work having similarly focused on the perceptions of institutional reputability among potential undergraduates (Carroll, 2014; Drewes & Michael, 2006), as well as academic identity and learning satisfaction in current undergraduates (Huang et al., 2015). As such, research to date on how university rankings correspond with the psychological experiences of those who participate in these institutions has looked almost exclusively at how undergraduates and potential applicants perceive the institution with respect to reputability and likelihood of attendance (for a review, see Espeland & Sauder, 2016). Although this focus is to be expected given its direct relevance to student recruitment efforts and a consumer satisfaction framework being increasingly adopted by universities, it does not account for the lived psychological experiences of other populations who directly enable the reputability of postsecondary institutions, namely faculty and graduate students.

Case Study: THE World University Rankings

As one of the most widely used and comprehensive rankings of post-secondary institutions internationally, the Times Higher Education (THE) World University Rankings have since 2011 attempted to quantify and rank the teaching and research success of over 1,000 institutions worldwide across thirteen performance indicators. With respect to teaching quality, the THE ranking incorporates institutional data concerning student demographics (e.g., international to domestic student ratio) and classroom composition (e.g., staff to student ratio). To assess research output, the THE ranking further includes non-self-report markers of research productivity (e.g., income, publication counts) and impact (e.g., citations, industry transfer). Taken together, the THE ranking algorithm compiles varied publicly observable, quantitative measures of teaching and research success to create a simplified omnibus metric of institutional quality with which universities can be compared internationally by potential students, university administrators, and funding agencies.

However, despite institutional ranking systems being largely informed by the teaching and research efforts of faculty at these institutions, empirical research has not yet extensively examined how university rankings correspond with the psychological experiences of *faculty members* who work at these institutions. For example, whereas the THE teaching rankings do address classroom composition (e.g., smaller classes being of greater benefit to students), they do not address associated teaching demands faced by faculty (e.g., greater burnout due to higher teaching loads; Watts & Robertson, 2011). Similarly, whereas THE research metrics do account for research productivity (e.g., publications) and income (e.g., grants), they do not reflect the pressure experienced by faculty to "publish or perish" and secure external funding despite increasing competition (Fernet et al., 2004).

This lack of consideration for the lived experiences of faculty is perhaps best reflected by an interesting paradox in how "reputability" is assessed in the THE rankings. More specifically, perceived reputability of a given institution within the academic community represents the largest THE ranking component (≈33%) and is based exclusively on the perceived excellence in teaching and research as reported by "experienced, published scholars" (Times Higher Education, 2016). However, because faculty respondents to the annual THE

Reputation Survey (from which this THE ranking component is derived) are prohibited from reporting on the qualities of their own institution, these reputability indicators thus *by design* do not account for the internal institutional insights of the very faculty upon whose teaching and research efforts the THE rankings are based. Moreover, given long-standing research showing persistent discrepancies in how individuals report on their own experiences (e.g., nuanced personal and situational factors) as compared to those of others (e.g., actor-observer bias; Jones & Nisbett, 1971), this exclusion of faculty reports of their own institution also precludes a more nuanced, realistic assessment of critical social-environmental factors that may contribute to or impede academic productivity (e.g., resources, collegiality, support).

In addition to underexplored implications for post-secondary faculty, university rankings are similarly informed by the teaching and research activities of *graduate students*. For example, the THE rankings for teaching quality have consistently incorporated the ratio of doctoral students to bachelor's students based on the assumption that "a high proportion of postgraduate research students also suggests the provision of teaching at the highest level that is thus attractive to graduates and effective at developing them" (Times Higher Education, 2016). Although this ratio does reflect basic enrolment/completion rates, it does not account for the impact of available institutional resources (e.g., professional development, financial support) on graduate student motivation and productivity (Litalien & Guay, 2015). Similarly, whereas the "doctorates awarded to academic staff" ratio does attempt to capture the capability of institutions to train larger numbers of graduate students in a timely manner, it does not address the lived experiences of students in large graduate programs (e.g., lack of personalized supervision; Hein et al., 2011) or the psychological impact on faculty of training large numbers of graduate students (e.g., exhaustion; Lackritz, 2004).

Accordingly, although university rankings such as the THE are used internationally to help students and their parents choose quality institutions, and are supported by institutions to maintain viability and visibility in a competitive higher education marketplace, these metrics tend to employ simplified indicators of teaching efficacy (e.g., class size, demographic proportions) and research productivity (e.g., rate of publications, grants) that do not reflect the lived experiences of faculty or graduate students at these institutions. Moreover, whereas these rankings do reflect some engagement with these critical stakeholders by incorporating doctoral student ratios and perceptions of excellence by external established scholars (e.g., tenured faculty), this psychological aspect is limited due to excluding (a) perceptions of pre-tenure and non-tenure-track (e.g., adjunct) faculty, (b) perceptions of graduate students, and (c) other psychological variables involving motivation and well-being known to correlate with performance in faculty and graduate students. To address this research gap, this chapter outlines preliminary empirical evidence from three recent international pilot studies with pre-tenure faculty, open-rank faculty (e.g., contingent through full professor status), and graduate students (both master's and PhD) to explore how the THE university rankings correspond with various established indicators of motivation and psychological health in these under-examined stakeholder populations.

Motivation and Well-Being of Faculty

Owing in large part to steadily increasing institutional demands for productivity and documented excellence in disparate teaching, research, and service obligations, recent international surveys of well-being in post-secondary faculty show stress levels to have increased significantly over the past two decades (Kinman & Jones, 2004; Rothmann & Barkhuizen, 2008; Watts & Robertson, 2011). Empirical research further indicates that faculty stress levels exceed those of other university staff, various other professional occupations (e.g., white-collar and social services workers, health professionals, military staff), and the general population (Goodwin et al., 2013; Tytherleigh et al., 2005). The current academic employment climate has also been found to contribute to high levels of occupational burnout and psychological health challenges (Watts & Robertson, 2011; Zhong et al., 2009). Given direct links between faculty well-being and research and teaching performance (Blix et al., 1994), research in this domain has focused on identifying critical antecedents and correlates of well-being and burnout in post-secondary faculty including both external, social-environmental factors (e.g., institutional demands) and internal, psychological variables (e.g., achievement motivation; for reviews, see Sabagh et al., 2018; Salimzadeh et al., 2017).

Social-Environmental Factors

Considering the extensive nature of existing empirical research showing that various elements of the academic work environment significantly impact faculty well-being, it stands to reason that university rankings as a proxy for institutional demands and resources should similarly correspond with psychological health indicators in this post-secondary community. For example, international findings consistently demonstrate the harmful effects of excessive job demands and overwork on burnout in faculty (Barkhuizen et al., 2014; van Emmerik, 2002; Zhong et al., 2009). Additionally, whereas high teaching loads and large class sizes have typically been found to negatively impact faculty well-being (Gonzalez & Bernard, 2006; Lackritz, 2004; Watts & Robertson, 2011), recent studies further highlight the psychological costs of contentious interactions with students (Frisby et al., 2015) and online instruction (Hogan & McKnight,

2007), as well as demands for research productivity and administrative service (Gomes et al., 2013; Vera et al., 2010).

Research with post-secondary faculty also underscores the critical role of social support in mitigating experiences of burnout (Otero-López et al., 2008; Singh & Bush, 1998; van Emmerik, 2004), with findings showing higher burnout levels among faculty who report unsupportive relationships with administrators or colleagues (Barkhuizen et al., 2014; Rothmann et al., 2008; van Emmerik, 2002). Beyond the psychological strain of balancing disparate academic and professional responsibilities in terms of role conflict (Fernet et al., 2004; Ghorpade et al., 2011; van Emmerik, 2004), findings show balancing one's academic work with personal or family obligations to be a particularly salient contributor to faculty burnout (Hogan et al., 2014; Kinman, 2008).

Psychological Correlates

Given the extent to which various psychological variables involving motivation and emotional well-being have been empirically observed to correspond with stress and burnout in faculty populations, it was expected that university rankings should similarly be related to these critical psychological processes. For example, motivational beliefs reflecting perceived competence (Navarro et al., 2010), perceived control over academic stressors (Gomes et al., 2013), and intrinsic motivation (Li et al., 2013; Singh & Bush, 1998) have consistently been found to correspond with lower psychological strain in faculty. Similarly, emotional experiences pertaining to academic work have been shown to correspond with psychological health in faculty, including not only general measures of job satisfaction (Lundberg & Cooper, 2010; Zhang & Zhu, 2008) but more specific measures assessing discrete emotions such as enjoyment, pride, anger, or anxiety related to teaching (Gates, 2000; Hagenauer & Volet, 2014) or to research activities (Stupnisky et al., 2019; Stupnisky et al., 2016).

With respect to more serious psychological adjustment correlates of burnout and stress in the context of academic employment, studies show specific coping strategies to correspond with faculty well-being (e.g., humour, emotional labour; Blix et al., 1994; Tümkaya, 2007; Zhang & Zhu, 2008) as well as job engagement and quitting intentions (e.g., Barkhuizen et al., 2014; Li et al., 2013). Findings also show links between stress and depression in post-secondary faculty (e.g., Shen et al., 2014; Zhong et al., 2009), with poor psychological health among faculty further linked to greater physical illness symptoms (Dreyer et al., 2010; Sang, Teo, Cooper, & Bohle, 2013). Taken together, considering the scope of social-environmental and psychological variables found to overlap empirically with stress and burnout in faculty members, it was hypothesized that university rankings should similarly correspond with these critical occupational and psychological indicators.

Potential Relations with University Rankings

Given the current lack of research exploring the linkages between university rankings and the psychological experiences of faculty who work at these institutions, with the notable exception of recent work exploring rankings-related anxiety experienced by university administrators (Espeland & Sauder, 2016), the specific expected magnitudes and directions of these relations remain unclear. For example, to the extent that higher THE rankings reflect optimal teaching environments and research productivity, faculty at higher-ranked institutions should report greater motivation for teaching and research than faculty at lower-ranked institutions. Alternatively, should higher THE rankings also reflect greater pressure for high-profile publications and grant funding (e.g., at the expense of quality instruction), faculty at higher-ranked institutions may experience poorer psychological well-being than their colleagues at lower-ranked, teaching-focused institutions. Similarly, whereas faculty at higher-ranked universities may perceive greater internal support for their teaching and research efforts (e.g., resources, collegiality), they may also experience a more individualistic, competitive, and performance-focused work environment that could mitigate or override the psychological benefits of available supports. Thus, given the speculative and potentially mixed nature of relations between university rankings and the psychological experiences of faculty, the present studies aimed to shed some light on if and how such relations may be observed on an international scale.

Motivation and Well-Being of Graduate Students

In stark contrast to the extensive extant literature on the interplay between structural and personal variables in undergraduate populations, research on the educational, social, and psychological experiences of graduate students is surprisingly limited. Over the past fifty years, attrition from graduate programs has remained consistently high (e.g., ≈50%; Lovitts, 2001) as have the rates of graduate students reporting high stress levels (Virtanen et al., 2017; Wyatt & Oswalt, 2013), psychological health concerns (Hyun et al., 2006; Pallos et al., 2005), and physical illness (Juniper et al., 2012). Beyond the obvious challenges of graduate education with respect to completing program requirements (e.g., coursework, thesis) and developing professional competencies (e.g., synthesis, analysis, dissemination, instruction), graduate students also face ever-increasing demands for research excellence and productivity in a context of heightened competition (e.g., financial support, employment) that further threaten their performance and well-being (Geraniou, 2010; Tanaka & Watanabea, 2012).

Social-Environmental Factors

Given existing research on graduate student development showing that various external, social-environmental factors contribute to stress and well-being levels (for a review, see Sverdlik et al., 2018), it was expected that university rankings, as a proxy for quality training and resources for doctoral students, should similarly correspond with motivation and psychological health in graduate students more generally. For example, findings show quality of supervision to be consistently cited by graduate students as impacting their satisfaction, persistence, and performance (Gube et al., 2017; Solem et al., 2011), with supervisors who exhibit distinct mentorship characteristics (e.g., timely feedback, regular meetings, clear expectations, equitability) proving optimal for student development (Hein et al., 2011; McAlpine & McKinnon, 2013). Research with graduate students further illustrates the importance of institutional support, with clear performance expectations (Gardner, 2013; Hoskins & Goldberg, 2005; Lin, 2012) and greater opportunities for skill and career development being particularly critical for mitigating stress in graduate students (Austin, 2009; O'Meara et al., 2014). Graduate students at institutions that provide greater financial support also tend to report greater well-being and persistence (Leijen et al., 2016; Litalien & Guay, 2015), with studies further showing the struggle to balance academic work with personal obligations to negatively impact persistence and well-being (Castelló et al., 2017; Levecque et al., 2017).

Psychological Correlates

Considering the aforementioned research showing how specific aspects of graduate education contribute to greater stress, significant relations were also expected between university rankings and other psychological variables associated with stress in graduate students. With respect to motivational beliefs, studies have found graduate students' perceptions of personal competence to correlate with motivation and productivity (Lambie & Vaccaro, 2011; Litalien & Guay, 2015), and research also highlights the importance of intrinsic motivation in response to educational challenges (Devos et al., 2017; Flynn et al., 2012). Recent research has further explored graduate students' motivational beliefs concerning their skill development (De Welde & Laursen, 2008; Stubb et al., 2012) and extrinsic concerns (e.g., employability; Brailsford, 2010). More serious indicators of well-being have also been examined in graduate students, including coping strategies (e.g., self-talk, help-seeking; Geraniou, 2010; Sala-Bubaré & Castelló, 2016), as well as burnout and depression (Galdino et al., 2016; Uqdah et al., 2009).

Potential Relations with University Rankings

As existing research on the correspondence between university rankings and the lived experiences of graduate students is regrettably limited, the magnitude and direction of potential relations between rankings and psychological adjustment in graduate students remains an open question. For example, although THE rankings explicitly incorporate doctoral student graduation rates to represent quality of training, they do not account for the experiences of master's students or the perceptions of graduate students concerning their own or other institutions (e.g., reputability). Relatedly, whereas graduate students at higher-ranked institutions could be expected to receive higher-quality supervision leading to greater motivation and persistence, they may also experience poorer well-being resulting from pressure to publish repeatedly before graduation (e.g., manuscript-based dissertations), in addition to satisfying degree requirements (e.g., coursework). As noted above, although it is possible that larger graduate programs are better equipped to train students in a timely manner, it is also possible for graduate students in large programs at high-ranking institutions to experience less personalized supervision, leading to feelings of demotivation and isolation. In sum, considering the growing literature showing academic demands faced by both graduate students and faculty to correspond significantly with various facets of psychological health, the present research aimed to further explore the extent to which university rankings, as an assumed indicator of institutional quality, corresponded empirically with established measures of motivation and well-being across three pilot studies conducted with pre-tenure faculty, faculty across ranks, and graduate students internationally.

Study 1: Pre-tenure Faculty

Studies consistently show pre-tenure faculty to be particularly susceptible to impaired psychological health due to heightened demands for teaching excellence (Simmons, 2011; Solem & Foote, 2004) and research productivity (Boice, 1991; Greene et al., 2008) as part of the often ambiguous and anxiety-provoking nature of the tenure process (Mullen & Forbes, 2000; Nir & Zilberstein-Levy, 2006). Nevertheless, the psychological experiences of pre-tenure faculty have to date been largely excluded from consideration in the THE rankings, that are instead informed by the perceptions of senior scholars with greater experience and job security (tenure). Thus, considering that pre-tenure scholars have been overlooked in the rankings calculations and corresponding literature, despite being especially likely to be impacted by the pressures for teaching and research excellence implied by university rankings, further research on how those rankings correspond with the psychological experiences of this particularly vulnerable faculty population is clearly warranted.

To address this research gap, an exploratory study was conducted to assess potential relations between THE rankings and a range of motivational and well-being indicators specifically in pre-tenure faculty. This pilot study sample consisted of eighty-six pre-tenure faculty (66% female) employed at thirty-four ranked institutions across Canada and the US, with 27% recruited by mass email via the faculty association at a research-intensive Canadian university and the remaining participants recruited via social media (Twitter, Facebook). Consistent with recent research with pre-tenure faculty (Stupnisky et al., 2015) and the THE rankings comprising specifically teaching- and research-specific indicators, teaching vs. research versions of multiple self-report measures were examined so as to examine potentially differential relations between rankings and teaching vs. research outcomes.

Motivation and Well-Being Measures

Following from the long-standing expectancy-value framework for conceptualizing achievement motivation constructs (Eccles, 2005), motivational beliefs in pre-tenure faculty were assessed with respect to their expectations for success as afforded by their perceptions of personal competence, using faculty-specific measures adapted from established scales. Administered scales included measures of *self-efficacy* informed by social cognitive theory (Schunk & Pajares, 2009) that were specific to teaching (sample item: "I feel competent in clearly communicating ideas during in class lectures"; Busch et al., 1998) or research activities (sample item: "I feel competent in gathering reliable and valid research data"; Hardré et al., 2011). Also assessed were *perceived control* over teaching/ research activities (e.g., "The more effort I put forth, the better I do"; Stupnisky et al., 2015) and *perceived competence* in teaching/research based on self-determination theory (Ryan & Deci, 2009; e.g., "In my [teaching/research], I feel capable at what I do"; Van den Broeck et al., 2010). Participants' personal values underlying their teaching vs. research efforts were also examined using an adapted measure of subjective *task value* (intrinsic, attainment, utility, and cost; Eccles, 2005; e.g., "It is important to me that I do well on this task"). We further administered more specific value-related measures specific to teaching vs. research informed by self-determination theory, assessing *intrinsic motivation* (e.g., "Because it is pleasant to carry out this task"), *introjected motivation* (e.g., "Because I would feel guilty not doing it"), and *external motivation* (e.g., "Because I am paid to do it"; Fernet et al., 2004).

Beyond cognitively oriented measures of achievement motivation, participants' emotional experiences specific to engaging in teaching vs. research were also assessed. More specifically, three scales based on the control-value theory of achievement emotions (Pekrun et al., 2011) assessed the emotions of *anxiety* (e.g., "I get tense when [teaching/doing research]"), *boredom* (e.g., "I get so bored while [teaching/conducting research] that my mind begins to wander"), and *enjoyment* (e.g., "I look forward to [teaching/working on research]). Faculty emotions and commitment concerning their academic employment were further assessed using adapted versions of constructs commonly examined in occupational psychology research (see Stupnisky et al., 2017; Stupnisky et al., 2015). These measures included *perceived success* in teaching vs. research (e.g., in relation to self-standards, departmental tenure expectations, other faculty), *job satisfaction* (e.g., salary, teaching load, social relationships, job security), *work-life balance* (e.g., "I have been able to balance my work and home/personal life"), and a single-item measure of *intention to quit* one's current academic position (for a position at another institution). Finally, psychological well-being in pre-tenure faculty with respect to social aspects of the academic work environment were assessed, including perceived *autonomy* (e.g., "In my [teaching/research], I feel a sense of choice and freedom") and *relatedness* (e.g., "When [teaching/conducting research], I feel close with people who are important to me"), based on self-determination theory. Faculty perceptions of *collegiality* (e.g., "My department is very supportive"), *clarity of tenure expectations* (e.g., "I received sufficient feedback on my progress towards tenure and promotion"), and *professional balance* were also assessed (e.g., "I have been able to balance my teaching, research, and service duties"; see Stupnisky et al., 2015).

Analysis and Results

To evaluate the anticipated relations between university rankings and psychological variables in pre-tenure faculty, participants' self-reported institution of employment was recoded to a numeric variable reflecting the 2014–15 THE World University Ranking of that institution. This numeric variable was subsequently assessed as a predictor of the aforementioned self-report measures in a hierarchical linear regression analysis. To provide a suitably conservative analysis of ranking effects, indicators of engagement with the online survey protocol were controlled for as background covariates in step 1 of the regression (i.e., order in which participants completed the survey, elapsed survey completion time; see Hall et al., 2017). Participants' age and gender were also controlled for in step 1, given existing research showing younger faculty and female faculty to report poorer well-being levels (Ghorpade et al., 2011; Li et al., 2013; Rothmann & Barkhuizen, 2008). University rankings were then introduced in step 2 of the regression analysis to evaluate the unique additional variance explained in each of the psychological outcomes beyond that explained by the background variables.

The regression results showed no statistically significant relations with university rankings for any of the *teaching-related* motivation and well-being measures. Although preliminary correlations suggested that pre-tenure faculty at lower-ranked institutions placed lower value on teaching ($r(81) = -0.28$, $p = 0.011$) and were more bored with their teaching activities ($r(78) = 0.19$, $p = 0.100$), these relations were not significant in regressions controlling for background variables ($\beta = -0.23$, $p = 0.071$; $\beta = 0.13$, $p = 0.306$, respectively). In contrast, multiple significant regression effects showed pre-tenure faculty at higher-ranked institutions to report greater perceived control ($\beta = -0.27$, $p = 0.025$) and competence ($\beta = -0.29$, $p = 0.021$) concerning their *research activities*, with university rankings explaining an additional 4.9% and 5.6% of variance in these motivation variables beyond background covariates, respectively (i.e., increase in adjusted R^2). Given that the THE university rankings are applied exclusively to research-intensive institutions, these relations underscore the research-related criteria of this ranking system in showing higher rankings to principally predict greater faculty confidence in their ability to conduct quality research. Although an additional correlational finding showed pre-tenure faculty at lower-ranked institutions to also report lower anxiety concerning research activities ($r(77) = -0.25$, $p = 0.031$), this finding was not significant in the more conservative regression analysis ($\beta = 0.20$, $p = 0.123$).

In summary, these preliminary findings show that university rankings indeed correspond empirically with specific psychological variables in pre-tenure faculty, with the most robust relations observed reiterating the utility of the THE rankings as an indicator of faculty potential for quality research. More specifically, whereas suggestive preliminary correlations showed university rankings to additionally correspond with more values-oriented motivational beliefs (i.e., that teaching is enjoyable, important, useful, and worthwhile), as well as multiple indicators of emotional well-being (i.e., boredom, anxiety), these relations were not statistically significant in more intensive regression analyses controlling for age, gender, and survey engagement. However, as the largely nonsignificant rankings effects across the motivation and well-being outcomes in this study may have also resulted from insufficient power due to the small sample size and restrictive recruitment parameters (i.e., pre-tenure rank, Canada/US only), a more inclusive, larger-scale analysis was warranted to better examine how university rankings interact with motivation and well-being internationally in both faculty and graduate students. To address this research gap, Study 2 and Study 3 recruited faculty across ranks (e.g., tenure-track, contingent) and graduate students from various countries, respectively, to complete an even more comprehensive survey assessing both motivational variables (e.g., causal attributions, self-determined motivation) and various indicators of psychological well-being ranging from achievement emotions (e.g., hope, guilt) to more serious mental and physical health challenges (e.g., depression, illness).

Study 2: Open-Rank Faculty

Although the psychological experiences of post-secondary faculty have been previously addressed in relation to THE rankings, the scope of these variables has been limited specifically to the general perceptions of more *senior faculty* concerning the teaching and research reputability of *other* institutions. Accordingly, further research is needed with faculty across ranks to examine how important psychological variables beyond perceived reputability may also correspond with the international ranking of one's own institution. To address this research objective, a second exploratory pilot study was conducted with faculty across ranks (both non-tenure and tenure-track) at institutions around the world to examine empirical relations between the THE rankings and an expanded set of motivation and psychological health measures.

The second study sample consisted of 884 faculty (66% female) employed at 114 ranked institutions across 26 countries, with most participants employed at universities in the US (48%), UK (18%), Canada (14%), Australia (8%), and Europe (8%). In contrast to Study 1, faculty participants were employed across ranks (e.g., US/Canada: 30% contingent, 37% assistant, 24% associate, 10% full; UK/Australia: 48% lecturer, 21% senior lecturer, 13% reader, 10% professor, 4% tutor) and had been employed as academics for an average of seven years (*SD* = 6.65). Participants were predominantly recruited via social media (e.g., Facebook: 43%, Twitter: 49%) as part of a larger data-collection effort examining self-regulation and academic success in higher education (SAS Project; Hall, 2015, 2016, 2017). Although a subset of measures assessed were equivalent to those in Study 1, most scales in Study 2 examined additional motivational and well-being constructs using adapted versions of established self-report measures.

Motivation and Well-Being Measures

To more closely examine faculty motivation with respect to their perceptions of personal control, four measures based on Weiner's (2010) attribution theory were administered. Faculty first indicated the most likely reason behind their academic setbacks (e.g., rejected manuscripts, unsuccessful grant applications, low course evaluations) and then rated the reason according to *internality* (e.g., "inside/outside of you"), *stability* over time (e.g., "permanent/temporary"), *personal controllability* (e.g., "(not) manageable by you"), and *external controllability* (e.g., "others have (no) control"; see McAuley et al., 1992). Perceptions of value were also assessed using five measures based on self-determination theory that measured *intrinsic, introjected,* and *external motivation* for academic career pursuits, as well as *integrated motivation* (e.g., "My academic career is a fundamental part of who I am and my identity") and *identified motivation* (e.g., "Maintaining or improving my expertise in my field of research"; adapted from Litalien et al., 2015).

In addition to measures of achievement motivation, faculty emotions following academic career setbacks were explored using a modified measure assessing single-item indicators of both positive (*hope, pride*) and negative (*guilt, helplessness*) emotional responses (Hall et al., 2004). As in Study 1, measures of psychological well-being specific to personal work beliefs involving *job satisfaction, work-life balance,* and *intention to quit* were assessed, albeit using alternative measures (Gutek et al., 1991; Hackett et al., 2001; Moe et al., 2010). To further examine how faculty attempt to maintain their psychological well-being in response to stress through both adaptive and maladaptive coping strategies, a subset of participants (N = 185) also completed four, two-item self-report measures assessing *problem-solving* (e.g., "I made a plan of action and followed it"), *cognitive restructuring* (e.g., "I convinced myself that things weren't quite as bad as they seemed"), *wishful thinking* (e.g., "I wished that the situation would go away or somehow be over with"), and *social withdrawal* (e.g., "I avoided being with people") in response to a specific stressful academic situation experienced over the previous few months (Tobin, 1995). Finally, established measures addressing more serious psychological and physical health challenges were completed by the entire sample, including *impostor syndrome* (e.g., "I'm afraid people important to me may find out that I'm not as capable as they think I am"; Clance, 1985), *illness symptoms* (e.g., sleep problems, headaches, muscle tension, poor appetite; Cohen & Hoberman, 1983), *emotional exhaustion* (e.g., "I feel burned out from my work"; Maslach et al., 1996), and *depression* (e.g., "I felt that everything I did was an effort"; Andresen, 1994).

Analysis and Results

Similar to Study 1, hierarchical linear regressions (step 1: background variables; step 2: university rankings) were conducted to evaluate the hypothesized relations between the 2014–15 THE World University Ranking of faculty participants' self-reported institution and the psychological variables controlling for age, gender, and survey engagement (order of participation, elapsed completion time). Regression results showed university rankings to not correspond significantly with any of the motivational or work belief measures assessed. However, modest yet statistically significant ranking effects were consistently observed across measures reflecting how faculty responded to academic setbacks and stressors in terms of both their emotions and coping strategies.

As for their *emotional experiences,* findings showed faculty at lower-ranked institutions to experience slightly higher levels of guilt ($\beta = 0.10$, $p = 0.009$; 0.8% more variance explained) and hope ($\beta = 0.08$, $p = 0.041$; 0.5% more variance explained) in response to academic career setbacks (e.g., poor teaching evalu-ations, manuscript or grant rejections). Although these mixed emotions may appear contradictory, Weiner's (2010) attribution theory suggests that both emotions result from an underlying perception of personal control over a past event (guilt) and future occurrence of an event (hope). However, this interpre-tation is contradicted by a lack of significant effects on the causal attribution measure indicating perceived personal controllability, as well as findings from Study 1 showing higher (not lower) rankings to correspond with greater per-ceived control. This interpretation is also inconsistent with a marginally sig-nificant result showing lower university rankings to correspond with greater feelings of helplessness in faculty after academic setbacks ($\beta = 0.08$, $p = 0.057$; zero-order correlation: $r(669) = 0.08$, $p = 0.044$), an emotion consistently asso-ciated with a lack of perceived control (Weiner, 2010). In any case, these results suggest that academic setbacks may be more emotionally charged for faculty at lower-ranked universities.

Consistent with the results for emotions following career setbacks, the pres-ent results further showed university rankings to correspond with *coping strat-egies* reported by faculty in response to academic stressors. In addition to a marginally significant effect suggesting that faculty at lower-ranked institu-tions were less likely to use the typically adaptive coping strategy of cognitive restructuring ($\beta = -0.12$, $p = 0.103$), multiple significant effects showed faculty at lower-ranked institutions to be more likely to endorse maladaptive coping strategies involving wishful thinking (hoping the problem would go away; $\beta = 0.16$, $p = 0.041$; 1.8% more variance explained) and social withdrawal (inten-tional isolation; $\beta = 0.21$, $p = 0.006$; 0.6% more variance explained). Finally, although none of the ranking effects for more serious indicators of physical and psychological health were statistically significant, multiple marginally sig-nificant findings showed faculty at lower-ranked institutions more frequently report symptoms of both physical illness ($\beta = 0.08$, $p = 0.064$) and depression ($\beta = 0.07$, $p = 0.102$). In sum, despite a notable lack of empirical relations with motivational and work-related beliefs, findings for faculty across academic ranks and countries consistently indicated that those employed at lower-ranked universities experienced poorer well-being levels.

Study 3: Graduate Students

As outlined above, the psychological experiences of graduate students have been largely excluded to date, both in the calculation of university rankings and in the accompanying research literature on related psychological variables. More specifically, whereas non-self-report markers of graduate student par-ticipation in research and teaching activities are incorporated into the THE algorithm (e.g., doctoral to bachelor's student ratio, doctoral graduation to staff ratio, graduate student publications and citations), the perceptions of graduate students themselves concerning the quality of teaching, supervision, and research at their own or other institutions has not been assessed. Moreover, the extent to which university rankings correspond with psychological experiences of graduate students in both master's and PhD programs has yet to be empirically examined. To explore these research questions, a third pilot study was conducted to explore potential relations between THE university rankings and a range of motivational and mental health variables in graduate students.

The third study sample consisted of 2,173 graduate students (71% female) enrolled at 134 ranked universities across 32 countries including the US (51%), Canada (18%), UK (13%), Europe (11%), and Australia (5%). Participants were enrolled across graduate degree programs (e.g., master's: 18%; PhD: 58%, combined master's/PhD: 21%), with most required to complete a thesis or dissertation (96%), not being registered as an international student (81%), and not teaching post-secondary courses as the primary instructor (75%). As in Study 2, participants were predominantly recruited via social media (e.g., Facebook: 60%, Twitter: 28%) as part of a larger project on self-regulation and success in higher education (SAS Project; Hall, 2015, 2016, 2017). With the exception of job satisfaction (omitted) and quitting intention (an additional scale item was included), each of the self-report motivation and well-being measures in Study 2 was replicated in Study 3, with scale preambles and items modified as needed to refer to graduate education experiences (e.g., as encountered in one's "graduate studies" or "degree program").

Analysis and Results

Consistent with Studies 1 and 2, hierarchical regression analyses (step 1: background variables; step 2: university rankings) were conducted to examine expected empirical relations between the 2014–15 THE World University Ranking of the institution at which the participants reporting being enrolled as a graduate student and the self-report measures of motivation and psychological well-being. In addition to controlling for the potentially confounding effects of survey engagement (order of participation, elapsed completion time), participants' age and gender were once again included as covariates, following from existing research with graduate students showing motivation and well-being to vary significantly as a function of these demographic variables (Brown & Watson, 2010; Cao, 2012; Ellis, 2001; Kusurkar et al., 2010; Rosser & Lane, 2002).

Contrary to preceding findings with faculty, university rankings were not found to correspond with any of the *emotion* or *coping* measures related to academic setbacks for graduate students. In contrast, multiple weak yet significant results showed that graduate students at lower-ranked universities reported consistently higher levels across the varied types of *self-determined motivation*.

Poorer university rankings predicted not only higher levels of motivation for graduate study due to personal principles (integrated motivation: goals, values, identity; $\beta = 0.05$, $p = 0.041$; 0.2% more variance explained) and utilitarian concerns (identified motivation: development of skills, knowledge, opportunities; $\beta = 0.07$, $p = 0.002$; 0.5% more variance explained), but also greater motivation due to more extrinsic expected benefits (external motivation: prestige, employment, money; $\beta = 0.08$, $p = 0.002$; 0.5% more variance explained). Although similar effects for intrinsic motivation ($\beta = 0.04$, $p = 0.092$) and introjected motivation ($\beta = 0.04$, $p = 0.075$) were not statistically significant, these findings nevertheless show university rankings to have significant empirical relationships with a range of motivational reasons for pursuing graduate studies.

A second unique set of results was observed with graduate students: Poorer university rankings corresponded with a greater psychological focus on the role of external factors as contributors to academic performance and stress. More specifically, although the regression results for *causal attributions* to personally controllable factors ($\beta = -0.04$, $p = 0.104$) and externally controlled factors ($\beta = 0.04$, $p = 0.063$) were only marginally significant, a significant preliminary zero-order correlation between ranking and external attributions was observed (i.e., to others having control over reasons for failure experiences; $r(1,953) = 0.05$, $p = 0.031$). This latter result suggests that graduate students at lower-ranked universities were more concerned with their academic progress and performance being disrupted by factors external to and not controllable by themselves than were their counterparts at more prestigious institutions.

Finally, two additional weak yet significant effects were observed showing university rankings to also correspond with more serious indicators of *physical and psychological health* in graduate students. More specifically, not only were graduate students at lower-ranked universities more likely to report experiencing difficulty balancing their academic and personal responsibilities ($\beta = 0.06$, $p = 0.016$; 0.3% more variance explained), but they were also more likely to report experiencing multiple potentially critical illness symptoms ($\beta = 0.05$, $p = 0.049$; 0.2% more variance explained). Considered alongside the aforementioned findings for external types of motivation and causal attributions, the results for work-life balance further suggest that graduate students at lower-ranked universities are significantly more concerned with the impact of external factors on their academic success than are their peers at higher-ranked institutions. Moreover, findings showing university rankings to correspond with work-life balance and illness symptoms also suggest that the perceived quality of academic environment can have significant implications for non-academic aspects of graduate students' personal lives and well-being (e.g., health, relationships).

General Discussion

To summarize across the three sets of findings presented in this chapter, the present pilot study findings suggest that university rankings do indeed correspond empirically with a range of psychological variables involving motivation and well-being among both faculty and graduate students internationally. In Study 1, pilot results for pre-tenure faculty in Canada and the US mainly validated the research-specific emphasis of the THE rankings in showing higher-ranked institutions to employ pre-tenure faculty with greater confidence in their abilities to conduct quality research. Following from suggestive results showing pre-tenure faculty at lower-ranked universities to also report more maladaptive value levels and more negative emotions, Studies 2 and 3 offered a more extensive analysis of how university rankings correspond with well-being indicators in faculty across ranks, as well as graduate students, worldwide. Whereas Study 2 showed lower rankings to typically coincide with lower levels of adaptive emotions and coping responses to academic stressors among faculty, Study 3 showed lower rankings to correlate with higher levels of multiple types of motivation underlying academic persistence in graduate students, as well as a heightened awareness of how external factors (e.g., others, personal obligations) can interfere with academic success. Finally, pilot results from Studies 2 and 3 suggested that lower university rankings may additionally correspond with more serious psychological and physical health problems in both faculty and graduate students (i.e., illness, depression).

Accordingly, the present results contribute substantially to existing research on the psychological correlates of university rankings not only in expanding the scope of variables assessed (e.g., reputability perceptions) to include motivation and well-being, but also by exploring these variables in underexamined higher education communities, namely faculty and graduate students. Given that university rankings are composed largely of the teaching, research, and engagement efforts of faculty and graduate students, with these populations having a significant vested interest in the reputation and quality of their institution, these results highlight the importance of continued research on how rankings correspond with motivation, well-being, and health in these populations. However, despite these findings showing university rankings not to simply reflect non-emotional learning and achievement outcomes, but instead to correlate significantly with various indicators of motivation, emotional well-being, and quality of life in faculty and graduate students, they must also be considered in the context of multiple limitations of pilot research presented.

Study Limitations and Future Directions

First, considering the scope of analyses conducted in Study 1, due to assessing teaching-specific vs. research-specific versions of several self-report measures, it is possible that the two significant regression values may have resulted from capitalizing on Type I error. However, this possibility of random significance is mitigated by the regression analyses providing more conservative estimates than zero-order correlations due to controlling for potential confounds, with these exploratory findings also proving consistent with multiple marginally significant effects in Study 3 for causal attributions. Second, although multiple significant coefficients were observed in Studies 2 and 3, the proportion of additional variance explained by university rankings on psychological variables beyond that of background variables (e.g., age, gender) in these studies was consistently small, particularly in the graduate student study, where statistical significance was afforded mainly by the substantial sample size.

One possible reason for these weak effects may be the limited internal reliability of specific scales employed (e.g., self-determined motivation subscales developed for Study 2: $0.55 < \alpha s < 0.79$). Accordingly, continued research to develop more reliable motivation and well-being measures for these underexplored populations is encouraged. However, it is also possible that considerable variance in the structure and supports of doctoral training and academic employment internationally may have contributed to weaker findings for Studies 2 and 3. For example, whereas graduate programs in Germany are highly structured and similar to professorial employment with respect to mandated compensation and office space as well as teaching, supervision, and research demands (Thies & Kordts-Freudinger, 2019), graduate programs in North America can vary widely in both financial support (e.g., salary, awards, none) and academic obligations (e.g., teaching vs. thesis only). Similarly, further research is needed to explore how substantial international variability in professorial employment structures (e.g., academic ranks, administrative roles, job security) and region-specific faculty demands (e.g., UK Research Excellence Framework) may mitigate or moderate relations between university rankings and the lived experiences of academic staff.

Alternatively, it also possible that due to the omnibus nature of university rankings comprising divergent facets of institutional quality (e.g., teaching excellence, research productivity, international reputation, industry preparedness), further research employing disaggregated or more specific rankings may help clarify how rankings correspond with psychological outcomes in faculty and graduate students (e.g., UK: Teaching vs. Research Excellence Framework rankings). However, it should also be considered that university rankings may simply not correspond as strongly with motivation and well-being measures as with other variables that are more closely tied to academic performance. For example, whereas research has examined how rankings are related to learning-specific outcomes in undergraduates (e.g., satisfaction with learning; Huang et al., 2015), findings on how university rankings correspond with self-regulated learning (or teaching) in faculty and graduate students is lacking (e.g., planning, time management, self-monitoring; Zimmerman, 2011).

As for other potentially beneficial directions for future study, given that the THE university rankings comprise exclusively research-intensive universities, how the psychological experiences of faculty and graduate students correspond with other rankings systems would also be of interest. For example, it is possible that competing international rankings systems (e.g., ARWU, Leiden, QS, U-Multirank), other national ranking systems (e.g., Canada: Maclean's; US: *U.S. News & World Report*), rankings within disciplines (e.g., STEM vs. social sciences), or rankings of non-academic indicators (e.g., social mobility, Wolfston, 2016; environmental sustainability, Ragazzia & Ghidinia, 2017) would show different patterns of relations with motivation and well-being in faculty and graduate students. Consistent with the emerging importance of the "meta-science" discipline in which perceptions of academics concerning post-secondary structures are explicitly assessed (Ernst et al., 2018; Kousta et al., 2016), greater research on how faculty, graduate students, and other vested communities (e.g., administrators, staff, post-doctoral scholars) perceive the reputability and efficacy of rankings systems is also encouraged.

The present findings are also consistent with existing research showing significant psychological benefits of institutional support for both graduate students (e.g., career development, Austin, 2009; O'Meara et al., 2014; financial support: Leijen et al., 2016; Litalien & Guay, 2015) and faculty (Rothmann et al., 2008; van Emmerik, 2002). Hence, future research on the extent to which university rankings further reflect available institutional resources for students and faculty is needed to better examine institutional support as a mediating variable. For example, it is possible that highly ranked institutions providing more extensive support services to graduate students (e.g., career advising, financial aid, health services) could account for the pilot results showing positive relations between rankings and motivation and health. Although pilot results did not show rankings to be related to perceptions of workplace climate for pre-tenure faculty (i.e., perceived autonomy, relatedness, collegiality), it is nevertheless possible that higher-ranked universities provide greater levels of specific resources for faculty (e.g., teaching workshops, internal grants, health insurance) that could help explain the observed relations between rankings and mental health for faculty in Study 2.

Moreover, as the social-environmental climate of a post-secondary institution can be experienced differently as a function of personal characteristics (e.g., varying perceptions of inclusion or support as a function of gender, sexual, or racial minority status), more research on how rankings correspond with the lived experiences of under-represented and/or marginalized academic groups is warranted. For example, existing research shows female academics to be disadvantaged in hiring, tenure, promotion, and funding decisions (Baker, 2018) and to report less supportive work climates (e.g., collegiality) and poorer mental health (Hogan et al., 2014). Racialized scholars and Indigenous scholars also consistently report lower institutional support (Henry, Dua, James, et al., 2017; Henry, Dua, Kobayashi, et al., 2017), as well as workplace discrimination and harassment (Cropsey et al., 2008; Hurren, 2018). Sexual minority academics similarly report troubling rates of workplace harassment (e.g., one in five: American Physical Society, 2016; Rankin et al., 2010) and discrimination (David, 2017). As under-represented academics can be expected to experience the real-world implications of institutional reputability differently from their peers, further examination of how rankings correspond with the perspectives of marginalized faculty and students (as well as accompanying hiring, promotion, and equity practices) at these institutions is needed to provide a better understanding of the psychological and physical health implications of university rankings for marginalized academic groups.

Finally, future research should examine the relations between university rankings and psychological variables both longitudinally and as mediated by intervening variables to better address *how* rankings impact psychological experiences. Consistent with existing studies focused on undergraduate recruitment (Broecke, 2015; Drewes & Michael, 2006), longitudinal studies with faculty and graduate students about how they respond psychologically to changes in one's institutional ranking could be informative in terms of how personal psychological experiences (e.g., achievement emotions: pride, shame) or social-psychological variables (e.g., collective self-esteem; Crocker et al., 1994) potentially mediate the effects of these changes over time. In summary, the present findings provide initial evidence regarding the relationship between international university rankings and self-report indicators of motivation, health, and well-being in faculty and graduate students, with these novel results suggesting multiple intriguing avenues for future research on how rankings impact the lived experiences of these overlooked stakeholder populations.

REFERENCES

American Physical Society. (2016). Report: LGBT+ climate in physics. College Park, MD: American Physical Society Ad Hoc Committee on LGBT+ Issues (C-LGBT). https://www.aps.org/programs/lgbt

Anderson, G. (2006). Carving out time and space in the managerial university. *Journal of Organizational Change Management, 19*(5), 578–92. https://doi.org/10.1108/09534810610686698

Andresen, E.M. (1994). Screening for depression in well older adults: Evaluation of a short form of the CES-D. *American Journal of Preventive Medicine, 10*(2), 77–84. https://doi.org/10.1016/S0749-3797(18)30622-6

Austin, A. (2009). Cognitive apprenticeship theory and its implications for doctoral education: A case example from a doctoral program in higher and adult education. *International Journal for Academic Development, 14*(3), 173–83. https://doi.org/10.1080/13601440903106494

Baker, K.J. (2018). *Sexism ed: Essays on gender and labor in academia.* Raven Books.

Barkhuizen, N., Rothmann, S., & van de Vijver, F. (2014). Burnout and work engagement of academics in higher education institutions: Effects of dispositional optimism. *Stress and Health, 30,* 322–32. https://doi.org/10.1002/smi.2520

Biron, C., Brun, J.-P., & Ivers, H. (2008). Extent and sources of occupational stress in university staff. *Work: A Journal of Prevention, Assessment and Rehabilitation, 30*(4), 511–22.

Blix, A.G., Cruise, R.J., Mitchell, B.M., & Blix, G.G. (1994). Occupational stress among university teachers. *Educational Research, 36*(2), 157–69. https://doi.org/10.1080/0013188940360205

Boice, R. (1991). New faculty as colleagues. *International Journal of Qualitative Studies in Education, 4*(1), 29–44. https://doi.org/10.1080/0951839910040103

Brailsford, I. (2010). Motives and aspirations for doctoral study: Career, personal, and inter-personal factors in the decision to embark on a history PhD. *International Journal of Doctoral Studies, 5,* 15–27. https://doi.org/10.28945/710

Broecke, S. (2015). University rankings: Do they matter in the UK? *Education Economics, 23*(2), 137–61. https://doi.org/10.1080/09645292.2012.729328

Brown, L., & Watson, P. (2010). Understanding the experiences of female doctoral students. *Journal of Further and Higher Education, 34,* 385–404. https://doi.org/10.1080/0309877X.2010.484056

Busch, T., Fallan, L., & Pettersen, A. (1998). Disciplinary differences in job satisfaction self-efficacy, goal commitment and organizational commitment among faculty employees in Norwegian colleges: An empirical assessment of indicators of performance. *Quality in Higher Education, 4*(2), 137–57. https://doi.org/10.1080/1353832980040204

Cao, L. (2012). Differences in procrastination and motivation between undergraduate and graduate students. *Journal of the Scholarship of Teaching and Learning, 12*(2), 39–64.

Carroll, D. (2014). An investigation of the relationship between university rankings and graduate starting wages. *Journal of Institutional Research, 19*(1), 46–54.

Castelló, M., Pardo, M., Sala-Bubaré, A., & Suñe-Soler, N. (2017). Why do students consider dropping out of doctoral degrees? Institutional and personal factors. *Higher Education, 74*(6), 1053–68. https://doi.org/10.1007/s10734-016-0106-9

Clance, P.R. (1985). *The impostor phenomenon: When success makes you feel like a fake.* Bantam Books.

Clarke, M. (2007). The impact of higher education rankings on student access, choice, and opportunity. *Higher Education in Europe, 32*(1), 59–70. https://doi.org/10.1080/03797720701618880

Cohen, S., & Hoberman, H. (1983). Positive events and social supports as buffers of life change stress. *Journal of Applied Social Psychology, 13*, 99–125. https://doi.org/10.1111/j.1559-1816.1983.tb02325.x

Crocker, J., Luhtanen, R., Blaine, B., & Broadnax, S. (1994). Collective self-esteem and psychological well-being among White, Black, and Asian college students. *Personality and Social Psychology Bulletin, 20*(5), 503–13. https://doi.org/10.1177/0146167294205007

Cropsey, K.L., Masho, S.W., Shiang, R., Wikka, V., Kornstein, S.G., & Hampton, C.L. (2008). Why do faculty leave? Reasons for attrition of women and minority faculty from a medical school: Four-year results. *Journal of Women's Health, 17*(7), 1111–18. https://doi.org/10.1089/jwh.2007.0582

David, T.D. (2017). *Contextualizing LGBTQ faculty experiences: An account of sexual minority perceptions* (doctoral dissertation). University of New England, ME. https://dune.une.edu/theses/147

Davies, S., Maldonado, V., & Zarifa, D. (2014). Effectively maintaining inequality in Toronto: Predicting student destinations in Ontario universities. *Canadian Review of Sociology, 51*(1), 22–53. https://doi.org/10.1111/cars.12032

Devos, C., Boudrenghien, G., Van der Linden, N., Azzi, A., Frenay, M., Galand, B., & Klein, O. (2017). Doctoral students' experiences leading to completion or attrition: A matter of sense, progress and distress. *European Journal of Psychology of Education, 32*(1), 61–77. https://doi.org/10.1007/s10212-016-0290-0

De Welde, K., & Laursen, S.L. (2008). The "ideal type" advisor: How advisors help STEM graduate students find their "scientific feet." *Open Education Journal, 1*, 49–61. https://doi.org/10.2174/1874920800801010049

Drewes, T., & Michael, C. (2006). How do students choose a university? An analysis of applications to universities in Ontario, Canada. *Research in Higher Education, 47*(7), 781–800. https://doi.org/10.1007/s11162-006-9015-6

Dreyer, S., Dreyer, L.I., & Rankin, D.M. (2010). The health and wellbeing of staff members at a tertiary institution in New Zealand. *ICHPER-SD Journal of Research, 5*(1), 45–53.

Eccles, J.S. (2005). Subjective task value and the Eccles et al. model of achievement-related choices. In A.J. Elliot & C.S. Dweck (Eds.), *Handbook of competence and motivation* (pp. 105–21). Guilford Press.

Ellis, E.M. (2001). The impact of race and gender on graduate school socialization, satisfaction with doctoral study, and commitment to degree completion. *Western Journal of Black Studies, 25*, 30–45.

Ernst, A.F., Hoekstra, R., Wagenmakers, E.-J., Gelman, A., & van Ravenzwaaij, D. (2018). Do researchers anchor their beliefs on the outcome of an initial study? Testing the time-reversal heuristic. *Experimental Psychology, 65*(3), 158–69. https://doi.org/10.1027/1618-3169/a000402

Espeland, W., & Sauder, M. (2016). *Engines of anxiety: Academic rankings, reputation, and accountability*. Russell Sage Foundation.

Fernet, C., Guay, F., & Senécal, C. (2004). Adjusting to job demands: The role of work self-determination and job control in predicting burnout. *Journal of Vocational Behavior, 65*, 39–56. https://doi.org/10.1016/S0001-8791(03)00098-8

Flynn, S.V., Chasek, C.L., Harper, I.F., Murphy, K.M., & Jorgensen, M.F. (2012). A qualitative inquiry of the counseling dissertation process. *Counselor Education and Supervision, 51*, 242–55. https://doi.org/10.1002/j.1556-6978.2012.00018.x

Frisby, B.N., Goodboy, A.K., & Buckner, M.M. (2015). Students' instructional dissent and relationships with faculty members' burnout, commitment, satisfaction, and efficacy. *Communication Education, 64*(1), 1–18. https://doi.org/10.1080/03634523.2014.978794

Galdino, M.J.Q., Martins, J.T., Haddad, M.D.C.F.L., Robazzi, M.L.D.C.C., & Birolim, M.M. (2016). Burnout syndrome among master's and doctoral students in nursing. *Acta Paulista de Enfermagem, 29*, 100–6. https://doi.org/10.1590/1982-0194201600014

Gardner, S.K. (2013). Women faculty departures from a striving institution: Between a rock and a hard place. *Review of Higher Education, 36*, 349–70. https://doi.org/10.1353/rhe.2013.0025

Gates, G.S. (2000). Teaching-related stress: The emotional management of faculty. *Review of Higher Education, 23*(4), 469–90. https://doi.org/10.1353/rhe.2000.0016

Geraniou, E. (2010). The transitional stages in the PhD degree in mathematics in terms of students' motivation. *Educational Studies in Mathematics, 73*, 281–96. https://doi.org/10.1007/s10649-009-9205-1

Ghorpade, J., Lackritz, J., & Singh, G. (2011). Personality as a moderator of the relationship between role conflict, role ambiguity, and burnout. *Journal of Applied Social Psychology, 41*(6), 1275–98. https://doi.org/10.1111/j.1559-1816.2011.00763.x

Gomes, A.R., Faria, S., & Gonçalves, A.M. (2013). Cognitive appraisal as a mediator in the relationship between stress and burnout. *Work & Stress, 27*(4), 351–67. https://doi.org/10.1080/02678373.2013.840341

Gonzalez, S., & Bernard, H. (2006). Academic workload typologies and burnout among faculty in Seventh-Day Adventist colleges and universities in North America. *Journal of Research on Christian Education, 15*(1), 13–37. https://doi.org/10.1080/10656210609484992

Goodwin, L., Ben-Zion, I., Fear, N.T., Hotopf, M., Stansfeld, S.A., & Wessely, S. (2013). Are reports of psychological stress higher in occupational studies? A systematic review across occupational and population based studies. *PLOS ONE, 8*(11), e78693. https://doi.org/10.1371/journal.pone.0078693

Greene, H.C., O'Connor, K.A., Good, A.J., Ledford, C.C., Peel, B.B., & Zhang, G. (2008). Building a support system toward tenure: Challenges and needs of tenure-track faculty in colleges of education. *Mentoring & Tutoring: Partnership in Learning, 16*(4), 429–47. https://doi.org/10.1080/13611260802433791

Gube, J., Getenet, S., Satariyan, A., & Muhammad, Y. (2017). Towards "operating within" the field: Doctoral students' views of supervisors' discipline expertise. *International Journal of Doctoral Studies, 12*, 1–16. https://doi.org/10.28945/3641

Gutek, B.A., Searle, S., & Klepa, L. (1991). Rational versus gender role explanations for work-family conflict. *Journal of Applied Psychology, 76*, 560–8. https://doi .org/10.1037/0021-9010.76.4.560

Hackett, R.D., Lapierre, L.M., & Hausdorf, P.A. (2001). Understanding the links between work commitment constructs. *Journal of Vocational Behavior, 58*, 392–413. https://doi.org/10.1006/jvbe.2000.1776

Hagenauer, G., & Volet, S. (2014). "I don't think I could, you know, just teach without any emotion": Exploring the nature and origin of university teachers' emotions. *Research Papers in Education, 29*(2), 240–62. https://doi.org/10.1080/02671522.2012 .754929

Hall, N.C. (2015, 1 July). @AcademicsSay: The story behind a social-media experiment. *Chronicle of Higher Education.* http://chronicle.com/article/AcademicsSay -The-Story/231195

Hall, N.C. (2016, July). *The SAS Project: A case study of motivation research recruitment via social media.* Paper presented at the annual meeting of the Society for the Study of Motivation, Gdansk, Poland.

Hall, N.C. (2017, April). *@AcademicsSay: A case study in faculty engagement via Twitter.* Paper presented at the annual meeting of the American Educational Research Association, San Antonio, TX.

Hall, N.C., Hladkyj, S., Perry, R.P., & Ruthig, J.C. (2004). The role of attributional retraining and elaborative learning in college students' academic development. *Journal of Social Psychology, 144*, 591–612. https://doi.org/10.3200/SOCP.144.6.591 -612

Hall, N.C., Hubbard, K.A., & Copeland, L. (2017, April). *Interventions gone wild: Achievement effects of online control- and value-enhancing programs for first-year students.* Paper presented at the annual meeting of the American Educational Research Association, San Antonio, TX.

Hardré, P.L., Beesley, A.D., Miller, R.L., & Pace, T.M (2011). Faculty motivation to do research: Across disciplines in research-extensive universities. *Journal of the Professoriate, 5*(1), 35–69.

Hein, S.F., Lawson, G., & Rodriguez, C.P. (2011). Supervisee incompatibility and its influence on triadic supervision: An examination of doctoral student supervisors' perspectives. *Counselor Education and Supervision, 50*, 422–36. https://doi.org /10.1002/j.1556-6978.2011.tb01925.x

Henry, F., Dua, E., James, C.E., Kobayashi, A., Li, P., Ramos, H., & Smith, M.S. (2017). *The equity myth: Racialization and Indigeneity at Canadian universities.* UBC Press.

Henry, F., Dua, E., Kobayashi, A., James, C., Li, P., Ramos, H., & Smith, M.S. (2017b). Race, racialization and Indigeneity in Canadian universities. *Race Ethnicity and Education, 20*, 300–14. https://doi.org/10.1080/13613324.2016.1260226

Hogan, R.L., & McKnight, M.A. (2007). Exploring burnout among university online instructors: An initial investigation. *Internet and Higher Education, 10*(2), 117–24. https://doi.org/10.1016/j.iheduc.2007.03.001

Hogan, V., Hogan, M., Hodgins, M., Kinman, G., & Bunting, B. (2014). An examination of gender differences in the impact of individual and organisational factors on work hours, work-life conflict and psychological strain in academics. *Irish Journal of Psychology, 35*(2–3), 133–50. https://doi.org/10.1080/03033910 .2015.1011193

Horstschräer, J. (2012). University rankings in action? The importance of rankings and an excellence competition for university choice of high-ability students. *Economics of Education Review, 31*(6), 1162–76. https://doi.org/10.1016 /j.econedurev.2012.07.018

Hoskins, C.M., & Goldberg, A.D. (2005). Doctoral student persistence in counselor education programs: Student–program match. *Counselor Education and Supervision, 44*(3), 175–88. https://doi.org/10.1002/j.1556-6978.2005.tb01745.x

Huang, L.L., Chen, S.W., & Chien, C.L. (2015). The effect of university ranking on learning satisfaction: Social identities and self-identity as the suppressor and mediators. *Asian Journal of Social Psychology, 18*(1), 33–42. https://doi.org/10.1111 /ajsp.12064

Hurren, W. (2018, July). Breaking the code of silence on sexual harassment within the faculty. *University Affairs*. https://www.universityaffairs.ca/opinion/in-my-opinion /breaking-the-code-of-silence-on-sexual-harassment-within-the-faculty

Hyun, J.K., Quinn, B.C., Madon, T., & Lustig, S. (2006). Graduate student mental health: Needs assessment and utilization of counseling services. *Journal of College Student Development, 47*, 247–66. https://doi.org/10.1353/csd.2006.0030

Jones, E.E., & Nisbett, R.E. (1971). The actor and the observer divergent perceptions of the causes of behavior. In E.E. Jones, D.E. Kanouse, H.H. Kelley, R.E. Nisbett, S. Valins, & B. Weiner (Eds.), *Attribution: Perceiving the causes of behavior* (pp. 79–94). General Learning Press.

Juniper, B., Walsh, E., Richardson, A., & Morley, B. (2012). A new approach to evaluating the well-being of PhD research students. *Assessment & Evaluation in Higher Education, 37*, 563–76. https://doi.org/10.1080/02602938.2011.555816

Kinman, G. (2008). Work stressors, health and sense of coherence in UK academic employees. *Educational Psychology, 28*(7), 823–35. https://doi.org/10.1080 /01443410802366298

Kinman, G., & Jones, F. (2004). *Working to the limit*. AUT Publications.

Kousta, S., Ferguson, C., & Ganley, E. (2016). Meta-research: Broadening the scope of *PLOS Biology*. *PLOS Biology, 14*(1), e1002334. https://doi.org/10.1371/journal .pbio.1002434

Kusurkar, R., Kruitwagen, C., ten Cate, O., & Croiset, G. (2010). Effects of age, gender and educational background on strength of motivation for medical school. *Advances in Health Sciences Education, 15*, 303–13. https://doi.org/10.1007/s10459-009-9198-7

Lackritz, J.R. (2004). Exploring burnout among university faculty: Incidence, performance, and demographic issues. *Teaching and Teacher Education, 20*(7), 713–29. https://doi.org/10.1016/j.tate.2004.07.002

Lambie, G.W., & Vaccaro, N. (2011). Doctoral counselor education students' levels of research self-efficacy, perceptions of the research training environment, and interest in research. *Counselor Education and Supervision, 50,* 243–58. https://doi .org/10.1002/j.1556-6978.2011.tb00122.x

Leijen, Ä., Lepp, L., & Remmik, M. (2016). Why did I drop out? Former students' recollections about their study process and factors related to leaving the doctoral studies. *Studies in Continuing Education, 38*(2), 129–44. https://doi.org/10.1080/015 8037X.2015.1055463

Levecque, K., Anseel, F., De Beuckelaer, A., Van der Heyden, J., & Gisle, L. (2017). Work organization and mental health problems in PhD students. *Research Policy, 46*(4), 868–79. https://doi.org/10.1016/j.respol.2017.02.008

Li, Y., Li, J., & Sun, Y. (2013). Young faculty job perceptions in the midst of Chinese higher education reform: The case of Zhejiang University. *Asia Pacific Journal of Education, 33*(3), 273–94. https://doi.org/10.1080/02188791.2013.787388

Lin, Y. (2012). Life experiences of dissatisfied science and engineering graduate students in Taiwan. *College Student Journal, 46,* 51–66.

Litalien, D., & Guay, F. (2015). Dropout intentions in PhD studies: A comprehensive model based on interpersonal relationships and motivational resources. *Contemporary Educational Psychology, 41,* 218–31. https://doi.org/10.1016 /j.cedpsych.2015.03.004

Litalien, D., Guay, F., Morin, A.J.S. (2015). Motivation for PhD studies: Scale development and validation. *Learning and Individual Differences, 41,* 1–13. https:// doi.org/10.1016/j.lindif.2015.05.006

Lovitts, B.E. (2001). *Leaving the ivory tower: The causes and consequences of departure from doctoral study.* Rowman & Littlefield.

Lundberg, U., & Cooper, C.L. (2010). *The science of occupational health: Stress, psychobiology, and the new world of work.* Wiley-Blackwell.

Mangan, J., Hughes, A., Davies, P., & Slack, K. (2010). Fair access, achievement and geography: Explaining the association between social class and students' choice of university. *Studies in Higher Education, 35*(3), 335–50. https://doi .org/10.1080/03075070903131610

Maslach, C., Jackson, S.E., & Leiter, M.P. (1996). *Maslach burnout inventory manual* (3rd ed.). CPP, Inc.

McAlpine, L., & Akerlind, G. (Eds.) (2010). *Becoming an academic: International perspectives.* Palgrave Macmillan.

McAlpine, L., & McKinnon, M. (2013). Supervision – the most variable of variables: Student perspectives. *Studies in Continuing Education, 35,* 265–80. https://doi.org/10 .1080/0158037X.2012.746227

McAuley, E., Duncan, T.E., & Russell, D. (1992). Measuring causal attributions: The revised Causal Dimension Scale (CDSII). *Personality and Social Psychology Bulletin, 18,* 566–73. https://doi.org/10.1177/0146167292185006

Moe, A., Pazzaglia, F., & Ronconi, L. (2010). When being able is not enough: The combined value of positive affect and self-efficacy for job satisfaction in teaching. *Teaching and Teacher Education, 26,* 1145–53. https://doi.org/10.1016/j.tate.2010.02.010

Mullen, C.A., & Forbes, S.A. (2000). Untenured faculty: Issues of transition, adjustment and mentorship. *Mentoring and Tutoring, 8*(1), 31–46. https://doi.org/10.1080/713685508

Navarro, M.L.A., Mas, M.B., & Jiménez, A.M.L. (2010). Working conditions, burnout and stress symptoms in university professors: Validating a structural model of the mediating effect of perceived personal competence. *Spanish Journal of Psychology, 13*(1), 284–96. https://doi.org/10.1017/S1138741600003863

Nir, A.E., & Zilberstein-Levy, R. (2006). Planning for academic excellence: Tenure and professional considerations. *Studies in Higher Education, 31*(5), 537–54. https://doi.org/10.1080/03075070600922725

O'Meara, K., Jaeger, A., Eliason, J., Grantham, A., Cowdery, K., Mitchall, A., & Zhang, K.J. (2014). By design: How departments influence graduate student agency in career advancement. *International Journal of Doctoral Studies, 9,* 155–77. https://doi.org/10.28945/2048

Otero-López, J.M., Mariño, M.J.S., & Bolaño, C.C. (2008). An integrating approach to the study of burnout in university professors. *Psicothema, 20*(4), 766–72.

Pallos, H., Yamada, N., & Okawa, M. (2005). Graduate student blues: The situation in Japan. *Journal of College Student Psychotherapy, 20*(2), 5–15. https://doi.org/10.1300/J035v20n02_02

Pekrun, R., Goetz, T., Frenzel, A.C., Barchfeld, P., & Perry, R.P. (2011). Measuring emotions in students' learning and performance: The Achievement Emotions Questionnaire (AEQ). *Contemporary Educational Psychology, 36*(1), 36–48. https://doi.org/10.1016/j.cedpsych.2010.10.002

Pollitt, C., & Bouckaert, G. (2004). *Public management reform: A comparative analysis.* Oxford University Press.

Ragazzia, M., & Ghidinia, F. (2017). Environmental sustainability of universities: Critical analysis of a green ranking. *Energy Procedia, 119,* 111–20. https://doi.org/10.1016/j.egypro.2017.07.054

Rankin, S., Weber, G.N., Blumenfeld, W.J., & Frazer, S. (2010). *2010 state of higher education for lesbian, gay, bisexual and transgender people.* Q Research Institute for Higher Education. https://www.campuspride.org/wp-content/uploads/campuspride2010lgbtreportssummary.pdf

Rosser, S.V., & Lane, E.O.N. (2002). Key barriers for academic institutions seeking to retain female scientists and engineers: Family-unfriendly policies, low numbers, stereotypes, and harassment. *Journal of Women and Minorities in Science and Engineering, 8*(2), 161–89. https://doi.org/10.1615/JWomenMinorScienEng.v8.i2.40

Rothmann, S., & Barkhuizen, N. (2008). Burnout of academic staff in South African higher education institutions. *South African Journal of Higher Education, 22*(2), 439–56. https://doi.org/10.4314/sajhe.v22i2.25796

Rothmann, S., Barkhuizen, N., & Tytherleigh, Y.M. (2008). Model of work-related ill health of academic staff in a South African higher education institution. *South African Journal of Higher Education, 22*(2), 404–22. https://doi.org/10.4314/sajhe.v22i2.25794

Ryan, R.M., & Deci, E.L. (2009). Promoting self-determined school engagement: Motivation, learning, and well-being. In K.R. Wentzel & A. Wigfield (Eds.), *Handbook of motivation at school* (pp. 171–96). Routledge.

Sabagh, Z., Hall, N.C., & Saroyan, A. (2018). Antecedents, correlates, and consequences of faculty burnout. *Educational Research, 60*(2), 1–26. https://doi.org/10.1080/00131881.2018.1461573

Sala-Bubaré, A., & Castelló, M. (2016). Exploring the relationship between doctoral students' experiences and research community positioning. *Studies in Continuing Education, 39*(1), 16–34. https://doi.org/10.1080/0158037X.2016.1216832

Salimzadeh, R., Saroyan, A., & Hall, N.C. (2017). Examining the factors impacting academics' psychological well-being: A review of research. *International Education Research, 5*(1), 13–44. https://doi.org/10.12735/ier.v5n1p13

Sang, X., Teo, S.T., Cooper, C.L., & Bohle, P. (2013). Modelling occupational stress and employee health and wellbeing in a Chinese higher education institution. *Higher Education Quarterly, 67*(1), 15–39. https://doi.org/10.1111/j.1468-2273.2012.00529.x

Schunk, D.H., & Pajares, F. (2009). Self-efficacy theory. In K.R. Wentzel & A. Wigfield (Eds.), *Handbook of motivation at school* (pp. 35–53). Routledge.

Shen, X., Yang, Y.L., Wang, Y., Liu, L., Wang, S., & Wang, L. (2014). The association between occupational stress and depressive symptoms and the mediating role of psychological capital among Chinese university teachers: A cross-sectional study. *BMC Psychiatry, 14*(1), 329. https://doi.org/10.1186/s12888-014-0329-1

Simmons, N. (2011). Caught with their constructs down? Teaching development in the pre-tenure years. *International Journal for Academic Development, 16*(3), 229–41. https://doi.org/10.1080/1360144X.2011.596706

Singh, S.N., & Bush, R.F. (1998). Research burnout in tenured marketing professors: An empirical investigation. *Journal of Marketing Education, 20*(1), 4–15. https://doi.org/10.1177/027347539802000102

Solem, M.N., & Foote, K.E. (2004). Concerns, attitudes, and abilities of early-career geography faculty. *Annals of the Association of American Geographers, 94*(4), 889–912. https://doi.org/10.1080/03098260600717299

Solem, M.N., Hopwood, N., & Schlemper, M.B. (2011). Experiencing graduate school: A comparative analysis of students in geography programs. *Professional Geographer, 63*, 1–17. https://doi.org/10.1080/00330124.2010.533547

Stubb, J., Pyhältö, K., & Lonka, K. (2012). The experienced meaning of working with a PhD thesis. *Scandinavian Journal of Educational Research, 56,* 439–56. https://doi.org /10.1080/00313831.2011.599422

Stupnisky, R.H., Hall, N.C., Daniels, L.M., & Mensah, E. (2017). Testing a model of pretenure faculty members' teaching and research success: Motivation as a mediator of balance, expectations, and collegiality. *Journal of Higher Education, 88*(3), 376–400. https://doi.org/10.1080/00221546.2016.1272317

Stupnisky, R.H., Hall, N.C., & Pekrun, R. (2019). The emotions of pretenure faculty: Implications for teaching and research success. *Review of Higher Education, 42*(4), 1489–1526. https://doi.org/10.1353/rhe.2019.0073

Stupnisky, R.H., Pekrun, R., & Lichtenfeld, S. (2016). New faculty members' emotions: A mixed-method study. *Studies in Higher Education, 41*(7), 1167–88. https://doi.org /10.1080/03075079.2014.968546

Stupnisky, R.H., Weaver-Hightower, M., & Kartoshkina, Y. (2015). Exploring and testing predictors of new faculty success: A mixed-method study. *Studies in Higher Education, 40*(2), 368–90. https://doi.org/10.1080/03075079.2013.842220

Sverdlik, A., Hall, N.C., McAlpine, L., & Hubbard, K.A. (2018). The PhD experience: A review of the factors influencing doctoral students' completion, achievement, and well-being. *International Journal of Doctoral Studies, 13,* 361–88. https://doi .org/10.28945/4113

Tanaka, M., & Watanabea, Y. (2012). Academic and family conditions associated with intrinsic academic motivation in Japanese medical students: A pilot study. *Health Education Journal, 71,* 358–64. https://doi.org/10.1177/0017896911401004

Thies, K., & Kordts-Freudinger, R. (2019). German higher education academic staff's positive emotions through work domains. *International Journal of Educational Research, 98,* 1–12. https://doi.org/10.1016/j.ijer.2019.08.004

Times Higher Education (2016, September). *World University Rankings 2016–2017 methodology.* https://www.timeshighereducation.com/world-university-rankings /methodology-world-university-rankings-2016-2017

Tobin, D.L. (1995). *Coping Strategies Inventory: Short form.* Unpublished scale. http://www.ohioupsychology.com/files/images/holroyd_lab/ CopingStrategiesInventory32item.pdf

Tümkaya, S. (2007). Burnout and humor relationship among university lecturers. *Humor, 20*(1), 73–92. https://doi.org/10.1515/HUMOR.2007.004

Tytherleigh, M., Webb, C., Cooper, C., & Ricketts, C. (2005). Occupational stress in UK higher education institutions: A comparative study of all staff categories. *Higher Education Research & Development, 24*(1), 41–61. https://doi .org/10.1080/0729436052000318569

Uqdah, A.L., Tyler, K.M., & DeLoach, C. (2009). Academic attitudes and psychological well-being of Black American psychology graduate students. *Negro Educational Review, 60,* 121–2.

Van den Broeck, A., Vansteenkiste, M., De Witte, H., Soenens, B., & Lens, W. (2010). Capturing autonomy, competence, and relatedness at work: Construction and initial validation of the Work-Related Basic Need Satisfaction Scale. *Journal of Occupational & Organizational Psychology, 83*, 981–1002. https://doi .org/10.1348/096317909X481382

van Emmerik, H. (2002). Gender differences in the effects of coping assistance on the reduction of burnout in academic staff. *Work and Stress, 16*(3), 251–63. https://doi .org/10.1080/0267837021000034593

van Emmerik, H. (2004). For better and for worse: Adverse working conditions and the beneficial effects of mentoring. *Career Development International, 9*(4), 358–73. https://doi.org/10.1108/13620430410526157

Vera, M., Salanova, M., & Martín, B. (2010). University faculty and work-related well-being: The importance of the triple work profile. *Electronic Journal of Research in Educational Psychology, 8*(2), 581–602. https://doi.org/10.25115/ejrep.v8i21.1373

Virtanen, V., Taina, J., & Pyhältö, K. (2017). What disengages doctoral students in the biological and environmental sciences from their doctoral studies? *Studies in Continuing Education, 39*(1), 71–86. https://doi.org/10.1080/015803 7X.2016.1250737

Watts, J., & Robertson, N. (2011). Burnout in university teaching staff: A systematic literature review. *Educational Research, 53*(1), 33–50. https://doi.org/10.1080/00131 881.2011.552235

Weiner, B. (2010). The development of an attribution-based theory of motivation: A history of ideas. *Educational Psychologist, 45*(1), 28–36. https://doi .org/10.1080/00461520903433596

Wolfston, J. (2016, 5 July). College admissions favor the rich. *Hechinger Report*. http:// hechingerreport.org/college-admissions-favor-rich-lets-turn-around-taxpayer -funded-tuition-relief-becomes-another-handout-wealthy

Wyatt, T., & Oswalt, S.B. (2013). Comparing mental health issues among undergraduate and graduate students. *American Journal of Health Education, 44*(2), 96–107. https://doi.org/10.1080/19325037.2013.764248

Zhang, Q., & Zhu, W. (2008). Exploring emotion in teaching: Emotional labor, burnout, and satisfaction in Chinese higher education. *Communication Education, 57*(1), 105–22. https://doi.org/10.1080/03634520701586310

Zhong, J., You, J., Gan, Y., Zhang, Y., Lu, C., & Wang, H. (2009). Job stress, burnout, depression symptoms, and physical health among Chinese university teachers. *Psychological Reports, 105*(3), 1248–54. https://doi.org/10.2466 /pr0.105.3F.1248-1254

Zimmerman, B.J. (2011). Motivational sources and outcomes of self-regulated learning and performance. In B.J. Zimmerman and D.H. Schunk (Eds.), *Handbook of self-regulation of learning and performance* (pp. 49–64). Routledge.

10 Beyond Rankings and Impact Factors

MICHELLE STACK AND ANDRÉ ELIAS MAZAWI

The recent university admissions scandal in the US demonstrates the risks wealthy parents are willing to take to ensure their offspring are admitted to top-ranked schools. In 2019, thirty-three parents were indicted for bribing coaches and college admissions officers to get their children into top-ranked schools. Thirteen coaches at schools, including Stanford, Yale, and UCLA were charged in federal court for participating in what the US attorney general for the District of Massachusetts called a nationwide conspiracy (United States Attorney's Office for the District of Massachusetts, 2019). This is not to say that only top-ranked schools participate in such activities, but the rankings hold these institutions up as something all others should aspire to. One wonders then, what do rankings tell us about the politics and ethics of ranked institutions?

Geopolitics and Rankings

Stromquist (2013) points to the influence of the World Bank in promoting the idea of world-class universities and its belief in the need to pick winners and losers to produce competitive knowledge economies. Rankings, therefore, must be approached in relation to broader geopolitical dynamics, which have implications for how universities organize themselves, shape their governance structures, and position themselves concerning research, labour market opportunities, and recruitment of faculty and students. While neo-institutional theory would consider these isomorphic processes as part of the influences that rankings exert on organizational policies and practices, the chapters in this volume indicate that the effects of rankings are far from uniform, neither within institutions nor across institutions, or even countries. Rather, what emerges are highly contextualized dynamics, in which rankings shape the operation and governance of higher education research in multifaceted ways. What is clear, however, is that rankings – as semiotic systems of representation – have become sites of struggle and competition, and intense ones at that, in which vying for visibility and legitimacy is paramount. This view is supported by Meyer (2017) who points out that today's rankings have parallels to battles of the past:

> The spirit in which these reforms are pursued bears an uncanny resemblance not to the celebrated reforms of a Wilhelm von Humboldt, but to Humboldt's competitor Napoleon Bonaparte, who engineered France's polytechnical university reforms, designed to harness the power of the intellect to the project of national economic and military strength. Ironically, though, even in the realm of promoting economic and social development, the Napoleonic polytechnics were decidedly less successful than the Humboldtian universities built on the integration of teaching with research, autonomy with community, and moral formation with scientific research. (p. 4)

As sites of struggles and competitive advantages, rankings – and the hierarchies they seek to capture and institutionalize – are potent geopolitical tools. They shape higher education recruitment strategies and the economic horizons associated with them. They also offer venues for the exertion of soft power and the articulation of hegemonic positions in the determination of particular visions of the university and its roles in society.

While the ubiquity and influence of rankings mark the growing centrality of higher education in domestic and international forms of stratification, they also signal the emergence of what Walter Mignolo (2002) refers to as the "geopolitics of knowledge." To understand the implications of these geopolitical dynamics, it is important to reflect critically, less on the rankings as indicators of value, quality, reputation, and scholarly output and more on rankings as multifaceted geopolitical codes that work to naturalize inequity as necessary for the development of society and human knowledge.

Yet, the geopolitics of knowledge conceal more complex, contradictory, and ambivalent webs of power relations and struggles that underpin the emergence and consolidation of regional and global articulations of competing higher education opportunities. As Weiler (2005) states, this "ambivalence" is a "function of societal and political contradictions about the role of knowledge and the purposes of the university" (p. 177). Thus, on the one hand, university rankings claim to measure aspects associated with the quality of higher education, while on the other they are blurring what these measures of quality stand for within the broader competition over resources, recruitment, and the marginalization of competing conceptions of research and knowledge. This second aspect associated with rankings is well captured by Robertson and Keeling (2008). They observe that, with the emergence of competitive international higher education networks, "policies, programmes and practices have been increasingly co-opted and shaped by wider geo-strategic political and economic interests" (p. 221). These processes underpin the formation of a "multi-scalar, multi-centric relation within and across spaces" of higher education, "where new capabilities are emerging to disrupt – and reconfigure – the balance of power" (p. 236). The contributions in this book are indicative of what we call "the mechanics of disruption," effected by university rankings in relation to the plurality of purposes served by higher education institutions. In this regard, Shahjahan and Morgan (2016) point out that studies of higher education have not yet fully clarified how differential geographies of power and dependency emerge among higher education institutions and that these "remain largely unaddressed" (p. 92). This observation is relevant, we argue, to the study of university rankings and their geopolitical implications. While rankings are frequently framed within economic, managerial, or policymaking narratives, the impacts of geopolitics, military conflicts, and political and ideological rivalries on higher education are simply ignored, dismissed, or belittled. Clearly then, considered geopolitically, the nexus between university rankings, higher education governance, the organization of academic work, and modes of knowledge generation cannot be fully appreciated without accounting for the ways in which university rankings complicate the contested aims of higher education. Moreover, drawing on Novelli and Cardozo (2012), we argue that policymakers build on these articulations of university rankings as "a key discursive justification" (p. 197) for strategically promoting higher education recruitment in different parts of the world. Not less, considered from a perspective of geopolitics of knowledge, tensions over the enactment of hegemonic "spaces" or "regions" through higher education signal the "crucial role of 'educational diplomacy' for imperialism of the capitalist sort" (Hartmann, 2008, p. 208) in view of facilitating foreign policy goals and the configuration of highly appealing university recruitment hubs (Altbach, 1995, p. 455; El-Khairy, 2010). As shown by Lee (2015), in the Asia-Pacific region, university "hubs" reflect a "strong desire to parlay leadership in higher education into geopolitical influence" (p. 85). Lee notes that political elites seek to leverage "economic interests and soft power rationales" in ways that "amplify the impact of an education hub" (p. 86) on the state's perception as a "global superpower" and as an "indispensible ... regional broker ... through education, training, research, and norm dissemination" (p. 87). The role played by university dynamics in sustaining such strategic visions is crucial. The implications of these processes transcend questions regarding higher education governance reforms in relation to the "immediate returns on neoliberal pursuits" (Lee, 2015, p. 86). Rather, as Mignolo (2003) suggests, these processes necessitate an examination of the involvement of higher education in enacting modes of coloniality and geo-epistemic marginality between and within societies and world regions as part of wider geographies of power difference that shape their relations. Contributors to this book suggest that university rankings could be approached as manifest articulations of coloniality. Quijano (2007) explains that coloniality refers to the "history of power" (p. 168) that continues to operate across geographical spaces and organizational sites, long after the disappearance of colonialism, in the guise of projects of modernity and progress. One could argue that the coloniality promoted by university rankings is thus "constitutive" of a "form of domination" – epistemic, institutional, and material – that shapes "subordinate relations, not only in the European view but also in the eyes of their own bearers" (pp. 168, 170). In that sense, university rankings enact the"logic of coloniality" precisely on the basis of a "measurable" ordering of quality. University rankings thus impose as universal what is effectively a culturalized mode of knowledge generation (see Mignolo, 2003, p. 100). The result of this "geopolitics of knowledge" is a double "fracture," epistemic and spatial, which reproduces the "dependence" of Global South societies on universities located in industrialized societies, "while at the same time disrupting the memories of the colonies." University rankings thus impose an "internal colonialism" that marginalizes the relevance and pertinence of Indigenous knowledges in higher education institutions and the possibilities associated with their mobilization towards meaningful development (p. 102). This "double fracture" has material and institutional consequences. Within higher education, it "manifests itself at the level of the disciplines" (p. 110), particularly in how the social sciences and humanities are organized in relation to the sciences and how both marginalize Indigenous ways of knowing. It also inscribes within higher education institutions an academic epistemic culture that consecrates the hegemony of Eurocentric systems of classification through which academics come to perceive, understand, and research themselves, their cultures, and societies using knowledge generated by centres of power (Mignolo, 2009). One could argue that these systems of classification operate as "normative vocabularies" (Skinner, 1999): in the hands of policymakers, they serve as ideological and rhetorical "tools and weapons of debate" (p. 62) within which knowledge can be enunciated, sanctioned, and appraised under the claim of objectivity and credibility. Ultimately, the vocabularies promoted by university rankings shape the way academics embody their coloniality within the context of geopolitics, impacting their institutional and social statuses and their freedoms. Such an analytical view resonates with Mignolo's (2009) observation that "the geopolitics of knowledge goes hand in hand with the geopolitics of knowing" (p. 2).

The significance of the above observations transcends the bounds of how neo-liberal policy pursuits or globalization (however defined) impact higher education. Rather, these observations focus on how university rankings are involved in producing material and symbolic geographies of power by promoting university models that actively shape the world's regional landscapes in higher education, as well as their external relations among various world regions. In sum, based on the chapters included in this volume, university rankings operate as proxies of coloniality, through which the hegemonic positions of Global North higher education institutions are reproduced within ever-shifting configurations of international relations and political economies. The geopolitics of rankings indicate that higher education institutions are part of the broader shifting terrain between territory, authority, and rights, as articulated by Saskia Sassen (2006). What this means for Global South universities is that the knowledge they produce remains largely confined to the margins of the world economy and in knowledge mobilization (Aliet, 2007; Mazrui, 2003; Santos, 2005).

One should note that efforts to rank higher education institutions for particular attributes of quality operate subtle agendas of modernity. Such efforts are nothing new. For instance, Hammarfelt et al. (2017) observe that Cattell, who invented a 1905 ranking of "eminent men," was a supporter of eugenics. At the time, there was great concern about the decline of the British Empire and a sense that "the fate of the national was dependent on the overall quality of 'men' and the measurement and promotion of eminence was deemed as an important task" (p. 396). Cattell set out to find the "eminent men" and develop ideas around how to bring them all into the same institutions that would allow them to flourish and regenerate what he considered a superior society based, primarily, on notions of masculinity and whiteness. He developed surveys and ways of testing reputation that became rankings.

In approaching rankings, and what they stand for in the broader order of things, the challenge is to learn from such constructions of higher education at different points of human history and in different world regions. While not dealing directly with rankings, the works of Linda T. Smith, Sandra Harding, and Linda Alcoff, to name but a few, are distinctively relevant to understanding the geopolitical and political-economic codes that underpin the current constructions of rankings from an Indigenous, feminist, and civil rights movements perspectives. These works raise critical questions about whose science and whose knowledge (Harding, 1991) do particular constructions of scholarship and knowledge privilege and serve. In the following pages, we extend our discussions, unpacking each of the above aspects.

University Rankings and Beliefs

Raewyn Connell (2014) observes that university rankings would make sense if there is a belief in a

> homogeneous domain of knowledge on which the measuring operations may be performed. In this model, there is a single domain of biochemistry, on which all biochemistry journals and their contributors can be arrayed and ranked. There is a single domain of sociology, a single domain of philosophy and so on. The Web

of Knowledge stretches out smoothly in all directions, embracing all countries and connecting all practitioners in a global, homogeneous tissue. (p. 211)

Connell, citing the work of social scientists on six continents, points to the falsehood of such an assumption and its premises. In the case of the top-ranked, wealthiest universities, the "rules of the game" (Bourdieu, 1990) continue to provide them with a large piece of the pie. Nevertheless, for the vast majority of universities that do not make it into world university rankings, the "game" frequently means spending a large chunk of limited resources on marketing rather than on students.

It is also important to consider this dynamic over the backdrop of the emergence of internationalization as a driving force in the repositioning of higher education institutions towards recruitment. Tamrat and Teferra (2018) point to a change in how internationalization has been operationalized since the 1990s. Prior to the 1990s, internationalization was based more in academic exchange and cooperation; however, for the most part, higher education institutions in the Global North have "shifted to a more competitive posture as compared to those in the developing world that had not yet abandoned their cooperative stance" (p. 439). Brendan Cantwell (2017) argues that global university rankings are both symptom and cause of global competition and that "rankings also provide a set of metrics that facilitate competition, define competitiveness, normalize and celebrate competition" (p. 311). Cantwell's argument can be extended to analysing the rankings industry as part of global trading arrangements that encompass educational programs and services (e.g., offshore campus), which is similar to the movement of other forms of industrial goods. In the context of the now superseded North American Free Trade Agreement (NAFTA), for example, the aim was "to eliminate barriers in trade, and facilitate the cross-border movement of goods and services between Parties" (Article 102, section A). This movement of goods included, among other things, "the accreditation of schools or academic programs" at the post-secondary level, their licensing, and the mutual determination of their ethical standards and codes of conduct of their members (see Annex 1210.5, section A).

Notwithstanding this connection, rankings play out within contexts and dynamics that transcend the political economy of competitive advantages over recruitment. The search for channels of soft power, through rankings and their cultural impacts, represents important foreign policy goals, whether in relation to national universities in Latin America, Africa, or the Middle East (Altbach, 1995). For instance, the first world university ranking was developed in China as part of Chinese government policy. The policies aimed to increase the influence of Chinese universities through modelling their institutions after universities in America that were seen as powerful drivers in the twentieth century. A century earlier, America modelled their universities on the influential German universities of the nineteenth century (Jöns & Hoyler, 2013). Jöns and Hoyler (2013) argue that disparities between have and have-not regions of the world provide evidence producing "highly partial geographies of global higher education," based partly in broader inequity and a narrow focus on scholarship and science, privileges an Anglo-American audit culture. However, as Beck (2012) reminds us, this is not inevitable. Currently, there are many examples of internationalization based in gaining even more resources for the Global North; however, it is possible to look to paths towards ethical engagement. Part of this process entails questioning the dissonance of rankings that prize capitalist accumulation as world class and looking at the commitments of higher education institutions towards sustainability of the planet. The challenges posed by the COVID-19 pandemic since late 2019 and widespread environmental crises, for example, can serve as a good illustration. Ilieva et al. (2014) point to how current forms of internalization cannot be sustainable from a climate change viewpoint or the point of view of human language and cultural sustainability. Sustainability also refers to diversity within humans, and here they note the destruction of language and ways of learning.

In this collection, Lloyd and Ordorika examine rankings in relation to the Global South and argue that the focus on rankings has narrowed who and what counts, claiming that this has implications that go far beyond higher education to the role of the state in facilitating collective goals. Sá, Kachynska, Sabzalieva, and Martinez also take a comparative approach (Central Asia, CEE, and Latin America) and point to the GURs both rewarding and reinforcing a particularly Anglo-European university tradition as world class. They show how rankings become normalized and condition the policymaker concerning "the way problems are framed and the policy alternatives to address them, which become articulated through the assumption of inter-institutional competition." However, they reveal differences in how global policy diffusion occurs and how governments respond to rankings. Shahjahan, Estera, and Vellanki look at how the geopolitics of knowledge that privilege the Global North are visualized and spatialized on the websites of the *Times Higher Education* rankings and the *U.S. News* rankings. As the authors demonstrate, not only do rankings privilege territorial destinations of higher education, but they also link subtle forms of territorial primacies that reinforce the construction of where legitimate science and scholarship is located and produced. Together the three chapters elucidate the role of rankings in reinforcing economic, spatial, visual, and symbolic geopolitics of knowledge that privilege the Global North.

Knowledge and Rankings

The chapters in this section of the book make evident that university rankings and journal impact factors are interconnected. Academics and non-academics alike are often incredulous concerning who and what counts in determining a university's ranking and the influence of publishing monopolies on rankings.

The three chapters in this section illuminate how rankings influence the cost of knowledge and what knowledge is represented as valuable. When global rankings become central to policy and practices, journal impact factors come to dominate the story of who and what is excellence and where excellence exists. As Morrison demonstrates, academics are pressured to publish in major journals that are owned by one of five companies. They do this for free. They also peer-review the articles of others for free, and some serve as editors for the journals. Some universities give various incentives to encourage academics to publish more in top journals. The public pays for much of this research in several ways, including taxes, but they hit an expensive paywall if they try to access research. Universities also invest millions of dollars to secure access to research produced by their own faculty and that of other institutions. Universities supply data to rankings corporations (e.g., number of international students, faculty-to-student ratio) for free. Rankings corporations use this data to generate an ever-growing list of profitable rankings products. They have developed an integrated business model that is beneficial for interconnected rankers and companies but less profitable for education or the dissemination of accessible research. In his chapter, St. Clair shows how the focus on Global North metrics further marginalizes local knowledge and regional tertiary educational development in the Global South. Rankings and journal impact factors are essential to understanding why universities are competing to be the same globally. It is important to capture how the local and the regional are impacted in different ways by metrics claiming to be neutral and global. In her chapter, Chou argues the greater losses of this competition for regions that do not use English as a first language and are located outside of the Global North.

Larivière et al. (2015) demonstrate that the academic publishing industry is profitable economically yet obsolete from a technological point of view. It fulfills mainly symbolic functions (p. 12) needed by scholars – both senior and junior – to amass academically sanctioned forms of capital necessary for tenure and to receive or maintain grant funding and status. These authors observe:

> The negative effect of various bibliometric indicators in the evaluation of individual researchers cannot be understated. The counting of papers indexed by large-scale bibliometric databases – which mainly cover journals published by commercial publishers ... creates a strong incentive for researchers to publish in these journals, and thus reinforces the control of commercial publishers on the scientific community. (Larivière et al., 2015, p. 12)

It is crucial to reflect on the implications of Larivière et al.'s observation, which addresses the centrality of quantitative measures in the valuing of scholarship. It points to the circularity of the rationale that underpins such measures and how such measures become, in turn, nested within ranking systems. This circularity normalizes a computational system which equates mathematical and statistical formulaic configurations while rendering invisible the organizational and institutional practices that underpin their production. It also blurs the overt or covert interests within which such configurations are produced, choreographed visually, and disseminated as objective knowledge. The consequences transcend the question of "reinforced control" – true as it is – signalling the colonization of the higher education life-world (to draw on Jürgen Habermas) and its subjugation, as a field, to industrial relations of production. The main implication of this view – again, to draw on Habermas – is the disruption of the communicative capacities within the higher education field in elaborating its own ontological and epistemic frameworks and conversations regarding the value of education, knowledge, and their role in contemporary societies. The *Guardian*'s editorial of 4 March 2019 on academic publishing and "disastrous capitalism" is quite indicative in that regard. It documents the massive profits made by companies, such as Elsevier, and the impact this has on knowledge generation, dissemination, and mobilization. The editorial poignantly noted,

> In some ways the scientific publishing model resembles the economy of the social internet: labour is provided free in exchange for the hope of status, while huge profits are made by a few big firms who run the market places. In both cases, we need a rebalancing of power.

The *Guardian*'s view, it is worth noting, reflects broader concerns regarding the closing of the scholarly endeavour, not because of its embrace of "moral relativism," as suggested by Allan Bloom (1987), but rather because of the hegemonic position the publishing and rankings industries exert in determining how scholarship is made (or not made) public. These Janus figures have resulted in a higher education field that is repositioning itself as a primarily privatized and privatizing capitalist endeavour. Questions are thus raised concerning the public good and the roles of knowledge and education in a democratic and pluralistic society (Slaughter & Rhoades, 2004).

Against this backdrop, some European and North American countries mandate that knowledge paid for by public dollars be accessible through open access means. In 2019 the University of California System, with its ten campuses, pulled out of its contracts with Elsevier (Fox & Brainard, 2019). By 2020, eleven European countries will require all published research they fund to be made publicly available (Yeager, 2018). These actions demonstrate the ability of countries and universities to challenge multinational corporate control of knowledge. What is less discussed is the role academics could play in revamping existing practices regarding open access publications and their relation to promotion and tenure.

The focus of journal impact factors, which are used by rankers, is based on publication counts in high-impact journals. However, absent is an indicator for the percentage of the work published by these journals which ends up being retracted. Some rankers, such as the *Times Higher Education*, use indicators related to the industry-university partnership. Not included are indicators that analyse the ethics of these partnerships. Lindsay McKenzie (2018), for example, attempted to acquire information from sixteen top-ranked universities who receive funding through Facebook as part of the Sponsored Academic Research Agreement, which is managed by a Facebook unit known for its secrecy. Many questions arise here: Are universities using public resources and trust to conduct corporate research that is corroding human rights and democratic institutions? What are universities for in relation to the public good? Can universities be trusted to provide independent and rigorous research if they are funded by companies such as Facebook? Richard Horton, editor of the prestigious medical journal the *Lancet*, shocked many when he stated that most medical research is flawed. He argues,

> Our acquiescence to the impact factor fuels an unhealthy competition to win a place in a select few journals. Our love of "significance" pollutes the literature with many a statistical fairy-tale. We reject important confirmations. Journals are not the only miscreants. Universities are in a perpetual struggle for money and talent, endpoints that foster reductive metrics, such as high-impact publication. National assessment procedures, such as the Research Excellence Framework, incentivize bad practices. (Horton, 2015, p. 1380)

Research on rankings, and the rankings of research, needs to more clearly make connections to their impacts on research integrity, dissemination, and mechanisms of appropriation in which research becomes locked to serve particular beneficiaries. This concern resonates strongly with Arjun Appadurai's (2006) call to consider research as a human right, central to the opportunities to preserve the vitality, equity, and political engagements of communities and individuals in determining the values on which social and political organization lies. Appadurai (2006) more specifically points this out:

> It is important to deparochialise the idea of research and make it more widely available to young people with a wide range of interests and aspirations. Research, in this sense, is not only the production of original ideas and new knowledge (as it is normally defined in academia and other knowledge-based institutions). It is also something simpler and deeper. It is the capacity to systematically increase the horizons of one's current knowledge, in relation to some task, goal or aspiration. (p. 176)

Appadurai's call to "deparochialise" research – as both cultural practice and social and political emancipation – emphasizes the need to conceive of research not just regarding its political economy and competitive economic advantages. In addition, research – and its outcomes in terms of knowledge articulations – must sustain a viable political culture that can best position individuals and groups to address the vexing issues of the time. Appadurai's call also has important implications for academic and their accountability to the public. Currently, academics at top-ranked universities are held accountable by the number of articles published in highly ranked journals, which most audiences who need such knowledge cannot afford to access. In other words, as the world's problems are developing into persistent wicked problems and populism and fascism are on the rise, academics are evaluated based on how well they communicate to each other within the framework of metrics owned and operated mainly by media and publishing oligarchies.

Influence of Rankings on Institutional and Individual Well-Being

The contributions in this section of the book demonstrate that rankings influence how people see themselves and the higher education institutions that employ them. Hall's chapter shows us that rankings can impact their denizens' health in many ways. Ishikawa's chapter further highlights how rankings impact the employment prospects of domestic students upon graduation. Barron's chapter reminds us that the effect of rankings is not homogeneous, though. Individuals and institutions might both acquiesce to the demands of rankings while at the same time attempting to resist. Slaughter and Rhoades (2004), in their seminal study of academic capitalism, show how universities have moved to compete in the global marketplace for high-ability students. While the "academic capitalism" thesis has received a wide range of discussions, the effects of such dynamics on the well-being of students, staff, and faculty remain relatively much less studied.

To appreciate the questions associated with well-being, it is important to recall that rankers and publishing monopolies are powerful, and mostly hidden, decision-makers. They may not be in the room when university leaders or faculty members are deciding on strategic directions, but they have framed the parameters of what would be seen as possible and desirable. As the contributors in this section demonstrate, scholars, students, and university leaders are not mere executors. Rather, as core players and enactors of the life of the university, they participate in hierarchies that are gendered, racialized, ableist, and based in class. Rankings and other metrics require attention to the impact they have on staff, students, and faculty from equity-seeking groups. What the chapters in this section show clearly is that the impact of rankings, and the alignment of university practices and internal governance, exerts a heavy toll on faculty and on their capacity to sustain pedagogically viable professional relationships with students and colleagues.

Considering the well-being of faculty and students when discussing rankings remains an understudied and marginalized area. In that sense, Hall's chapter opens up new lines of inquiry regarding the modalities through which rankings competitions trickle down to the university and the epistemic obedience and disobedience they trigger. While more research is needed to unpack the dynamics at stake, and their impacts, it is important also to extend the discussion to the impacts associated with the use of different social media on the way rankings about institutions are handled, disseminated, and communicated – whether within or across institutions – and the effects of this mediatized practice on faculty, student, and staff wellness and sense of affiliation and belonging.

Must Rankings Be Here to Stay?

Neo-liberalism, new public management, marketization, corporatization, and mediatization all play a role in rankings and journal impact factors. However, education is a contested space, and with debate and struggle more inclusive and democratic spaces are possible. A way to limit discussion is to assert that an organization or system is so powerful and natural that is cannot be changed. However, history is replete with examples of change aimed at challenging exclusion. Civil rights, feminism, and disability rights normalized the right to inclusion. Of course, pushes for equity are contested and the fight for equitable education is ongoing and forevermore complex. Understanding neo-liberalism is key to understanding where we stand today in terms of the challenges facing higher education institutions, their governance, and how they position themselves in relation to market economies. That said, this also requires an assessment of the role of social movements and activism, within and outside academe, and the roles they have come to play in calling for an inclusive education. This is well captured by Robertson and Olds (2016), who, drawing on Santos, point to how universities have responded, so far, to "strong questions with weak answers. Weak answers are technical answers devised of the moment. They are answers that focus on the problem as if it were disconnected from wider social, economic and political phenomena" (p. 25). They argue that higher education institutions and their denizens need to provide strong answers that are theoretically robust and attuned to context and that "advance an agenda and set of strategies, institutionally and sectorally, that seeks to challenge and if necessary change the current state of affairs" (p. 26). The education industry cradle-to-grave is a massive market, but for most educators and advocates education is siloed – early childhood, primary, secondary, adult, tertiary, etc. An education movement is needed that crosses these boundaries. Given that the aims of education heavily hinge on values, beliefs, hopes, and aspirations of diverse people, answers require approaches that start with democratic governance and participation. Building on these chapters, further research is needed to examine the interconnected geographies across staff and advisories to rankings, publishing, technology, supranational organizations, and media industries. Research that examines the circulation of rankings products through websites and social and legacy media is also needed. How does one story about what a world-class university stands for normalize a global governance model of education? How might the introduction of multilayered stories become part of public debate and policy over the goals and ends of higher education?

Who Counts and Why?

An area requiring far more attention is rankings and journal impact factors in relation to how they frame ableism and racism. Disability studies scholars have repeatedly demonstrated the ways disabled students and faculty are excluded from higher education institutions. Taylor and Shallish (2019) provide an insightful analysis of how equity discourses are often rooted in ableism: a belief that the good mind, the good body, can be objectively measured and perform to a normal standard. They write:

> Higher education equity for students positioned as outside the racialized construct of bodily and mental normalcy must begin with locating disability in the social structures of higher education itself and as conditioned by forces of intellectual, economic, and social normalization that reinforce some bodies as worthy and others as liabilities. (p. 1219)

According to the World Health Organization (WHO) 15 per cent of the population has a disability. Yet they are under-represented in scholarship about rankings and impact factors. A number of scholars have shown how disabled scholars are excluded from universities through arbitrary performance metrics and through spatial and temporal arrangements (Brown & Leigh, 2018; Janz & Stack, 2020; Pearson & Boskovich, 2019; Stapleton, 2015; Titchkosky, 2010; Waterfield et al., 2018). Current ways of assessing who and what counts as world class arguably amplify these structural inequities. What would it look like to create higher education institutions that are based in diverse positionalities as a way to improve the rigour of scholarship and teaching?

Richards et al. (2018) provide an urgently needed analysis of rankings on institutions they refers to as "Minority-Serving Institutions" (MSIs). While these authors focus on MSIs in the US, the critique they advance applies to rankings more broadly:

> To the extent that a college ranking represents a normative judgment, the question of what is normative may follow a familiar dynamic, well-characterized by Ladson-Billings (1998), "In a racialized society where whiteness is positioned as

normative, everyone is ranked and categorized in relation to these points of opposition" (p. 9). Thus, the norms for excellence in higher education, as defined in college rankings, are largely based on metrics biased against the forms of capital particular to MSIs. (p. 270)

For the contributors to this volume, a core concern about rankings is, therefore, the extent to which rankings obstruct alternative voices and the epistemic and ontological views that underpin them. Central to the rankings stand notions of excellence. Excellence, far from being a science, is primarily grounded in culturally sensitive and culturally dependent practices, views, habits, and beliefs. How specific constructions of "excellence" – as rhetorical devices – come to operate as a platform for the subordination of the different Other emerges as a central concern.

In a country like Canada, and in countries in which Indigenous communities have long been marginalized, oppressed, and dispossessed, debates on rankings acquire paramount importance and particular meanings which remain overlooked. In challenging Canadian higher education institutions to move beyond their role in colonization, Kirkness and Barnhardt (1991) identify the "4Rs" – respect, reciprocity, relevance, and responsibility – that pertain to research. These 4Rs all require time for relationship-building, respect for land, sharing knowledge, and giving back to the community. None of these requirements matches with the scholarship required to do well in rankings. There is much to learn from institutions with governance structures grounded in lifelong education and accountability to community and land. Many Māori universities, Tribal colleges in the United States, and Indigenous universities in Canada and worldwide provide ways of thinking and acting outside of a winners and losers approach to education. Notwithstanding, the relevance of their work and knowledge remains outside the bounds of interest of established rankings systems.

Critical questions arise at this juncture, questions which remain largely unattended either by rankings or by university leaderships: How do Indigenous scholars in top-ranked universities navigate these contradictory demands? Given the United Nations Declaration of the Rights of Indigenous Peoples, what responsibilities do institutions and governments have to ensure rankings and other new managerial processes are not negatively impacting Indigenous education and research? How can higher education institutions be structured to deeply engage with decolonizing efforts that acknowledge and respect land and Indigenous peoples' land?

In conclusion, rankings and journal impact factors are not abstract in their effects. They represent products that change what diverse publics perceive as good education and research that they want access to. Alternative models grounded in educational, democratic, and participatory principles should include students and the diverse publics that work within universities, and those who support educational institutions or depend on them. This requires students, faculty, staff, and diverse publics to consider these institutions as theirs and to demand they be governed as such.

This book highlights aspects of higher education that have been left to fend for themselves when it comes to discussing the material impacts of rankings on both higher education and wider social and political questions. What the contributions assembled in this book do show is that rankings are not just – if ever – about excellence and quality of higher education, as the admissions' scandal we started with suggests. Rather, rankings and associated products (e.g., journal impact factors) require an in-depth reclaiming of the roles and purposes of higher education institutions in contemporary societies. If our thinking about rankings remains locked in the circular rationalities of formulaic measurements, we are bound to lose whatever freedoms and participatory horizons are still available to us, as both academics and community members.

REFERENCES

Aliet, J. (2007). Convergence and glocalization – not counter-penetration and domestication: A response to Prof. Ali Mazrui. *Alternatives: Turkish Journal of International Relations, 6*(1&2), 1–14. https://dergipark.org.tr/en/download/article-file/19489

Altbach, P.G. (1995). Education and neocolonialism. In B. Ashcroft, G. Griffiths, & H. Tiffin (Eds.), *The post-colonial studies reader* (pp. 452–6). Routledge.

Appadurai, A. (2006). The right to research. *Globalisation, Societies and Education, 4*(2), 167–77. https://doi.org/10.1080/14767720600750696

Beck, K. (2012). Globalization/s: Reproduction and resistance in the internationalization of higher education. *Canadian Journal of Education, 35*(3), 133–48.

Bloom, A. (1987). *Closing of the American mind*. Simon and Schuster.

Bourdieu, P. (1990). *The logic of practice*. Stanford University Press.

Brown, N., & Leigh, J. (2018). Ableism in academia: Where are the disabled and ill academics? *Disability & Society, 33*(6), 985–9. https://doi.org/10.1080/09687599 .2018.1455627

Cantwell, B. (2017). The geopolitics of the education market. In E. Hazelkorn (Ed.), *Global rankings and the geopolitics of higher education* (pp. 309–23). London: Routledge. https://doi.org/10.4324/9781315738550

Connell, R. (2014). Using southern theory: Decolonizing social thought in theory, research and application. *Planning Theory, 13*(2), 210–23. https://doi .org/10.1177/1473095213499216

El-Khairy, O. (2010). American dreams of reinventing the "Orient": Digital democracy and Arab youth cultures in a regional perspective. In A. Mazawi & R. Sultana (Eds.), *World yearbook of education: Education and the Arab "world"* (pp. 319–34). New York: Routledge. https://doi.org/10.4324/9780203863596

Fox, A., & Brainard, J. (2019). University of California boycotts publishing giant Elsevier over journal costs and open access. *Science*. https://www-sciencemag-org.ezproxy.library.ubc.ca/news/2019/02/university-california-boycotts-publishing-giant-elsevier-over-journal-costs-and-open

Guardian. (2019, 4 March). Editorial: View on academic publishing: disastrous capitalism. https://www.theguardian.com/commentisfree/2019/mar/04/the-guardian-view-on-academic-publishing-disastrous-capitalism

Hammarfelt, B., de Rijcke, S., & Wouters, P. (2017). From eminent men to excellent universities: University rankings as calculative devices. *Minerva, 55*(4), 391–411. https://doi.org/10.1007/s11024-017-9329-x

Harding, S.G. (1991). *Whose science? Whose knowledge? Thinking from women's lives*. Cornell University Press.

Hartmann, E. (2008). Bologna goes global: A new imperialism in the making? *Globalisation, Societies and Education, 6*(3), 207–20. https://doi.org/10.1080/14767720802343308

Horton, R. (2015). Offline: What is medicine's 5 sigma? *Lancet, 385*(9976), 1380. https://doi.org/10.1016/S0140-6736(15)60696-1

Ilieva, R., Beck, K., & Waterstone, B. (2014). Towards sustainable internationalisation of higher education. *Higher Education, 68*(6), 875–89. https://doi.org/10.1007/s10734-014-9749-6

Janz, H., & Stack, M. (2020). Thinking through a course on educational technology and ableism: Implications for syllabus design. In A.E. Mazawi & M. Stack (Eds.), *Course syllabi in faculties of education: Bodies of knowledge and their discontents, international and comparative perspectives* (pp. 187–202). Bloomsbury.

Jöns, H., & Hoyler, M. (2013). Global geographies of higher education: The perspective of world university rankings. *Geoforum, 46*, 45–59. https://doi.org/10.1016/j.geoforum.2012.12.014

Kirkness, V.J., & Barnhardt, R. (1991). First Nations and higher education: The four R's – respect, relevance, reciprocity, responsibility. *Journal of American Indian Education, 30*(3), 1–15.

Larivière, V., Haustein, S., & Mongeon, P. (2015). The oligopoly of academic publishers in the digital era. *PLOS ONE, 10*(6), e0127502. https://doi.org/10.1371/journal.pone.0127502

Lee, J. (2015). The regional dimension of education hubs. *Higher Education Policy, 28*(1), 69–89. https://doi.org/10.1057/hep.2014.32

Mazrui, A.A. (2003). Towards re-Africanizing African universities: Who killed intellectualism in the post colonial era? *Alternatives: Turkish Journal of International Relations, 2*(3&4). https://dergipark.org.tr/en/download/article-file/19428

Mckenzie, L. (2018, 21 May). Research universities quietly collaborate with Facebook. What are they working on? *Inside Higher Education*. https://www.insidehighered

.com/news/2018/05/21/research-universities-quietly-collaborate-facebook-what
-are-they-working

Meyer, H.-D. (2017). *The design of the university: German, American, and "world class."* Routledge.

Mignolo, W.D. (2002). The geopolitics of knowledge and the colonial difference. *South Atlantic Quarterly, 101*(1), 57–96. https://doi.org/10.1215/00382876-101-1-57

Mignolo, W.D. (2003). Globalization and the geopolitics of knowledge: The role of the humanities in the corporate university. *Nepantla: Views from South, 4*(1), 97–119.

Mignolo, W.D. (2009). Epistemic disobedience, independent thought, and de-colonial freedom. *Theory, Culture & Society, 26*(7–8), 1–23.

Novelli, M., & Cardozo, M.L. (2012). Globalizing interventions in zones of conflict: The role of Dutch aid to education and conflict. In A. Verger, M. Novelli, & H.K. Altinyelken (Eds.), *Global education policy and international development: New agendas, issues and policies* (pp. 193–208). Bloomsbury.

Pearson, H., & Boskovich, L. (2019). Problematizing disability disclosure in higher education: Shifting towards a liberating humanizing intersectional framework. *Disability Studies Quarterly, 39*(1). https://doi.org/10.18061/dsq.v39i1.6001

Pennock, L., Jones, G.A., Leclerc, J.M., & Li, S.X. (2016). Challenges and opportunities for collegial governance at Canadian universities: Reflections on a survey of academic senates. *Canadian Journal of Higher Education, 46*(3), 73–89. http://search .proquest.com/docview/1863560396/abstract/C88CC6F2D0F94906PQ/1

Quijano, A. (2007). Coloniality and modernity/rationality. *Cultural Studies, 21*(2–3), 168–78. https://doi.org/10.1080/09502380601164353

Richards, D.A.R., Awokoya, J.T., Bridges, B.K., & Clark, C. (2018). One size does not fit all: A critical race theory perspective on college rankings. *Review of Higher Education, 42*(1), 269–312. https://doi.org/10.1353/rhe.2018.0030

Robertson, S.L., & Keeling, R. (2008). Stirring the lions: Strategy and tactics in global higher education. *Globalisation, Societies and Education, 6*(3), 221–40. https://doi .org/10.1080/14767720802343316

Robertson, S.L., & Olds, K. (2017). Rankings as global (monetising) scopic systems. In E. Hazelkorn (Ed.), *Global rankings and the geopolitics of higher education* (pp. 78–100). Routledge. https://doi.org/10.4324/9781315738550

Santos, B. De S. (Ed.). (2005). *Democratizing democracy: Beyond the liberal democratic canon.* Verso.

Sassen, S. (2006). *Territory, authority, rights: From medieval to global assemblages.* Princeton University Press.

Shahjahan, R.A., & Morgan, C. (2016). Global competition, coloniality, and the geopolitics of knowledge in higher education. *British Journal of Sociology of Education, 37*(1), 92–109. https://doi.org/10.1080/01425692.2015.1095635

Skinner, Q. (1999). Rhetoric and conceptual change. *Redescriptions: Political Thought, Conceptual History and Feminist Theory, 3*(1), 60–73.

Slaughter, S., & Rhoades, G. (2004). *Academic capitalism and the new economy: Markets, state, and higher education.* JHU Press.

Stapleton, L. (2015). The disabled academy: The experiences of Deaf faculty at predominantly hearing institutions. *Thought & Action,* 55–69. http://eric.ed.gov /ericwebportal/detail?Accno=EJ1086943

Stromquist, N.P. (2013). Globalization and "policyscapes": Ruptures and continuities in higher education. In P. Axelrod, R.D. Trilokekar, T. Shanahan, & R. Wellen (Eds.), *Making policy in turbulent times* (Vol. 1, pp. 221–48). McGill-Queen's University Press.

Tamrat, W., & Teferra, D. (2018). Internationalization of Ethiopian higher education institutions: Manifestations of a nascent system. *Journal of Studies in International Education, 22*(5), 434–53. https://doi.org/10.1177/1028315318786425

Taylor, A., & Shallish, L. (2019). The logic of bio-meritocracy in the promotion of higher education equity. *Disability & Society, 34*(7–8), 1200–23. https://doi.org /10.1080/09687599.2019.1613962

Titchkosky, T. (2010). The not-yet-time of disability in the bureaucratization of university life. *Disability Studies Quarterly, 30*(3/4). https://doi.org/10.18061/dsq .v30i3/4.1295

United States Attorney's Office for the District of Massachusetts. (2019). Investigations of college admissions and testing bribery scheme. https://www.justice.gov/usao-ma /investigations-college-admissions-and-testing-bribery-scheme

Waterfield, B., Beagan, B.B., & Weinberg, M. (2018). Disabled academics: A case study in Canadian universities. *Disability & Society, 33*(3), 327–48. https://doi.org/10.1080 /09687599.2017.1411251

Weiler, H.N. (2005). Ambivalence and the politics of knowledge: The struggle for change in German higher education. *Higher Education, 49,* 177–95. https://doi .org/10.1007/s10734-004-2921-7

Yeager, A. (2018, 4 September). Open-access plan in Europe bans publishing in paywalled journals. *Scientist.* https://www.the-scientist.com/news-opinion/open -access-plan-in-europe-bans-publishing-in-paywalled-journals-64748

Contributors

Advisory Editors

André Elias Mazawi is a professor in the Department of Educational Studies at the University of British Columbia. A sociologist of education by training, he is interested in understanding how state policies, geopolitics, and popular culture contribute to the construction of imaginaries of schooling and higher education and their effects on the articulation of governance regimes and policyscapes. He has published widely on these issues, with particular reference to Mediterranean and Middle Eastern societies. He is also an affiliate professor with the Euro-Mediterranean Centre of Educational Research at the University of Malta and serves on the Advisory Editorial Board of Postcolonial Directions in Education.

Mayumi Ishikawa is a professor of anthropology at the Center for Global Initiatives, Osaka University, Japan. Her research interests include the globalization of higher education and ethnographic studies of universities and of Malaysian Borneo, the internationalization of higher education, transnational mobility of students and scholars, world university rankings and the emergence of hegemony in academia, and power in the construction of knowledge. She edited *Sekai daigaku ranking to chi no joretsuka* (World University Rankings and the hegemonic restructuring of knowledge), a volume in Japanese published in 2016 by Kyoto University Press. Email: ishikawa@cgin.osaka-u.ac.jp

Chuing Prudence Chou (周祝瑛) received her PhD in comparative and international education from the University of California, Los Angeles (UCLA) and is a professor in the Department of Education at National Chengchi University (NCCU), Taiwan. Her edited book entitled *Chinese Education Models in a Global Age* (Singapore: Springer) was published in 2016 and its Chinese version has been available since 2018. Another edited book, *Cultural* *and Educational Exchanges between Rival Societies*, was also published in 2018 (Singapore: Springer). Website: http://www3.nccu.edu.tw/~iaezcpc/en. Email: iaezcpc@nccu.edu.tw

Contributors

Gary R.S. Barron is a generalist sociologist who is very interested in how categories and numbers are made and what they do once they are brought into the world. More traditionally stated, his scholarly interests are oriented around the politics and organization of knowledge, science and technology studies, health and illness, mental health and illness, and the intersections of these with law, organizations, performance, and strategy. He uses his sociological toolbox for subsistence purposes and to satisfy his curiosity with the world. Email: gary.barron@lethbridgecollege.ca

Annabelle Estera is a doctoral candidate in higher, adult, and lifelong education (HALE) at Michigan State University. Her research interests include decolonizing higher education, discourses of diversity and multiculturalism, and staff in higher education. Her dissertation work looks at the personal and professional meanings of decolonization for Filipinx higher education staff. She also holds an MA in higher education and student affairs from Ohio State University. Email: esteraan@msu.edu

Nathan C. Hall is an associate dean in the Faculty of Graduate and Postdoctoral Studies and associate professor in the Department of Educational and Counselling Psychology at McGill University. As director of the Achievement Motivation and Emotion Research Group (www.ame1.net), he examines in his research the role of motivation, self-regulation, and emotions in learning, achievement, and well-being in both learners and educators from K–12 to post-secondary contexts. Email: nathan.c.hall@mail.mcgill.ca

Nadiia Kachynska is a PhD candidate in comparative and international higher education at the University of Toronto. Her broad research agenda focuses on the impact of global trends on higher education systems and universities, the shifting role of universities in societies, and new models of higher education governance and evaluation. Her thesis research investigates organizational dynamics at universities in Central and Eastern Europe influenced by the emerging global norms of research excellence.

Marion Lloyd is a research professor at the Institute for the Study of the University and Education (IISUE) at the National Autonomous University of Mexico (UNAM). She holds a PhD in sociology and a master's in Latin

American studies from UNAM, as well as a BA in English and Spanish literature from Harvard University. Her research interests include comparative higher education policy, international university rankings, affirmative action in Brazil and the United States, and intercultural universities in Mexico. From 1995 to 2011 she was a foreign correspondent in Latin America and South Asia. Website: https://www.researchgate.net/profile/Marion_Lloyd

Magdalena Martinez is a PhD candidate in comparative and international higher education and an SSHRC scholar at the University of Toronto. Her research interests are access to post-secondary education and the development of community engagement policy and programs in Brazil and Latin America. She is also a research assistant in the Centre for the Study of Canadian and International Higher Education, where she collaborates on various projects relating to international research collaboration, national and international rankings, and research performance.

Heather Morrison is an associate professor at the University of Ottawa's School of Information Studies and cross-appointed to the Department of Communication since 2013. In 2012 she completed a doctorate in communication from Simon Fraser University on the topic of freedom for scholarship in the internet age. Currently, she is the principal investigator of the SSHRC Insight Project Sustaining the Knowledge Commons (2016–2021), which seeks to transition the economics underlying scholarly communication from the demand to the supply side to support an inclusive, open access global knowledge commons in the public interest. Website: https://uniweb.uottawa.ca/?lang=en#/members/706. Email: Heather.Morrison@uottawa.ca

Imanol Ordorika (PhD Stanford, 1999) is a professor of social sciences and education at the Universidad Nacional Autónoma de México. He is the author of *Power and Politics in Higher Education* (Routledge, 2003) and coeditor of ASHE reader *Comparative Education* (2010) and *Universities and the Public Sphere* (2011); he has also authored the chapters "Mexico: Dilemmas of Federalism in a Highly Politicized and Semi-decentralized System" in *Higher Education in Federal Countries: A Comparative Study* (with Rodríguez and Lloyd, SAGE, 2018) and "Field of Higher Education Research in Latin America" in *Encyclopedia of International Higher Education Systems and Institutions* (with Rodríguez, Springer, 2018), and the articles "The Academic Publishing Trap" in *Revista Española de Pedagogía* (2018) and "International Rankings and the Contest for University Hegemony" in *Journal of Education Policy* (with Lloyd, 2015).

Emma Sabzalieva (PhD Toronto, 2020) is a policy analyst at the UNESCO International Institute for Higher Education and Research Associate at York

University. Her core research interests are the new geopolitics of higher education and the effects of globalization on education policy. She researches a range of global settings and has regional expertise in the study of Central Asia and the former Soviet space, which she blogs about at http://emmasabzalieva.com.

Ralf St. Clair is a professor and the dean of education at the University of Victoria. He is a member of the Canadian Commission to UNESCO and the BC Teachers' Council. Dr. St. Clair is an active teacher, focusing on the education of adults, literacy, research methods, curriculum studies, and international education. Dr. St. Clair has been an active researcher for several decades, having studied adult education and literacy, educational aspirations, and Indigenous education. The common thread running through his work is a concern with equity and accessibility in education.

Creso M. Sá is a Distinguished Professor of Science Policy, Higher Education and Innovation at the University of Toronto. He is also director of the Centre for the Study of Canadian and International Higher Education (CIHE). His work focuses on science and technology policy, the evolving role of universities in the economy, and the organization of science. He is associate editor of *Studies in Higher Education* and editor-in-chief of the *Canadian Journal of Higher Education*.

Riyad A. Shahjahan is an associate professor of higher, adult, and lifelong education (HALE) at Michigan State University. He is also a core faculty member of Muslim studies, Chicano/Latino studies, and the Center for Advanced Study of International Development. His areas of research interest are globalization of higher education policy, temporality and embodiment in higher education, cultural studies, and de/anti/postcolonial theory. He is also coeditor of the blog http://lazyslowdown.com.

Michelle Stack is an associate professor, former senior policy adviser, and public commentator on education. Her research interests include university rankings and the role of media in the policymaking process. She is the author of *Global University Rankings and the Mediatization of Higher Education*. Michelle has led numerous courses and workshops focused on building the capacity of scholars to engage media to expand research-informed policy debates.

Vivek Vellanki is a visiting assistant professor in the Department of Curriculum and Instruction and a postdoctoral fellow in the Center for Research on Race and Ethnicity in Society at Indiana University. His scholarly and artistic works are centred on issues of migration, transnationalism, and youth identity/culture. He draws on visual methodologies and research-creation in order to question the boundaries between scholarly and creative work.

Index